Modernist Avant-Garde Aesthetics and
Contemporary Military Technology

Modernist Avant-Garde Aesthetics and Contemporary Military Technology

Technicities of Perception

Ryan Bishop and John Phillips

Edinburgh University Press

© Ryan Bishop and John Phillips, 2010, 2011

Edinburgh University Press Ltd
22 George Square, Edinburgh

www.euppublishing.com

First published in hardback by Edinburgh University Press in 2010

Typeset in Janson
by Servis Filmsetting Ltd, Stockport, Cheshire, and
printed and bound in Great Britain by
CPI Antony Rowe, Chippenham and Eastbourne

A CIP record for this book is available from the British Library

ISBN 978 0 7486 3988 5 (hardback)
ISBN 978 0 7486 4319 6 (paperback)

The right of Ryan Bishop and John Phillips
to be identified as authors of this work
has been asserted in accordance with
the Copyright, Designs and Patents Act 1988.

Contents

Acknowledgements   vi

List of Figures   viii

Part I Aesthetics, Poetics, Prosthetics   1
  1 The Slow and the Blind: Unhinging the Senses to Harness
     Them   3
  2 Sighted Weapons and Modernist Opacity: Aesthetics,
     Poetics, Prosthetics   25
  3 We Make It Beautiful   49
  4 We Don't Make It Beautiful   68

Part II Broadcast, Hinge, Emergency   93
  5 Ventriloquism, Broadcast and Technologies of Narrative   95
  6 The Military Body and the Curious Logic of the Hinge   117
  7 Manufacturing Emergencies   135
  8 Among the Blind and the Delay   147

Part III Surveillance, Targeting, Containment   167
  9 Strategies and Technologies of Containment: Containing
     the Political   169
 10 Scoping Out   197
 11 Satellites of Love and War   213

Index   229

Acknowledgements

This book has been several years in the making, and we have presented material related to it in numerous venues. Being able to air the ideas presented here to engaged and stimulating audiences has helped shape the project beyond measure. The authors would especially like to thank the following people and institutions for their support and intellectual engagement: Dean Tan Tai Yong in the Faculty of Arts and Social Sciences at the National University of Singapore (NOS); Robbie Goh and John Richardson, heads of the Dept of English at NUS; the faculty seminar participants over the years in the Dept of English at NUS; Tim Barnard and Greg Clancey in the Dept of History, NUS; the Science, Technology and Society research cluster participants at NUS; our graduate students; Lily Kong, Vice-President of NUS and the director of the Asia Research Institute; Caren Kaplan, Fran Dyson and the Cultural Studies Program at UC Davis; Doug Kellner and his graduate seminar at UCLA; The City as Target and Derrida workshop participants at NUS; Mac Daley and the Graduate Programme in Critical Theory and Cultural Studies at the University of Nottingham; Peter Stokes and the International Critical Management Studies Conference organisers in Cambridge and Budapest; and Jonathan Arac, John Armitage, Paul Bove, Mike Featherstone, and Couze Venn amongst leagues of others for constant intellectual support and arguments. A very special thanks is owed to Wong May Ee, who tirelessly helped us with endless details related to finalising the manuscript; without her, deadlines would never have been met. Parts of this book have appeared in significantly different forms in the following journals: *Boundary2*, *Body & Society*, *Cultural Politics*, *Theory Culture & Society*, *Culture and Organization*, *Critical Perspectives on International Business*, and *Social Identities*. We would like to thank the editors and reviewers of those journals for their intelligent engagement with this material. Finally, we owe a special thanks to Jackie Jones, editor without compare, at Edinburgh University Press, her fantastic team of colleagues, and the excellent reviewers of the manuscript.

Ryan would like to give special thanks to friends, colleagues, students and family members who provided immeasurable support while I was working on this material, especially my father Steve, my stepfather Chuck, my two brothers Eric and Steve, my lovely daughters Sarah and Sophia, and my dearest collaborator Adeline.

John gives thanks to friends, teachers, colleagues and students and family members who have helped and contributed to the writing of this book in various ways, especially to Barty, Pearson, Jane, Phil, Charlie, Phillipa, to my son Alex and most of all to Chrissie for her love and unflagging emotional and intellectual support.

List of Figures

Chapter 1

Figure 1.1	Keystone Image, "She Sees Her Son in France", advert for Stereopticon images during World War I.	3
Figure 1.2	Pablo Picasso, *Les Demoiselles d'Avignon* (1907).	10
Figure 1.3	Pablo Picasso, *Portrait of Olga in an Armchair (Portrait d'Olga dans un fauteuil)* (1917).	14
Figure 1.4	Pablo Picasso, *Portrait of Igor Stravinsky (Portrait d'Igor Stravinsky)* (1920).	15
Figure 1.5	Marcel Duchamp, *Network of Stoppages* (1914).	17
Figure 1.6	Network Centric Warfare.	18

Chapter 2

Figure 2.1	Apache Longbow Cockpit, AH-64D.	26
Figure 2.2	*The Blind Man* Cover.	40

Chapter 3

Figure 3.1	'We Make It Beautiful', Apache Longbow advert.	51
Figure 3.2	Eadweard Muybridge, *Nude Descending a Staircase*.	59
Figure 3.3	Marcel Duchamp, *Nude Descending a Staircase, No. 2* (1912).	59
Figure 3.4	Marcel Duchamp, *The Bride* (1912).	62
Figure 3.5	Apache Gunship on Tarmac.	63
Figure 3.6	Marcel Duchamp, *The Bride Stripped Bare by Her Bachelors, Even (The Large Glass)* (1915–23).	64
Figure 3.7	Apache Longbow in Flight.	65

Chapter 5

Figure 5.1   IHADSS Helmet.   111

Chapter 6

Figure 6.1   Transformer Toy as Soldier and Transport.   127
Figure 6.2   Soldier of the Future.   127

Chapter 7

Figure 7.1   'Big Joe' Chrysler Siren Advert.   139

Chapter 8

Figure 8.1   Marcel Duchamp, *Etant Donnés: 2. The Illuminating Gas* (1946–66).   161
Figure 8.2   Decoy.   163

Chapter 10

Figure 10.1   Guillaume Apollinaire, 'Visée'.   210

Chapter 11

Figure 11.1   Marcel Duchamp, *The Bride Stripped Bare by Her Bachelors, Even (The Large Glass)* (1915–23).   222

Part I

Aesthetics, Poetics, Prosthetics

Chapter 1

The Slow and the Blind: Unhinging the Senses to Harness Them

Figure 1.1   Keystone Image, "She Sees Her Son in France", advert for Stereopticon images during World War I. From the private collection of Bob Boyd, image supplied by Bob Boyd

"She Sees Her Son in France", explains the advert for the Keystone View Company.[1] Linking with the current innovations of commercial telephony that allowed voice and hearing to overcome time-space divisions, the advert uses the very popular mid-nineteenth century technology of stereoscopy to provide images of "the war zone". World events and military actions might have divided mother and son, but the ad suggests a host of technologies ease the pain of separation. The Keystone View Company can provide stereoscopic, three-dimensional images of the front. With the ad, we see what she sees: an image of a large cannon being aimed and ready for fire. An image of offensive weapons being readied for deployment distracts attention away from the defensive needs met by the trench (itself the target of German guns, undoubtedly pictured on stereoscopic cards for consumption in Berlin). Because the ad must represent what occurs visually in the mother's brain, we see the stereoscope projecting outward, away from the viewing machine towards a wall (as with cinema) rather than toward the lonely mother huddled in isolation. The direction of stereoscopic projection is as ambivalent in the representation as the analogy between telephony and stereoscopy is in the ad's logic.[2] The telephone's bidirectional, real-time aural flow is nothing like the stereoscope's unidirectional, past-tense optical illusion. But the ad's messages are quite clear: various forms of technologies fully functioning in the public sphere can serve as prosthetic extensions of the senses that can neatly erase the division between the domestic and military spheres. The state and the military might have cleaved mother and son, but they also provide the means for linking them up again while the separation remains intact.

The advert displays the then-contemporary manifestation of technologies long in the making. The visual capability afforded by the Keystone View Company in the first decades of the twentieth century reveals an extension of research into the senses and their operation that had served an essential component of scientific inquiry for well over 100 years, leading to a series of inventions and technologies that altered notions about the veracity of empirical knowledge while simultaneously revealing the gap between perceiver and perceived in the attempts to close this gap. The senses were unhinged from the corporeal body in specific ways that allowed their perceptive powers to be harnessed and enhanced in other ways. The unhinging and harnessing manifested itself in a multitude of consumer goods and gadgets (radio, telephones, gramophones, talking machines, photography, cinema, stereoscopes, and so on) and state-controlled military equipment (short-wave radio, sighting mechanisms, aerial photography, and so on). In both the content and the performative dimensions of their work, many modernist artists articulated this unhinging and relocation of sensory stimulation outside the body. Similarly, the technology that increasingly came to shape the public sphere also mobilised the power unleashed by the unhinging and reconnection of the senses, and nowhere was this more evident than in military technology and its increasing sophistication from the mid-nineteenth century and through the World Wars, technology that was trained increasingly on urban sites.

The early development of contemporary military technology coincides historically with an era that has been identified with a wide and complex array of active experimentation in the arts. It is difficult to find a satisfying consensus about what the overexposed terms modernism, modernity and postmodernism mean, and discussions today suffer from an unintentionally confusing metalanguage derived from otherwise contradictory elements of discourses from writers as disparate as Martin Heidegger, Walter Benjamin, Theodor Adorno and Max Horkheimer, Jürgen Habermas, Jacques Lacan, Jean-François Lyotard, Jean Baudrillard, Michel Foucault, Paul Virilio, and so on, who belong to a still-growing assembly of critical voices in contest. Yet the history of aesthetics since the middle of the eighteenth century forms a backdrop, a shadow attached to this critical tradition, attempting to establish aesthetic principles (grounded in experience as opposed to science or metaphysics) in accounting for personal and social activities as well as political organisation. The question of the artwork can no longer be dissociated (as in classical eras) from the sphere that nevertheless accounts for art and decides its place. But while the exhibited artwork continues to grow in stature, the sphere of techno-science seems all the more removed from it, despite obvious interactions and overlaps. The theatre of conflict is one thing. The museum of modern art is something else.

Modernist aesthetics emerges in works that in their production seem to engage destructively with an environment that has regulated in advance what an artwork should be (or what an artist should do or make). The "production of works", which remains today one of the most common assumptions about the function of artists, does not adequately describe the activities of the wide variety of artists and groups assembled uneasily under the banner of the modernist avant-garde. Rather than attempt yet another classification in this book we approach the intersection of modernist avant-garde aesthetics and contemporary military technology in specific readings of what, in the fortunate word of Marcel Duchamp, we may understand as the "operations" of art. An operation, rather than a work, does not leave untouched the sphere that attempts to regulate it. The evident works (the writings and exhibited objects) no longer settle easily under the association of art with questions concerning beauty, or fall prey to the confusion between the artwork and the object or the feeling it supposedly represents or expresses. But in identifying, experimenting with, and expanding the sphere that irreconcilably divides perception from its objects, the operations of modernist aesthetics inevitably expose the incipient development of technologies that are no less interested in this sphere. However, our readings show that the operations of technology are concerned at once to mobilise it, to control it, and at their most radical to be able to shut it down, reducing distance, delay and the hazards of chance absolutely rather than fostering their inevitable insistence. The delays, the experimental distortions, the disjunctions and the consistent destruction of expectations of continuity and coherence: all of this has its counterpart in contemporary, especially military, technology – more evident today in its late flowering under increasingly high stakes – but with the opposite target in view, to close the gap, to eradicate delay, to merge the image with the object.

Take-off in Slow Motion

An installation from 1997–8 by Graham Ellard and Stephen Johnstone, *The Geneva Express*, not only addresses the problem of the senses in technology but also provides us with a pattern that connects directly to avant-garde modernist aesthetics. The installation consists of videotapes of jet airplanes taking off and landing, which are projected in slow motion on opposite walls of a gallery space. John Gange, commenting on the installation, writes, "Slow motion is cinematography's inherent trace of its own prehistory".[3] In this trace the installation exemplifies the simultaneous running forwards and reaching back of the performative modalities of technology itself.

It is in fact a stock shot in many films: an airplane – a civilian jet or military fighter – lifts off its runway but does so in slow motion, so that viewers can revel in its technological glory. Two forms of technology make themselves evident in the slow motion take-off to create a moving image of the impossible – the simultaneous speeding up (the plane) and the slowing down of what is speeding up (of the plane by the film). One is the technology of speed and the other is the technology of visual culture. The harnessing of speed and technology (including visual culture) has emerged, and continues to do so, most readily in terms of military organisations and strategies. These technologies, organisations and strategies are almost immediately displaced into the rapid development of modern urbanism, for example mass rapid transport systems, communications systems, businesses and factories, urban architecture and housing. The functionality of technology throughout the modern era corresponds to the way the aesthetic is separated from the functional and rendered visible as evident object (*objet d'art*) separate and distinct from the instrumental (art for art's sake). The combining of the aesthetic and the technological in the slow-motion take-off reveals the equally, if not more powerful, function of the aesthetic in relation to the technological: in this instance, the evident miracle of technology. That is, the technology of visual culture – or rather the technology of the visual – represents the power of speed. In order to represent it, it must be slowed down. The example reveals very clearly a functional distinction between the technology of visual representation, which is capable of creating novel kinds of appearance, and the technology it represents, in this case the power and speed of the jet engine. The distinction is placed *en abyme*, to the extent that the *performance* is both the topic of this mode of technological representation and *the mode itself*.

This distinction between performance as visible power and performance as enunciative modality – made visible in the slow-motion take-off – functions as a kind of synecdoche of the modern era's representation of itself as supporting and supported by an increased functionality and instrumentality. In similar ways some strands of the avant-garde that respond to a sphere of overlapping aesthetic, social and technological activities allow us to analyse specific engagements with the conditions that give rise to technological, bureaucratic, institutional and spatial drives toward functionality and instrumentality. These engagements include those of the so-called avant-garde and high modernism. Unlike the standard self-representations of the modern, these attempt to manifest the *cleavage* between the technological and the aesthetic *as* the power of the modern manifesting itself. Although the modern era bespeaks the power of science, rationality and technology over a world of objects, its actual power resides in a capacity that can only be represented negatively, that of division, which tends to be manifested through the partition between the aesthetic and the functional. We need to draw on the peculiar history and fate of the two Greek terms *poiesis* and *techne* to illustrate what is at stake in the distinction.

For the Greeks, *techne*, which generally means *knowing how to make things* or *know-how with an end*, designates not only the range of skills belonging to any trained professional (Aristotle's examples include architects, ship builders, athletic trainers, generals, doctors and grammarians), but also to the principles of systematic treatment that are intensified in both industrial and post-industrial motorisation. *Techne* belonged to, and was one category of, a more general *poiesis*, which means *making, fabrication, production*, and more specifically it was the word for *poetry*. Aristotle, in the *Nicomachean Ethics*, distinguishes *techne*, as a *poiesis*, from *praxis*, on the grounds that *poiesis* has an end product (and all techniques are subservient to their end product), while *praxis* – or action – does not: "Making and acting are different," he says, using the example of architecture, which he describes as a rationally informed state of productive capability. The modern age erases this separation of *techne* from *praxis*, which plays a central role in Aristotle's account of the performative capacities of an ethical life as opposed to simply industrious activities.[4] It is now as if *techne*, especially in terms of its motorised and extended capabilities, has become the basis for *praxis* rather than being a function of *poiesis*, which must therefore be displaced or otherwise contained. In this respect, the modernist texts we examine in this book are especially significant for the ways in which they emphasise the non-productive aspects of life lived under technological domination, which technology tends to ignore, contain or – when these are not possible – destroy.

The division between *praxis* and *poiesis* is recast during the modern era in terms of technology and aesthetics, which has determining consequences for current distinctions between, say, experience and truth, the subject and the object, the visible and the invisible, the field of action and the horizon, and crucially the military and the civic. The recasting of this division establishes an ethical basis in usefulness and the result, while relegating the aesthetic to the realm of useless beauty. It is a division that based in *techne* turns on its source in *poiesis* to separate it out, leaving no sphere for *praxis* but the technological ethical environment. Action in all its traditional spheres – the political and ethical life of individuals, cities and states – has in this way been at least provisionally subordinated to a range of calculative, pragmatic, techno-logical principles that promise a perhaps infinitely extendible motorised functionality. Objections to these principles are many, of course; this follows because a place is reserved for ethical reactivity: the impoverished yet hypostatised sphere of what was once recognised as the productive force of *poiesis*. The division thus ensures healthy opposition, which through many kinds of strategy tends to be maintained in domesticated states (taking the forms, variously, of romanticism, liberal humanism, existentialism, democratic materialism, and critical theory). But the power of division, once activated, constantly creates new grounds and new conditions that, in turn, force new divisions. Reactive ethical and political positions may be contained but the force of the division itself will not. Optoelectronic technology, for example, constantly creates new demands for dividing the visible from the invisible because it consistently renders visible that which had been invisible – even when this is achieved through the erasure of earlier divisions. For instance, once light waves beyond the field of human vision have been discovered towards the end of the nineteenth century, the promise of an extension of the visible field becomes at once the promise of an absolute visibility, despite the fact that, in human terms, absolute invisibility still reigns amongst alternative sensations (hearing, smell, touch, muscular motion). In machinic terms these invisibilities can always be rendered somehow on a visible plane (sonority becomes visible as light-blip, and so on). But, as modernist aesthetics repeat-edly demonstrates, the synaesthetic qualities of sensate experience presup-pose a non-sensible "space" or "gap" of "exchange", which is nothing other than the division *itself*. A similar pattern holds in the related spheres of speed and time. As Paul Virilio argues, once the relative speeds of "the horse, the ship, the train, the automobile, the airplane" have been superseded by "the absolute speed of electromagnetic waves", new political questions inevitably arise:

> The question is whether we can actually democratize ubiquitousness and instan-taneity, which in fact are the prerogatives of providence, in other words, absolute autocracy? Today the tyranny of a dictator is being replaced by the tyranny of real time, which means that it is no longer possible to democratically share the time it takes to make decisions.[5]

Virilio's concern with the implications of electromagnetic technologies underlies a provocative and problematic series of critical interventions. The tyranny of real time, its ubiquity and instantaneity, operates according to (mechanically) antidemocratic assumptions (the absolute autocracy of a dictator). But in addition, if one acknowledges the impossibility of these absolute technocratisations (the statement of divine ubiquity falls foul of its divisive performance) we are faced with a potentially bleaker picture even than Virilio's fallen state: the failure of technocracy will ensure its continued incessant struggle with and against its outside.

The temporal and spatial lag that is always implied as the condition of human perception (if not always evident for experience) seems to have been simultaneously widened (by visual art) and erased (by visual technology) in the early years of the twentieth century. In his lecture on modern art, Paul Klee could observe: "Art does not reproduce what is visible, but *makes* visible. Formerly we used to represent things visible on earth. Today we reveal the reality behind visible things."[6] For the modern artist there would be nothing mysterious *in* this invisible reality made visible for it does nothing more than exploit the gap always implied by perception – as its possibility – thus bringing into play the mysterious *per se* and/or just the gap. The insistent yet always implicit logic of the operator *and/or*, as we will show, constitutes a hinge logic, according to which the mysterious can be regarded either as constituted by this gap or replaced by this gap or both (and both). The hinge thus offers a choice: the reality behind visible things can be made visible *or* the making visible of the reality behind visible things reveals that it cannot be made visible. The logic in fact offers this choice only by taking it away at the same time.

The experimental aesthetics of the modernist avant-garde can be connected, or hinged, according to the same logic, to the technologies of speed and optoelectronics. Pablo Picasso's early experiments, which preceded the development of what by convention becomes known as cubism, seem designed specifically to make this *gap* visible. If perception already implies the abstract representation of the visible earth (or the empirical) then the conventional aspects of the representation can themselves be made visible through the distortions to which Picasso increasingly subjects his experimental studies. These designs show how the mimetic line is maintained yet rendered in a way that gradually frees it from its mimetic function. It does not erase mimesis entirely but ironises it, creating a spatial dimension for art that, in relation to mimesis, has no business with it. The result, which seems to be based on a concerted analytical study of the gap of perception, has had an incalculable impact on the history of art in the twentieth century. The first major show of the Musée Picasso, organised by Hélène Seckel around *Les Demoiselles d'Avignon* in 1988, assembled a generous quantity of works associated with the famous painting, including notebooks, sketchbooks, studies, and designs in several media, whose production preceded and in a few cases postdated that of the painting. It is no longer feasible to view this painting in isolation, for its operations are now inextricably connected with the course of its emergence, and a vast scholarship has arisen (on the back of an already significant literature) in light of the exhibition and its multitude of materials.[7]

Demoiselles, begun early in 1907 and finished by June or July of that year, presents the culmination of months of studies. The five occupants of "the philosophical brothel" (Picasso's original title; it was renamed, to Picasso's distaste, for its first public exhibition in 1916), reduced from seven in earlier designs, gaze out in a way that challenges a spectator more used perhaps to gazing on the passivity of the classical nude. The metaphor of sexual relations, consistently troubled in modernist aesthetics, serves both to problematise the aesthetic and social themes of sex and gender and to implicate the spectator in a sphere disturbed by the no longer passive repose of the work itself. The painting combines, within the otherwise classical form of its composition, several disjunctive elements that can be traced individually to existing sketches or studies. If the studies represent incessant experiment with transformation or formal adventure (several series of line drawings reveal multiple modes of distortion in the mimetic function of the line), then the transformative tendency is continued on the canvas itself (executed in striking and specific ways in the faces and bodies of the women).

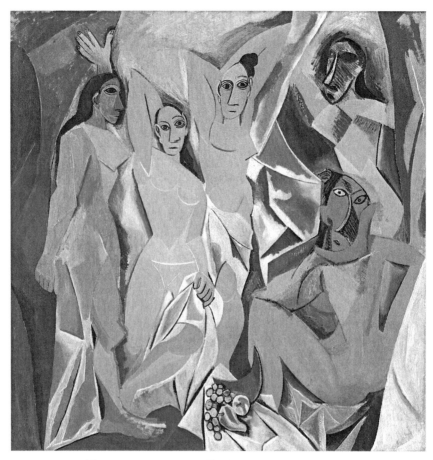

Figure 1.2   Pablo Picasso, *Les Demoiselles d'Avignon* (1907). Permission by the Picasso Estate, © Succession Picasso 2010; image provided by Scala 50 Group © Photo SCALA, Florence; The Museum of Modern Art, 2010

Critics divide the painting into a left side and a right "African" side, identifying the many allusions both to classical nudes and the so-called primitive images that at the time were provoking much ethnographic wonder. There is little doubt that this brothel, supplying material for philosophy (in the specialised form of aesthetics), offers art itself up in a confusing choice of spectacular options. The figure on the left stands next to a second figure who, on examination, turns out to be reclining, in repose, and viewed as if from above. The painting thus seems to be able to manipulate the spectator's eyes at will. The face in the upper right-hand corner (sometimes assumed to be influenced by an African mask but reminiscent in fact of a specific series of designs) seems especially to be reversing the work of the photographic image, inserting the distorting operations of an art no longer subservient to the mimetic aim into the space of representation, but also repeating nascent photographic possibilities by rendering what remains invisible to the naked eye visible, as if in competition with a technology also capable of catastrophic distortion.

Visual technology operates with material located in the same dimension (the gap of perception) yet exploits its apparent ability to abolish the gap, which amounts to nothing more than the abolition of the perception of the gap, rather than the abolition of the gap itself, which would, as we shall demonstrate, abolish the realm of organic perception altogether in order to replace it with a technological *super*-perception. Such a project, which none-theless forms one essential foundation for the development of military tech-nology in the twentieth century, must assume, therefore, that a rigorous and determinate division between the organic and the technological exists, that the organic is, for instance, too slow and thus fallible, as if its augmentation by prosthetic addition would ultimately require complete replacement, and so on. The technology of visual culture, in other words, duplicates the visible as if there was no gap – no part of representation that was *re*presentation.

The hold that the technology of representation has on observers – its ability to detach formal aspects of representation and reproduce them outside the observer's immediate gaze – can be demonstrated by still common reac-tions to Picasso's supposed "return to order" after World War I. Rosalind Krauss, for instance, sees Picasso's rapidly evolving cubist experiments as the transformation from the body to an arbitrary system of language, cul-minating in the techniques of collage, before he returns to a more classical, mimetic style. Nineteenth-century science, she claims, supports the artist's own perception of a loss of depth in the field of vision with the discovery that the retina could represent the world only in terms of its own limitations, as a two-dimensional plane, that is, as relentlessly flat: "That the carnal object-hood of the model was withdrawing progressively and that its loss was felt not as a triumph but as a kind of poignant tragedy is registered in Picasso's art of 1910 and 1911 by the way the work clings to the human figure," she argues, in what is an unashamedly psychoanalytical reading that supports the still dominant narrative of postmodernism's rising from the tragic ruined landscapes of modernist art.[8] David Joselit, drawing on Krauss but adding a twist of his own, reads cubism generally as an "epistemological transforma-tion of the biological body into a semiotic market place".[9] By submitting the nude to anatomical distortion and dissolution, Picasso thus responds to "two countervailing tendencies in the nineteenth century: the slipping away of the carnal body and the emergence of a full-scale semiotic market place" (Joselit, *Infinite Regress*, 45). However convincing and forceful the arguments of Krauss and Joselit might seem, our suspicion that some projection or at least appropriation has intervened is confirmed by Joselit's rather exaggerated speculations about Picasso's feelings on giving up the cubist distortions:

> acknowledging the loss of the body in his art was not easy for Picasso, and he quickly returned to it after World War I, never to lose his hold again. The

palpable relief and pleasure that he felt in his "return to order" is itself a dramatic gauge of how *necessary* cubism's gesture of liquidation must have felt to Picasso in 1910. (Joselit, *Infinite Regress*, 45)

The statement feels like a convenient fiction, with its rhetorically convincing but not actually existing "palpable relief" (if the relief existed, it is difficult to think of how it would be palpable, that is, as made available to the senses in the works themselves: but we will see). The myth produced by the Keystone postcard is reproduced here, the artist's work providing access to a *full* psychological dimension that is in fact projected *onto* the work rather than received from it.

Moreover, by the 1920s, Picasso's techniques had already surpassed the experimental distortions of his "cubist period" despite having passed through the period of apparent order that suits Joselit's questionable narrative well, drawing it to a close and bringing Picasso full circle: once more holding onto the voluble bodies of his nudes. But this is surely a fictional Picasso, quick to tears, trembling in the face of an unrelenting world made flat, a tragic, even Romantic Picasso. An alternative, more academic, reading of *Les Demoiselles d'Avignon* would see it as Carsten-Peter Warncke advises, that is, "as the programmatic statement of a new formal vocabulary, created from the systematic scrutiny of conventional representational approaches and the development of a new synthesis out of them".[10] The two Picassos: on one side, the tragic figure haunted by loss, at length relieved from and redeemed by his years of artistic suffering and abstention from the body; on the other side, the analyst, systematic experimenter with the techniques of representation, restlessly evolving through a lifetime of technical innovations. These two critical responses, which seem to offer a choice, can in fact be read together as exemplifying – even manifesting – the gap itself, dividing the world from the language that represents it, the organic from the semiotic (on one side) and the technological (on the other), the gap, in short, of perception itself.

So art history is caught in a logic it would attempt to apprehend theoretically but can only repeat differently. It functions as a hinge articulating the difference between the semiotic and the technological but in this way finds itself caught in a hinge logic that it cannot master. The currency of a post-Saussurean vocabulary (in texts that nonetheless fail to read this vocabulary with critical attention) generally escapes what is most pertinent in Saussure's linguistics: that it is not a linguistics at all but a metaphysics disguised as a theoretical linguistics, not able to maintain its determinate limitations, and in failing to do this producing an unintentional revision of metaphysics. The division between a body and a language would not, after all, be decisive, for, as Saussure laboriously taught, the unit of the language system would not have either a material or a semantic basis. Rather (as Saussure failed to acknowledge) it would be grounded in its own division from itself in its repetition, producing what we here recall as the gap in perception, an in principle *immediate* time lag without which there would be no perception whatsoever. Consequently, we would speak not of the materiality of the signifier but rather of the logic of the hinge.

The controversy can be put into perspective a little when, by turning to this apparent interruption by "order" (roughly between 1916 and 1924) of an otherwise exemplary experimentalist oeuvre, we find that the "return" to the human figure is no return at all but a further revolution of the previous revolution.[11] Picasso from about 1917 is no longer just painting from physical models visible on the earth but he is painting photographs. Not painting *from* photographs, either, but painting photographs themselves – or at least parts of them – the photographic image *qua*-image becomes the painter's model. It might also explain why these paintings are, as Krauss points out, "not just any set of figures but those of his friends and lovers." Contrary to the idea of the pathetic clinging to life that Joselit sees in these paintings, Picasso seems quite clearly to have been painting at least as if from photographs, portraits of friends and family, posed in the studio or at play outside, in ways that variously emphasise what the photograph (re)produces on its flat surface: the linear outline of his friend Stravinsky, or portraits of Olga, partly "coloured in" but partly "left" in a kind of tell-tale monochrome. Obviously this would not be any kind of departure from, even less an abandonment of, techniques of the collages of 1915 (sheets of yellowing newspaper pasted on paper and sketched upon with charcoal) but an extension of their idea. If the gap of perception in the cubist paintings and collages is rendered visible by their distortions, then, in this pure mimesis – or better, literal tracing – of the photographic image, the gap is in principle rendered absolute, in a relentless flattening not only of space but essentially of time too, where exposure replaces duration. Any re-placement of the physical body, any attempt at redemption, would only drive a further wedge between the body and its language of representation.

In these ways modernist aesthetics can reproduce the logic, laying it bare, of an optical technology that constantly creates new demands for dividing the visible from the invisible. The *secret* of Picasso's return to order is that the photograph itself – the visibility of the photograph – becomes invisible in its image, the painting. The photograph, in its evanescence as it fades into the coloured image, would therefore be the invisible representation, in Picasso's uncanny likeness, of a photo-electronic hinge connecting painting to its model in a comically ironic gesture that would occupy the artist off and on for several years. Painting had incorporated and modified the very thing that had hitherto remained external to it: the photograph.[12] The likenesses even reproduce – in a further comic twist – the effects variously of telephoto and wide angle lenses, which can enlarge extremities like hands and feet from certain perspectives: distorted perspectives of the lens and shutter as opposed to the mathematical quattrocento eye.

Similarly the conditions that allow the modern subject to understand itself as a subject constantly incorporate and modify those attributes previously

Figure 1.3   Pablo Picasso, *Portrait of Olga in an Armchair* (*Portrait d'Olga dans un fauteuil*) (1917). Permission by the Picasso Estate, © Succession Picasso 2010; image provided by RMN / René-Gabriel Ojéda

external to it. This power to divide, however, remains unpresentable, which is why it remains invisible even when it has been rendered somehow visible. Division per se would be uncontainable and incapable of being completely harnessed, because it is this power that brings the subject and its objects together in the synthesis of presence. Within the domain of technology the division most clearly emerges as the difference between the instrumental and predicative truth of technology, on one hand, and the modality of its enunciation, on the other. On one side the functionality of technology gains support from a notion of truth based upon modes of correspondence. That is, a statement that predicates some subject of some quality (for example, the jet engine is fast) corresponds to some state of affairs in terms of its truth or falsity. On the other side, the enunciative dimension, which falls on a rhetorical ground out of which all statements emerge but which bears no natural or necessary relation (whether of correspondence or anything else) to any other state of affairs, calls the performative level of address into play (who addresses whom and with what powers, with what effects). The modality of enunciation can be domesticated as a locus of *experience* and captured as a *poiesis* now *opposed* to *techne*. This process of framing the aesthetic text is maintained, looked after, and protected by those granted the responsibility for its guardianship: critics, historians, curators and the institutions that support them (the university, the museum, the archive), but which already manifest a framing on a greater scale. The modern milieu seems to be characterised by forms of framing; but where *poiesis* is concerned the very

Figure 1.4   Pablo Picasso, *Portrait of Igor Stravinsky* (*Portrait d'Igor Stravinsky*) (1920). Permission by the Picasso Estate, © Succession Picasso 2010; image provided by RMN / Béatrice Hatala

grounds of framing itself must be caught within a frame. Following this logic, then, according to which a power manifest in the modern age escapes that moment's attempt to capture it, the military operates with an aesthetics it often refuses to admit. The very constitution of the aesthetic is what makes the military and its functional instrumentalism possible.

Networks and Netwars

Deferment

Against compulsory military services: a "*deferment*" of each limb, of the heart and the other anatomical parts; each soldier being already unable to put his uniform on again, his heart feeding *telephonically*, a deferred arm, etc.

Then, no more feeding; each "*deferee*" isolating himself. Finally a Regulation of regrets from one "*deferee*" to another. (Marcel Duchamp)[13]

If the power that increasingly dominates modern global life is, as we have stated, the capacity to divide, especially, the aesthetic from the technological, then the military operates as a hinge linking divided regions. The military itself, of course, is manifestly capable of enforcing and making the many divisions essential to the modern milieu, in addition to its functioning as a hinge. The hinge provides the techne – without giving itself up *as* a techne – through which divisions are made. Consequently, such divisions would never be entirely accomplished. The logic of the hinge nonetheless allows this simultaneous linking and de-linking to occur, and thus allows the military as the crucial hinge between *praxis* and *poiesis* – now recast as operations and intelligence – to prosper in its ascendance. The hinge would therefore be the most basic component of the military body itself as well as its primary mode of operation.

When John Arquilla and David Ronfeldt, analysts at the National Defense Institute of the RAND Corporation, discuss "cyberwar" in their influential book *Networks and Netwars*, they do so *as if* the innovations of ICT and the network reveal a fundamental, futural shift in military planning and operations (despite the military's role in the development of these technologies). They describe the necessity of networks to "dissever and redisperse" when attacked in any manner, and to then "immediately recombine".[14] Late in their book, Arquilla and Ronfeldt ask "What holds a network together? What makes it function effectively?" (*Networks*, 323). The organisational answer to these questions about the mutability of a network and its infinite protean capacity resides in "the narratives or stories people tell". They conclude that it is "a 'story' expressing the netwar, and the doctrine guiding its strategy and techniques" that allows networks to function (*Networks*, 327). While fully agreeing with the explanatory power of narratives to organise and reveal links between events and ideas, we would argue that narrative is but another manifestation of the actual capacity that allows networks and the military body to function: the hinge, the *tache*. Narratives operate by linking together disparate elements, creating an effect of causality and sequence. The technics of narrative are those of the military body and the network insofar as the hinge allows narrative the power to connect events, spaces, and people in specific ways while disconnecting them in other strategic ways. The hinge at the material and immaterial levels, as a technology and technicity, provides the military body with all of its various capacities to sever, divide, recombine, attach, detach, and appropriate.

Marcel Duchamp's *Network of Stoppages* (*Réseaux des stoppages étalon*, 1914) superimposes four separate works: a version of *Young Man and Girl in Spring* (1911), a perspective study for *The Large Glass* (1913), a plan view drawing of *The Large Glass* (1913) and painted over these backgrounds three sets of the *Standard Stoppages* (*3 Stoppages étalon*) from 1913, also to be included in the *Large Glass* as its nine capillary tubes. *Network* thus experiments with the possibilities of attachment, detachment and delay that operate in a network through its illimitable combination of hinges. The work looks simultaneously back in time and forward, performing a kind of temporal hinging, and it experiments too with ideas of rotation, stitching and superimposition – spatial hinges. The hinge idea is provided literally by the *stoppages*, a French tailoring term for invisible repair, which operate together to revise inconclusively the metrical standard of measurement. A note by Duchamp from *The Box of 1914* describes the idea behind the *stoppages*: "If a straight horizontal thread one meter long falls from a height of one meter onto a horizontal

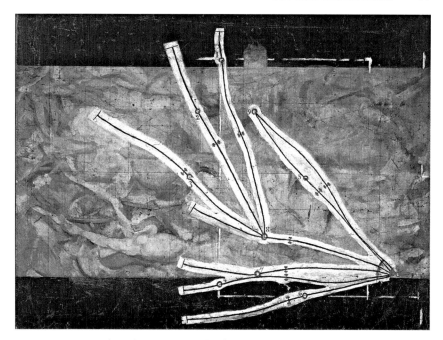

Figure 1.5   Marcel Duchamp, *Network of Stoppages* (1914). Permission by Adagp, © Succession Marcel Duchamp/ADAGP, Paris, 2010; image provided by Scala 50 Group © Photo SCALA, Florence; The Museum of Modern Art 2010

plane distorting itself as it pleases and creates a new shape of the measure of length" (Duchamp, *Writings*, 22). The relation between chance and will (the stoppage is described in terms of the thread falling "as it pleases"), which will be repeated throughout the works of this period, evokes the very idea of the hinge. In *Network* the painted threads connect three background images apparently unrelated to one another in any but the loosest fashion. Moreover, the layered images are connected by further invisible hinges, for two images beneath the *stoppages* (*Man and Girl* and *Perspective Drawing*) must be rotated ninety degrees, each in the opposite direction, to become properly visible. Integrating the layered images through the matrix of the *stoppages* or threads embedded in the painting, Duchamp illustrates, on the eve of World War I, both the material and immaterial powers of the hinge. The *stoppages* physically connect the superimposed images while evoking the idea of the hinge – or the *tache*, the bit – as simultaneous connection and disconnection. Looking like an aerial view of a network of roads or an anticipation of internet linkages and nodes, spectators glimpse vaguely sketched human bodies (the young man and girl reaching across the bush symbolising the passage from virgin to bride) beneath the linking strings. They have to look a bit harder to see the half-scale layout sketch for the *Large Glass*, also turned on its side.

The diffused bodies and the sketch are repaired, or (re)woven into each

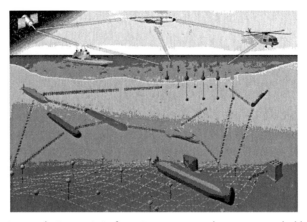

Figure 1.6   Network Centric Warfare. Permission and image provided by Jordan Crandall

other, as are the three layers of images through the clearly articulated linking power of network. The painting strings together a narrative of attachment that would perhaps threaten to be undone by the removal of the *stoppages*, were it not for the fact that each of the superimposed works, in only slightly different ways, tells the same tale of prosthetic attachment and detachment – mensurative and de-mensurated coordinates. Retrospectively, too, we can observe that the *Large Glass* will be *all* hinges, a neurotic repetition of hinge logic evoking an interminable cycle of failed connections.[15] Three dimensions (the area of the bride, the area of the bachelors, and the horizon that divides them) each operate according to internal and external connecting hinges, themselves each divided in threes or multiples of three (the bride's three windows, the nine malic moulds of the bachelors and their capillary tubes, the nine missed opportunities, or missed targets, represented by holes drilled by the bride's three "draft pistons", and so on). If one removed the hinges, joints and frames of the *Large Glass*, there would be nothing left.

Targets: Skopos and Episcopalism

A Flower, for example a tulip, is held to be beautiful because, in perceiving it, one encounters a finality which, judged as we judge it, does not relate to any end. (Immanuel Kant)[16]

I have a horror of people who speak about the beautiful. What is the beautiful? One must speak of problems in painting! Paintings are but research and experiment. I never do a painting as a work of art. All of them are researches. (Pablo Picasso)[17]

"Targeting recommends the best means to attain a goal", the USAF Intelligence Targeting Guide states, "it integrates intelligence information about the threat, the target system, and target characteristics with operations data on friendly force posture, capabilities, weapons effects, objectives, rules of engagement, and doctrine".[18]

At first sight nothing would seem more at odds with the impulse to aesthetics than military targeting. Kant and Picasso demonstrate two kinds of aesthetic resistance towards ends: on one side, Kant's attempt to establish the pure principle of beauty on moral grounds, with the notion of *Zweckmässigkeit ohne Zweck*, a finality without end, or the sense of having a view to an end without end, *without* an end in view – detached absolutely from an/the end; on the other, Picasso's restless experimentation with the forms, subjects and media of work – detached absolutely from its end. In each case the aesthetics must at all costs avoid having an end, an aim, in view. Targeting, on the other hand, would be all about putting an end into view. It would be a matter of combining two quite different notions of target, one belonging to an *operations community*, the other to an *intelligence community*:

> The operations community defines a target as: "a geographic area, complex, or installation planned for capture or destruction by military forces." The intelligence community definition is "a country, area, installation, agency, or person against which intelligence operations are directed." For targeting purposes, this definition must be expanded to include the contents of the area, complex, or installation (e. g., people, equipment, and, resources). Furthermore, capture or destruction must be expanded to include disruption, degradation, neutralization, and exploitation, commensurate with objectives and guidance. (USAF 8)

The two different definitions of target, which combine to provide the field of *targeting*, help to distinguish, yet also to blur the distinction between, *operators* and *targeteers*.[19] Intelligence provides mensurated coordinates for the operational capture or destruction of a geographical area.

However, between this pure *without-an-end* of the aesthetic ideology (which has as its end the pure *without* of ends per se) and targeting (which blurs the distinction between the mensurative intelligence and the operational attack in order to provide *only* ends) there lies a further deep complicity. Jacques Derrida's commentary on the *Third Critique*, which shows how deconstruction inevitably applies at the level of the *pivot*, the *without* or the *sans* of the pure cut,[20] borrows some terminology from artillery to help explicate Kant's logic:

> The feeling of beauty, attraction without anything attracting, fascination without desire have to do with this "experience": of an oriented, finalized movement, harmoniously organized in *view* of an end which is never *in view*, seen, an end which is missing, or a *but en blanc*. I divert this expression from the code of artillery: firing a *but en blanc* is to fire at a target [*blanc*] placed at such a distance that the bullet (or the shell) drops to intersect the prolongation of the line of sight. *But* refers here to the origin from which one fires *de but en blanc*: the gun barrel as origin of the drive. There must be finality, oriented movement, without which there would be

no beauty, but the orient (the end which originates) must be lacking. (Derrida, *The Truth in Painting*, 87).

Derrida's reading focuses on the hinge, *without*, in the phrase, *finality without end*, which allows the detachment of end from end in the pure work, and which falls outside, yet compromises this falling out, of the determinations of science, technology, anthropology and knowledge in general.[21] Kant's transcendental determination of pure art (or the determination of pure art *as* transcendental) relies upon an irreducible – yet not transcendental – hinge that connects the merely useful to the pure disinterested beautiful: connecting non-knowledge to knowledge and infecting it in principle at its, in this way, divided source. Derrida's commentary finds Kant's determination in the service of his morality, which, in the same way, is therefore also compromised. The compromise, nonetheless, remains powerful: the possibility of beauty resides strictly in its impossibility; the possibility of a just action resides strictly in its impossibility. He does not, of course, develop the reference to the code of artillery, but, via the hinge of an inevitable chiasmus, a complex of great difficulties can be engaged.

The French *but en blanc* evokes something close to the very essence of targeting (the targeting process comprising the full range of possible connections between targeting, targeteering, operations and targets) which involves a determination rendering a target that is never *in view* but nonetheless available for measured and calculated attack. Targeting brings targets into view, certainly, but the precondition would always be this relation of intelligence to targeting in *potentia*: call it the ideal beauty of targeting, severed absolutely from its end, so that it might have an end. The ultimate target would be entirely *without* the visible field. The two definitions of target must in this sense be maintained: the calculation – necessarily disconnected from anything that would actually *yet* be a target – must be able to range as widely as possible; and the operation – intrinsically unrelated to anything *but* the target – must be focused exclusively on the attack, the execution. Benign disinterest on one side can be merged with military operations on the other to produce interested, end-driven goals.

This double notion of the target can be regarded as a reduction of an older distinction that resides at the heart of the target concept and bears today, in this sediment form, the vestiges of an apparently archaic anxiety concerning the welfare of community in the face of what threatens it. The ancient concept *skopos* (from the ancient Greek, target) implies two functions: the scopic and episcopal, each of which serves in different yet inextricable ways to protect and threaten civic spaces. In its earliest manifestation, the *skopos* was a watchman, someone stationed on the *skopia* (the high ground) as a lookout. The *skopos*, first of all, is one who watches out for and looks after a community as its guardian, and in this role is a kind of *epi-scopus* or overseer. The term *episcopy* was then metonymically extended to include a range of civic duties crucial to the administration of early urban communities.

Later *skopos* became the name for that which seeks out and marks the object of some game, quest or contest/battle. The *skopos* hides out and marks the game. In a military idiom s/he is a spy or scout and, now increasingly so, a machine that acts as intelligence gatherer and surveyor of the battlefield. At the same time, the *skopos* is also the object on which one fixes one's eye, the mark itself, the target. In these senses, then, the scopic can both mark and target, as well as merge into the episcopal functions of governance and the military, an overseeing of the nation and its interests.

Targeting in its various different senses could not therefore be conceptually opposed to several functions that can be regarded as episcopal. These functions combine to characterise the basically benevolent caretaking and management of states and urban infrastructures: repair and maintenance, planning and building, policing, schooling, advising, protecting, the institutions of welfare, health (physical and emotional), insurance, social services of all kinds, churches, cemeteries, the media, distribution of goods and services, and so on. These episcopal functions imply specific kinds of targeting, and they also are designed to protect against more or less malevolent targeting of the cities. As such, these episcopal functions manifest the power to divide certain activities within the urban or nation-state domains into categories deemed benevolent or dangerous, generative or destructive. In this manner, the episcopal can mark through scopic technics those events, situations, conditions and people deemed threatening to the community and take action upon them: repair, removal, destruction, or diaspora.

Far from cancelling each other out, the determinate separation of the two dimensions of targeting (as manifested in the spear and the shield, the battlement and the cannon) intensifies and escalates the active levels of both the scopic technologies (ways of aiming and striking) and the episcopal ones. An example from Homer, in which the word for veil and battlement are the same (GK: Kredemnon), illustrates how both were always supposed to have functioned in the same way: as a type of defence that also attracts the very thing it is intended to defend against. The history of targeting (for example, ballistics and propulsion) is thus intrinsically connected with the rise and growth of urbanism as well as nation-states. The division between the two dimensions would be historical and very far from complete, implicating the military in the civic at all levels. And it would include the capacity to demarcate the military from the civic, as well as the capacity to erase and redraw that demarcation, as the situation demands.

By analysing the technological functionality of targeting, which includes a series of acts of indeterminate length but which at the very least divides intelligence, operation and target – for example, the marker from the striker and the striker from the mark as well as the mark itself into friend and foe or intended and accidental – targeting thus implies at its very basis the division between, and partial merging of, the scopic and the episcopal functions, which depend not only upon each other (in the familiar dialectic) but more crucially on the maintenance of the division. The maintenance of this division, as well as its occasional erasure or redrawing, embodies a kind of hinge logic. Thus enters the military body into the technologies of governance. Through the operation of the logic of the *tache*, the military and/or the nation-state through the military can attach to or detach itself from a host of technologies and technicities that provide each with scopic capacities and episcopal functions.

The separation of scopic and episcopal services lies at the heart of the increasing urbanisation of human society. The technologies and modes of social life addressed in various ways by modernist aesthetics, sometimes comically, often absurdly, but in some instances with unrestrained enthusiasm, are those of the processes of urbanisation in its escalating repetition. The scholarship on what has been labelled "modernity" is replete with paeans to the role of the city in its history and historicity. The city, always ambivalent, is regarded as a repository for individual freedom and alienation, of human progress and devolutionary mechanisation, of futural promise and rural ruin, of utopia and dystopia. The earliest glimpses of airpower prior to World War I and then deployed in that war reveal the shifting interest of military strategists away from the front and the trenches in rural areas to a more explicit targeting of cities through the technologies that help further produce urban space and existence.[22] If the two dimensions, scopic and episcopal, were now to merge completely, it would look quite serious: the total destruction that some people fear or the pastoral utopia that some people wish for. But the two do not cancel each other out. They – and their separation – are structurally necessary for one another.

Returning to our World War I Keystone card, "She Sees Her Son in France", we see an array of scopic and episcopal functions in operation, tracing the division via the hinge without which techno-science and the military body would not be what they are. Though her son is in the sights of a German *skopos* at the front in France, the episcopal function of the nation, aided and abetted by tele-technologies operating in both the civic and military spheres (the optics of sighting and stereoscopy), the maternal citizen can "see" in 3D that her son is fine. He might be standing next to a cannon and indeed be targeted by the enemy's cannons, but he is not cannon fodder. No fusillade assails him in the slowed down, frozen frame of the image, which produces the fiction of a re-assurance: the power of nation-state's techno-science to slow down the enemy's techno-science and thus protect its citizenry in their capacity as soldier. Though time and space may separate mother from son, tele-technologies can be deployed to overcome the division.

Notes

1. This image appear courtesy of Bob Boyd, from his private collection. Erkki Huhtamo discusses it in his study of virtual reality in "Media Art in the Third

Dimension: Stereoscopic Imaging and Contemporary Art" in Jeffery Shaw and Peter Weibel (eds) *Future Cinema* (Cambridge, MA: MIT Press 2003) pp. 466–473.

2. For an extended discussion of stereoscopes, see Jonathan Crary, *Techniques of the Observer* (Cambridge, MA: MIT Press, 1992).

3. John Gange, 'A Technics of Slow Motion', in John Gange (ed.), *Art, Technology, Technique* (London Pluto, 1998) pp. 147–9.

4. Aristotle, *Nicomachean Ethics*, Book 6, trans. H. Rackham (Cambridge: Harvard University Press, 1926) pp. 324–73.

5. Virilio, *Virilio Live: Selected Interviews*, ed. John Armitage (London: Sage, 2001) p. 92.

6. *The Thinking Eye: The Notebooks of Paul Klee*, ed. Jürg Spiller, trans. Ralph Manheim (London: Lund, 1961) p. 15.

7. For a survey of scholarship on *Demoiselles*, see Christopher Green (ed.), *Picasso's Demoiselles d'Avignon* (Cambridge: Cambridge University Press, 2001).

8. Rosalind Krauss, *The Picasso Papers* (Cambridge, MA: MIT, 1999) p. 271.

9. David Joselit, *Infinite Regress: Marcel Duchamp 1910–1941* (Cambridge, MA: MIT, 2001) p. 45.

10. Carsten-Peter Warncke, *Picasso* (London: Taschen, 2003) p. 64.

11. Warncke charts this period in Picasso's oeuvre as "Classicism and Surrealism" and establishes with exemplary clarity Picasso's development of technical means that in no way ever abandon the techniques of the so-called cubist era: there is rather an expansion of artistic techniques of production that directly engages contemporary technologies.

12. Picasso's apparent return to the order of a supposed neo-classicism has provoked, it seems, more controversy, and more wild psycho-biographical speculation, even than his cubist experiments. Even the most neutral commentators – the Musée Picasso, for instance – have to ask, in the light of paintings that exhibit conventionally detailed figuration, "could it be that the bold inventor of cubism had quieted down?" (Hélène Seckel, Musée Picasso Catalogue (Paris: Réunion des Musées Nationaux, 1996) p. 56). Yet photographic images that might plausibly have been the main source for these paintings have survived, suggesting not only particular sources but also a general idea – in the specifics of the photographic image – for the stylistic peculiarity of these undoubtedly odd works.

13. Marcel Duchamp, *Salt Seller: The Writings of Marcel Duchamp*, ed. Michel Sanouillet and Elmer Peterson (Oxford: Oxford University Press, 1973) p. 22.

14. John Arquilla and David Ronfeldt, *Networks and Netwars* (Santa Monica: RAND, 2001) p. 12. See also Samuel Weber's excellent discussion of Arquilla and Ronfeldt in "Targets of Opportunity: Networks, Netwar and Narratives". *Grey Room* 15 (2004) pp. 2–27.

15. Jean-François Lyotard's *Duchamp's Trans/Formers* treats the *Large Glass* systematically in terms of its hinge logic.

16. Immanuel Kant, *Critique of Judgement*, trans. Paul Guyer (Cambridge: Cambridge University Press, 2000) p. 179.

17. Interview with Lieberman, *Vogue*, 1 November, 1956.
18. http://www.fas.org/irp/doddir/usaf/afpam14-210/part01.htm#page7 (USAF).
19. "Targeteers provide the approved targets list, weaponeering, and target mate-rials, such as maps, charts, mensurated coordinates, and imagery. They assist operators in selecting mission routing, axis of attack, aimpoints, and fuze set-tings" (USAF 31).
20. Jacques Derrida, *The Truth in Painting*, trans. Geoff Bennington and Ian McLeod (London: Chicago, 1987). The *sans* ("without") retains the homophony with *sens* (sense as well as the senses) and manifests the inherent relation between sense and non-sense that the artwork reproduces.
21. The deconstruction of the absent end in the *quasi*-transcendental *without* impli-cates Kant's aesthetics not only in the series of divisions, cuts, differences named by Derrida, *trace*, *différance*, *hymen*, *brisure*, and so on, but it also aligns it with the irreducible divisions of modernist aesthetics that we explore in what follows.
22. See Ryan Bishop and Gregory Clancey "The City as Target, or Perpetuation and Death" in Bishop, Phillips and Yeo (eds), *Postcolonial Urbanism* (New York: Routledge, 2003) pp. 63–86.

Chapter 2

Sighted Weapons and Modernist Opacity: Aesthetics, Poetics, Prosthetics

Man has extended his means of perception and action much more than his means of representation and summation. (Paul Valery)[1]

If I had to sum up current thinking on precision missiles and saturation weaponry, I'd put it like this: once you can see the target, you can destroy it. (Former Under-Secretary of Defense, W. J. Perry)[2]

Who are you going to believe, me or your own eyes? (Chico Marx in *Duck Soup*)

The cockpit of the Apache helicopter, the US army's premier aerial fighting machine, reveals itself as a distillation of visual culture and visual prosthesis, for the pilot is encased in a virtual world and is allowed very limited use of his raw sensory organs. But while the electronically extended field of vision heightens and extends the illusion of agency, the pilot also becomes more instrumental and less responsible for decisions and actions. The emergence of the military machine, as Paul Virilio claims, was complemented by and synchronous with a watching (or seeing) machine.[3] The two machines conflate in the Apache cockpit, which resembles a flying camera obscura in several important ways. The resemblance between the cockpit and the darkroom of the camera obscura is not by chance nor is it only an analogy because the cockpit is only the most recent manifestation of the traditions of visual technology that link closely and inextricably the military, empirical science and the arts. What was of interest to early modern philosophers and scientists, in the camera obscura, for instance, remains in play in the most current versions of visual technology.

The Apache cockpit is a box that almost completely seals off all the senses but the visual, allowing a delimited but kinetic window on the world that appears simultaneous to the moment of perception. The interest and desire to understand how the eye perceives movement, which so enthralled early modern experimenters, leads to the development of instruments designed to close the gap between the perceiving subject and the visible world. While the medium of sensate vision is revealed as increasingly complex, technological visual media become more sophisticated, and the development of each

Figure 2.1   Apache Longbow Cockpit, AH-64D. Permission and image, copyright © Boeing

domain is overdetermined by the interactions between them. As intriguing as the links between the camera obscura and Apache cockpit are, the links are even more complex and intricate when one considers the relationships between visual technology and visual culture and aesthetics. It has become a common-place to relegate visual technology to the domain of the state/ private sector and visual aesthetics to the individual. But the moment at which this division becomes institutionalised, as well as some of the reasons why it occurs, reveals the two areas and enterprises as more interrelated than they might seem. The perverse underside of prosthetic technology's illusion of simultaneity, we argue, emerges in the way modernist aesthetics exploits the very gap that visual technology seeks to close. Modernism is thus revealed as the inverted image of modernity.

From World War I to the present, the story of military technology has been one of prosthetic extension, especially that of sight, with weapons becoming gifted with sensory perception and intelligence. This story is paralleled by the rise of visual mass media and their manipulation of the eye to create illusions of simultaneity, movement, and depth – a duplicity that resulted in the apparently increasing verisimilitude of the various media. Yet a third parallel appears with the concomitant increasing opacity found in modernist poetics. That is, all three stories tell the same paradoxical tale: the more we watch, the less we see.

Jonathan Crary identifies the move from the classical and Enlightenment understanding of the visual field to that posited by modernity as one that finds the *tabula rasa*, on which orderly representations of perception could be arranged, becoming a less reliable and simple mimetic phenomenon. He shows that modernity's visual field provided a surface of inscription capable of producing and incorporating a wide range of effects, including those that could lead to delusion and misunderstanding.[4] Crary's identification of post-Enlightenment trends concerning vision seems to us to be both accurate and insightful, though his understanding of the relations between modernity and Enlightenment seems questionable. Modernity in general, as a discursive ground of problems associated with, among other things, the secularisation of time consciousness, the intensification of questions of the empirical, and the proliferation of techniques, would thus include as one of its aspects the trends associated with Enlightenment. The shift from Enlightenment to post-Enlightenment might be better described in terms of the further intensification, a *surenchère*, of a general but increasingly technical drive for origins and originations. As Crary points out, the growing belief that vision involves a time lag of perception proves to be an essential aspect of this intensification. Unlike those sitting inside a camera obscura, the post-Enlightenment viewer can no longer believe that sight is instantaneous (Crary, *Techniques*, 96). The gap of apprehension provides both a challenge and an opportunity, a challenge to technology and an opportunity to those interested in aesthetics. As the history of visual technology manifests repeated attempts to increasingly narrow the gap, modernist aesthetics tries to highlight its unbridgeable nature.

The two fundamentally different approaches to the gap of perception began to define the division of the visual field in terms of the public and private realms. As a result, the "in-time" model of camera obscura observation became the lost origin that visual prosthetic technology, especially military applications of said technology, attempted to restore with "real-time" models. In some very profound ways, "real-time" technologies attempt to restore an Enlightenment viewing act to the viewing subject by collapsing distance and time. The "problem" posed by the gap of perception is solved by a return to a mythologised time of unproblematic perception, but this moment and condition are only regained through hyperactive optoelectronic prostheses.

The classical camera obscura provided a chamber within which "an orderly projection of the world, of extended substance, [was] made available for inspection by the mind" (Crary, *Techniques*, 46). Movement within the image added to the observer's sense of simultaneity and verity; in fact, many observers cited movement as the single most impressive feature of the camera obscura's representation, causing some to claim the image as more lifelike than the original (Crary, *Techniques*, 34) – a situation which signals the projective and prosthetic elements of originary perception. Contained in the camera obscura's image, then, is a nexus of apparent binary oppositions central to visual culture and visual prosthesis in art, science and military technology: time and space, vision and blindness, light and darkness, objects and processes, illusion and reality, space and movement, *kinesis* and *mimesis*. Despite the image's kinetic attributes, the camera obscura allowed the movement of matter to be contained enough to become the subject of contemplation. With long-range, visually prosthetic weaponry, a similar containment occurs, but with an altogether different goal. Rather than contemplation, manipulation and obliteration become the effects of both containment and observation. With such weaponry, to see the target is to destroy the target.

The relationship between the camera obscura, related visual manipulations and battlefield scoping for increasingly long-range weapons was understood early on. Cartographers had used it for civic and military planning but the military also found it useful for ordinance coordination in the seventeenth century. Later, in the early days of aviation, a camera obscura was erected at Langley Air Base to track the flight trajectories of two planes and analyse them for vehicle manoeurability.[5] Generating a stream of photographic images much like those created by Etienne-Jules Marey to document birds in flight, the US military published single-sheet images of tailspins, nose-dives and other abnormal flight trajectories to better analyse the planes it wished to use in battle. As with the slow-motion take-off, to understand the technology's speed, they had to slow it down. In this case, the breaking of motion into a series of static shots in relation to one another was achieved through the appropriation of camera obscura technology and photography.

But the way in which the camera obscura reappears in a military machine explicitly for targeting purposes is articulated by H. G. Wells in his 1903 tale about armoured land vehicles (that is, tanks) with a description of sighting and firing mechanisms uncannily like those found in the Apache. The gunners in the tanks "had the most remarkable sights imaginable, sights which threw a bright little camera-obscura picture into the light-tight box in which the rifleman sat", Wells writes. Anticipating too the conflation between scoping and targeting, further reducing gap of perception as well as visual data into action, Wells states that "this camera-obscura picture was marked with two crossed lines, and whatever was covered by the intersection of these two lines, that the rifle hit".[6] The precursor to the tank that Wells describes is not extraordinary for its prognosticative dimensions but rather for its historically conditioned ones. Wells was merely putting into practice in his short story the various trajectories of visual culture, visual technology and military technology that had coalesced with such frightening efficiency in the US civil war, and that had been intensified in the intervening decades as Europe hurtled toward World War I.

The desire to make target perception and target striking virtually the same act, as described by Wells, was essential to targeting systems throughout the twentieth century and remains firmly in play with current military technology. If one consults the plethora of official military-sponsored websites – sites that serve the dual purpose of information dissemination and high-tech showcase – one learns that essential to these results and to fulfilling "real-time" goals in the most recent Apache attack helicopter, the AH-64D, is its state-of-the-art MANPRINT (manpower and integration) cockpit. Much of this intricate integration encases the pilot's head. The IHADSS (integrated helmet and display sight system) manufactured by Honeywell provides the pilot with "a 40 [degree] by 30 [degree] field of view in a monocular video-with-symbology viewing system", according to one US Army website.[7] The key system of MANPRINT is the "Target-Acquisition Designation Sight and Pilot Night Vision Sensor" (TADS-PNVS), which, the words of a US military educational website, is "composed of a thermal imaging sight [that] is tied to the movement of the pilot's helmet".[8] According to this US military description, "the pilot receives all pertinent flight and target data through an eyepiece that is placed below the eye".

But the eye does more than merely receive information about targets with this system. Both pilot and gunner are provided with "the IHADSS collimated helmet mounted CRT projectors, designed to deliver raster scan camera imagery and calligraphic flight, weapon aiming and systems symbology *directly into the right eye*".[9] Much military technology, in its relentless pursuit of speed from World War II on, seeks to minimise human error in any given weapons system, often taking "the human element" out of the loop altogether. In the case of aircraft, humans remain an unavoidable part of the system, for the moment anyway. To avoid awkward or slow hand movements in attack situations, then, pilots and gunners can now use voice or gaze, speech input or eye input, to command the devices at their disposal – "this, thanks to *an infra-red sensor that recognizes direction of gaze by scanning the back of the pilot's retina*".[10] The IHADSS allows the crew to control "the sensors simply by looking at the point of interest, and the sensors can return information to their eyes".[11] The MANPRINT scheme brings the eye much closer to its military goal within the tradition of visual technology, a goal in which the outfitted organ receives and gives, aims and fires, reads and destroys, is passive and active. Visual prosthesis becomes more visually hands on by being tactilely hands off. The moment of perception approaches the moment of destruction, making the gap between apprehension and obliteration that much smaller. The distance between the visible text and the perceived object collapses in the blink of an eye *to* the blink of an eye, as does the erasure of the perceived object.

Head down in the Head Down Display (HDD), as the name indicates things should be, the gunner in the Apache attack helicopter uses "a monocle display unit surrounded by a rubber coaming [sic] which surrounds [his] eyes when his head is down in the unit. It is this section which gives the ORT (Optical Relay Tube) its periscope like appearance. With the gunner's head down in the display, video is placed before the right eye by means of a lens" (Aviation Encyclopedia). But, being biocular creatures, and having much of the verity of nineteenth-century pre-cinematic innovation manipulate this biocular field, we can safely say this is only half the story. The gunner's left eye is, in fact, "not in use", and the area it occupies is "sealed with a plastic cover" (Aviation Encyclopedia). The fate of the gunner's visual field in the HDD is a manifestation of the division of the visual domain since the turn of the century: one eye is prosthetically outfitted and extended far beyond its biological capacity; the other is sealed shut. The right eye is attached to the public domain; the left is abandoned to private darkness. The right is forced open to its technological prowess and control; the left is blinded.

Although the ORT may look like a periscope, the gunner bends into the eyepiece just as a viewer of early moving-picture exhibits did, as well as other visual consumerist gadgetry such as the *Kaiserpanorama* set up in Berlin in the 1880s by August Fuhrmann. The Berlin spectators sat in front of a lens similar to that found in the Apache cockpit and watched a regularly changing array of stereoscopic images intended to provide an illusion of depth. Though in and of themselves static, the images in the *Kaiserpanorama* moved in so far as they rotated along an axis allowing a change of scene every two minutes. The regulated movement of the images extended even further the industrialisation and commodification of movement, body position, sensory input and vision itself – each mechanically controlled for and by the regulation of time and payment.[12] The Apache gunner has somewhat more autonomy with regard to the visual field while also possessing more capacity to engage the image, in this case engage and destroy the image. To these ends, the HDD has a small screen that repeats the image/potential target, allowing the gunner to lose immediate visual contact with the screen display without losing the potential target-as-target. Similarly the right and left handgrips provide the gunner with the ability to change the image, the sensors deployed, tracking controls and weapon/laser triggers.

But what about the image? Does the image still exist? "*Can we still talk of images when there are no longer any pixels, the laser beam directly stimulating the retinal rods and cones of the eye?*"[13] Optoelectronic war, in fact, has eliminated the image. By reaching further than one could see unaided, one reduces the effect of eye-object time distancing. And by seeing further and quicker, by obliterating space and time, this technology has succeeded in destroying the very thing it hoped to magnify and control: the image. In an odd paradoxical twist, optoelectronics has achieved the opacity that modernist aesthetics so consistently pursued. The movement found in what-was-the image has resulted in blindness. The end of the image restores the opacity of distance; the clarity of vision uniformly pursued by the visual aesthetics of the military and the state has now resulted in an image-that-is-no-longer-an-image. This is why even the retinal rods of the pilot will no longer be trusted in future warfare. Currently the US military is attempting to procure what it claims publicly will be its "last manned fighter plane". Only computers and other machines will be able to read the non-image image of future warfare. Its targets, however, will not have this unmanned advantage.

But the MANPRINT leaves imprints elsewhere than on the retinal rods of pilots and gunners, or on the terrain of enemy territory, or the bodies of enemy soldiers. MANPRINT leaves an imprint on a poetic genre fundamental to understanding human mortality astride the earth and enmeshed in the diurnal cycle. In an almost negative version of the filmic technique known as "day for night", made famous by Truffaut's film with the same eponymous phrase, "the Pilot Night Vision System (PNVS) . . . turns night into day for the pilot" (Aviation Encyclopedia). The PNVS toggle switch creates an instant dawn song, heralding a new day of technological perception, which now means destruction. The new day is a day of destruction, a day that destroys as it comes into being, a day that turns back immediately into primal night by turning automatically from night into day.

The White Dawn of Modernity

It is possible to conceive of modernity, especially in its aspect as Enlightenment, as the repetition of false or phantom dawns. The phantom dawn constructs, literally builds through rhetoric, a new start that masquerades as a return to an origin in pure perception. In this case the PNVS can be regarded as a kind of fulfilment of modernity's quest for the immediate, a vast forgetting of the mediated processes that we sometimes experience as the build-up to awareness. Awareness, in this sense, can only be the consequence of an elaborate construction. G. W. F. Hegel gives a famous and graphic account of the western philosophical dawn. In a section of the preface to *The Phenomenology of Spirit*, entitled "Present Position of the Spirit", he sets out what he calls the current state of thought in its dialectical progress. Empiricism, it seems, was a necessary phase to get the eye to stop rising from the world in search of the clear glory of divine essence. The eye needed to be brought back down to earth before it could take off again with renewed clarity. But now, he explains, the spirit has rooted itself too deeply in experience. The uprooting of sense from the world will be gradual, he now tells us, but old, established patterns of thought will not appear changed until the transition – the "new birth" – has been achieved:

> This gradual crumbling, which did not alter the physiognomy of the whole is interrupted by the break of day that, like lightning, all at once reveals the edifice of the new world.[14]

It should be possible to see that the implication of rational historical progress that one can always read in Hegel can be grasped instead, just as easily, as a pattern of repetition, a repetition of the rhetoric of the dawn song – with all its conceits, the new birth, the new day, the new fashion out of old materials, and so on, and, hopefully, the moment of sunburst glory replacing anxious foreboding. The *Phenomenology* is Hegel's glorious dawn song and marks one aspect of modernity as something like the incessant repetition of phantom dawns.[15]

Hegel's mixed metaphors identify the roving eye of spirit with the passing of night into day – his eye might be like the sun as it rises and falls or like the waxing and waning moon. They suggest that the force needed to direct this eye first downwards and then back upwards can be regarded as if it was a work of cunning construction, the building going on all the time unnoticed until the moment of its glorious unveiling like an *aubade*, a song at dawn, a great morning erection. The building is the work of the night, the work of dreams and the work of anxious memory and mourning, while the dawn heralds a great awakening, an enlightenment and forgetting. This is the message of the last great modern dawn song before World War II – Book IV of James Joyce's *Finnegans Wake*. The call to all Finnegans becomes in book IV an explicit address not simply to dawn but to all dawns. An earlier, shorter version reads, "Calling all dawns. Calling all dawns to day", while the final published version melts dawn into down and day into dayne in the now classic: "Calling all downs. Calling all downs to dayne. Array! Surrection."[16] This is one example of many that show how Joyce was concerned, throughout the writing and re-writing of this text, with obfuscation, the entropic, metamorphosing process destroying its own traces in an explicit and increasing building-in of obscurity; he called the procedure "darkling". This section, furthermore, builds in an aesthetic reversal of its "topic", the arrival of the dawn. The whole paragraph is dotted with dawns – an aube, an alba, an aubade and the "sonne" rising as an erection – not so much a dawn song as a dawn chorale. As the light of the sun becomes evident – if not exactly visible – through the diaphanous stained glass windows of the village church, the figures in the window get into animated debate. One of the effects achieved here is the melting of light into sound, the opacity or invisibility of Joyce's night discourse – dawn comes but it does not get any brighter.

Three Kings: "Seeing Action"

The dawn song of *Finnegans Wake* represents the extreme form of a modernist trend that establishes a tradition going at least as far back as Chaucer, in the English tradition, and further, to the troubadours of the tenth century and to the dawn of the Romance languages. The song at dawn, or *alba*, incorporates certain highly charged transactions between sight and sound and between darkness and light. At its most orthodox the alba dramatises the regret felt by two lovers as the day comes so soon to separate them. The alba's potential was rediscovered in twentieth-century literary circles by, among others, Ezra Pound, who in 1905 translated the "Belangal Alba", and who returns to it in the first chapter of his first book of criticism, *The Spirit of Romance*, from 1910.[17] Here he identifies it with the beginning of Romance literature. But Romance literature, he argues, does not simply begin. Rather, a dawn – its ghostly entrance – can already be read in the Latin of sixth-century writers long before the romance tongues had developed much beyond the various corrupt ways of speaking the Latin of Romans. This phantom dawn, as he calls it, expresses "a foreboding of the spirit" that will become characteristic of the literature of the Middle Ages. As Pound is cheerfully aware, this dawn before dawn – an apparition as if from the future of a beginning that has not yet begun – rather suspiciously mirrors the concerns of the dawn song itself. At about this time Pound gave William Carlos Williams a volume of Spanish ballads, which Williams translated twice, in 1913 and again in 1936.[18] Williams would later, in *Desert Music*, return to the dawn song tradition to evoke a profound sense of foreboding towards the future, evoking a sun that must not at any cost be allowed to rise and looking forward in horror to the nuclear dawn and its light of 1,000 suns.[19]

But it is W. B. Yeats who makes possible a grand act of memory regarding the tradition – especially in the English idioms. When he published *The Winding Stair and Other Poems* in 1933, he included a poem in eleven parts, "A Woman Young and Old", which, he claims in the dedication, "was written before the publication of The Tower [1928] but left out for some reason I cannot recall".[20] If "A Woman Young and Old" properly belongs to the earlier collection, the poem itself, we quickly gather, echoes in at least some of its parts a canonical strain of English poetry, though his annotations clearly indicate an attitude to approaching day that increasingly characterises many modern writers into the 1930s and beyond. He writes, "I have symbolized a woman's love as the struggle of the darkness to keep the sun from rising from its earthly bed". Section VII, "Parting", is an admirable (and parodic) imitation of the alba. Yeats's version, which is as orthodox as one could wish, dramatises an elaborate rhetorical debate between lovers, the male recognising the first signs of dawn calling him from the bed to the world, the female setting up conceits in a futile if touching attempt to ward off the inevitability of parting and of day.

Paul Virilio echoes these sentiments in his epigraph to the 1997 *Open Sky*, "one day the day will come when the day will not come". One wonders, reading through this material, whether the day that Virilio projects into some unheard of future has already come about and modern existence occurs entirely within the rhetoric of the false dawn, warding off at all costs some actual dawn, some dawn that would end all dawns. It is with this sentiment in mind that we turn to contemporary cinema. David Russell's action film, *Three Kings*, engages both with the aesthetics of vision and blindness and with the Gulf War as an event that supposedly, in the hyperbole of Jean Baudrillard, did not happen.

Three Kings ostensibly addresses the Gulf War as it is most commonly analysed: as a media war. But it also, and more importantly, acts as a supplement to the television spectacle. This odd reversal of the one medium supplementing the other, in which cinema supplements television, performs its prosthetic function at the levels of content, ideology and theory. The fact that the film begins at the war's end signals its supplementary roles. We are told, therefore, that there is more to the Gulf War and its aftermath than meets CNN's eye.

Early in the film, the character Conrad Vig (Spike Jonze) complains that they are headed home without having seen any action, and the multiple ways in which one "sees action", or thinks one "sees action", becomes a *leitmotiv* of the film. Much as the French protagonist in Marguerite Duras' *Hiroshima Mon Amour* claims to have seen everything in Hiroshima while her Japanese companion tells her she has seen nothing, seeing and blindness, before and after war, dominate this film. Russell reminds us that although we believe we have seen everything of the war on telecommunications networks, our image needs supplementing. Upon hearing Vig's complaint that they "didn't get to see any action", Archie Gates (George Clooney) asks his gold-seeking partners: "Do you want to see action?" Vig replies, "Yes sir, I do. The only action we've seen is on CNN." Gates leaps from the parked jeep in the middle of the desert and shows them the sand-encrusted carrion of Iraqi soldiers buried alive by US tanks. But this is no revelation for his comrades in arms because they claim to have seen even this part of the war on CNN.

Just at this juncture, Gates, in full Virgil mode, reveals to his three Dantes exactly what happens when one "*sees* action". In this instance, he explains the effects of that most quotidian of the massive US armaments array: the humble bullet. CNN's broadcasts showed glowing streaks above Baghdad, Patriot missiles intercepting Iraqi rockets, laser-guided "smart bombs" flying through its video cross-hairs down a smoke stack, sighted US tanks wielding their sensory superiority over blind Iraqi tanks, pilot-less drones rounding up enemy soldiers – all of it with a profound lack of visible casualties. (Current military weaponry hides its human damage from the view of those inflicting the damage just as the telecommunications media elides specific elements from its coverage. Both traffic in absence and blindness.) The surface of the war appeared on the screen globally; the interior carnage of the war did not. *Three Kings* supplements the visual prosthesis that yields the aesthetics of television with that which yields the modernist aesthetics of blindness. *Three Kings* goes from the surface – the skin – through the cinematic cross-hairs to the hidden organs.

As Archie Gates explains the damage the one meagre bullet can inflict on the body, the cinema camera travels into the body with it. The skin disappears and we are below the epidermal level of television transmissions. "The worst thing about a gunshot wound, provided you survive the bullet," Gates details, "is a thing called sepsis." The camera reveals organs punctured by the penetrating bullet and bile seeping into the system. The camera, then, sees what those seeing action saw, and the cinema audience sees what it did not – indeed, could not – see as a television audience. The supplement unfolds the surface of the original, official narrative and prosthetically extends the corpus of the television narrative beyond its epidermal boundaries by going *inside* the narrative and the body. The action opens the body cinematically in exactly the same manner as military technology does, the camera becoming yet another "sighted" weapon. It reveals the casualties of military technology as the "causalties" they are, as the causal relationship between high-tech gear and high-yield kill. The video game war of massive yet unseen carnage becomes a cinematically visible individual death.

In this one brief gesture, Russell lifts the cathode rays from our eyes and lowers the IHADSS monitor to show what one mere bullet can do to one mere body. The scale moves from the macro technology of CNN/long-range weaponry to the micro technology of metal bullets hurling through space, most often evoked aurally rather than visually, thus creating a supplement of the miniature that throws the gargantuan into relief. Russell collapses the institutionalised visual aesthetics of the state and the military machine with that of the institutionalised visual aesthetics of the arts. *Three Kings* goes to great lengths to show us the very action long-distance weaponry hides from view. We see the weapons' effects not only from the furthest possible distance, as we always do, but also the closest possible distance by letting us view the insides that weapons violate. The camera reinstates the distance that the visual prosthesis of electromagnetic weapons eliminates. The film, as did modernist poetics, reinserts the gap closed by the state's institutionalised visual aesthetics.

As a result, the blinded youth flying sighted planes, shooting sighted weapons, killing sighted foes, finally see action. They see the action that the entire high-tech armaments complex would prefer they did not see (for a host of reasons). The blind youth in the audience learn that they have not seen it *all* on CNN, precisely because they have seen it *all* only on CNN. This is a prosthetic gesture Russell makes repeatedly, showing that the surface of the image is but the image of surface. The more action we see, the less we see action.

Black Light(e)ning

"What art is in reality is this missing link, not the links which exist. It's not what you see that is art, art is the gap." (Marcel Duchamp)[21]

Mina Loy has already examined the situation from a slightly different perspective in a poem from 1922, which first appeared in her *Lunar Baedeker* collection from that year. "Der Blinde Junge" dramatises an extraordinary transaction that occurs when the speaker comes across a blind war victim busking on a Vienna pavement.

> The dam Bellona
> littered
> her eyeless offspring
> Kriegsopfer
> upon the pavements of Vienna[22]

The first stanza leaves no doubt about what is at stake here – this is the result of war – but the personification of war and its victims in Bellona figured as a dam with a fresh litter already constitutes a quite complicated condensation. Bellona personified the force and the noise of battle for certain fanatical Roman cults, satirised by Juvenal, for instance, as clownishly subjecting themselves to horrific self-mutilations.[23] In the context of the poem, the Italian name "Bellona" chimes with the Austrian "Vienna", in one of the many sound effects of the poem, and contrasts with the German "*Kriegsopfer*," which echoes "offspring", reminding us that the essence of war is this difference – not just an abstract "war-in-general" but this Italian cult goddess personifying the energy and noise of battle and having German children. The pun on "litter" brings the Italian connection further into view with a less than oblique riposte to her ex-lover Marinetti's notorious 1909 glorification of war as "the sole hygiene of the world". It is also worth recalling what Marinetti had written at the start of the war, calling for a futurist expression of "the splendor of this conflagration . . . an expression so strong and synthetic that it will hit the eye and imagination of all intelligent readers".[24] Loy's poem has found a direct hit in this respect as the conflagration has literally hit the eye of the victim, rendering it "expressionless". And it is the idea that an eye – when it does work – is a vehicle for expression rather than a simple mechanical receptor of photons, as the post-Cartesian scientific world has always held, that is so suggestive here. What is remarkable about the poem is how the point of view of the speaker, the speaker's eye, becomes more and more focused on the single sightless eye of the victim. The poem draws attention to both these seers – the seeing and the unseeing – in a transaction that literally sparkles with darkness in an exchange between fundamentally incompatible elements as each of the drama's characters is reduced by synecdoche to an eye. The first stanza has already described the victim as eyeless, though the sense of this recalls Loy's earlier "Parturition", charting the experience of giving birth – a conceit that "Der Blinde Junge" maintains with admirable difficulty throughout. Three conceits that become interrelated in the later poem – those of birthing, the litter produced, and the blindness attendant in the process – can be found in the earlier poem, as the following lines observe:

> Impressions of a cat
> With blind kittens
> Among her legs (*Lunar*, 7)

The victim then is not so much eyeless as blinded, because the whole central section depends on the most condensed and opaque reflection upon his eye in order to achieve its surprising dawn at the end of the poem. But it is the sense of pushing against resistance – forces up against each other – that comes through most clearly. An eye, for which light is meaningless, gets involved by the light of day as an obstacle to light, producing several senses of the word "obstacle" at once.

Sparkling precipitate
the spectral day
involves
the visionless obstacle

At this stage the obstacle is at once the young war victim clotting up the arterial walkways of Vienna and his blind eye coming up meaninglessly, uselessly, against the sparkling day. The poem has so far succeeded in slowing down the reading process sufficiently to produce a powerful sense both of the struggle and the duration of the struggle, the gap between perception and its idea now properly unbridgeable. The next lines (four monosyllables followed by the verb) intensify the work of slowing things down:

this slow blind face
Pushing
its virginal nonentity
against the light (*Lunar*, 7)

The pushing is reminiscent also of her "Sketch of a Man on a Platform", supposedly Marinetti again, the genius of whose body (rather than mind):

Deals so exclusively with
The Vital
That it is equally happy expressing itself
Through the activity of pushing
THINGS
In the opposite direction
To that which they are lethargically willing to go
As in the amative language
Of the eyes (*Lunar*, 20)

The amative language of eyes comes up now against an unsurpassable hurdle – no communication occurs between an eye that looks and an eye that cannot see. But it is just at this point that a strange transaction begins to take shape – not so much face to face but eyeball to eyeball as the speaker, in what turns out to be a dialogue, attempts through description to make sense of this sight. The eye alone is in focus:

Pure purposeless eremite
of centripetal sentience

The language is marked less by the way it provides access to any simple sense or referent than by the sound effects it produces: 'eremite' sounds archaic in English and although it might once have been in common usage, by then the more common "hermit" would have done. This is a phrase you *hear* before any image comes to mind.[25] However, the sense is precise enough – this blind victim like his useless eye can be compared to a lonely recluse – the purity of its lack of purpose graces it with a kind of ironic sanctity. The next stanza provides more of the oddly undescriptive and archaic sounding English:

> Upon the carnose horologe of the ego
> the vibrant tendon index moves not
>
> since the black lightning desecrated
> the retinal altar (*Lunar*, 20)

Like the word "eremite" the obscure phrase "carnose horologe" would produce the same sense but more quickly for speakers of Italian, in which the phrase *carnoso orologo* simply means fleshy or muscular clock.[26] *Horologe* perhaps also, and most commentators point this out, echoes the French *horloge*, providing us with a reference to a whole range of mechanical time pieces, and to the Greeks, who came up with the term in the first place as a way of naming whatever instruments were available at the time for measuring the hours. A sundial would have been common, equating the measurement of time to light and to day as if blindness and the night were also hourlessness, temporality without division. The metaphoricity is powerful: the clock-face and the index-eye evoke an almost concrete condensation, like Umberto Boccioni's *Head + House + Light* and *Fusion of Head and Window*, which Angelo Bozzolla describes as "an extraordinarily inelegant attempt to fuse together elements of art and reality".[27] A real window crowns the sculptured head with its braided chignon of real hair.

An earlier poem by Loy, "Virgin Plus Curtains Minus Dots", has already played slightly mocking tribute to sculptures like these, echoing Boccioni's titles. And it is one of the many other occasions in Loy's writing where a transaction singularly *fails* to occur on the thematic level yet numerous transactions are being covertly made on an aesthetic one.

The Italian resonance provides the clearest indication for what may be a literal aspect of the highly condensed lines in "Der Blinde Junge". Boccioni's "Technical Manifesto of Futurism", from 1914, includes this statement:

> We cannot forget that the tick-tock and the moving hands of a clock, the in and out of a piston in a cylinder, the opening and closing of two cogwheels with the continual appearance and disappearance of their steel cogs, the fury of a flywheel or the turbine of a propeller, are all plastic or pictorial elements of which a futurist work in sculpture must take account. The opening and closing of a valve create a rhythm just as beautiful but infinitely newer than the blinking of an animal eyelid.[28]

Here the mechanical clock, in the spirit of the absolute value of newness, replaces the fleshy old eye. There is a peculiar literalness to Loy's language and while there is some satisfaction in the metaphoricity that allows us to see the eye as a kind of measurer of time passing, there is also a literal sense by which the eye simply *is* a gauge of time. Einstein was late on the scene in 1904 when, as part of his theory of relativity, he pointed out that time should be understood in terms of relative speeds, and that light is simply speed itself.[29] By the late nineteenth century, furthermore, the eye is known to be an extremely limited tool, hardly catching any of the light available, especially not the so-called black light that can be discovered off the visible parts of the spectrum. So when Loy writes, "black lightening" (with an *e*) we would guess that is exactly what she means.[30] Beyond the conventional oxymoron of black lightning – a sharp enough evocation of the effect of shrapnel from an explosive as it severs the connection between retina and optical nerve – Loy's original spelling, corrected in Conover's edition, allows the phrase to say much more than this (while saying that too, of course). The dawning of a light considered black opens the understanding to a field of vision that has nothing to do with the eye: rays that move outside the eye's spectrum – ultraviolet and infrared light waves – the electromagnetic waves that pass through telecommunications systems, through wired as well as wireless broadcasting, or X-rays, passing through solid objects like those Boccioni sculptures. The speed of light is time, so the eye is a particular if limited kinetic dial. The one we are focusing on here does not work.

The final section comes on a first reading like Hegel's daybreak. Having focused with increasing intensity on a single unseeing eye the speaker calls on another sense, this time one the victim also has the use of:

> Listen!
> illuminati of the coloured earth
> How this expressionless "thing"
> blows out damnation and concussive dark
>
> Upon a mouth-organ. (*Lunar*, 20)

Not only does the literal image (busking war victim) for the first time come into view opening our eyes to the scene of blindness, but also it comes into sound, opens our ears to the noise of the scene. The eye – blind as it is – expresses itself prosthetically. The condensation between the mouth of the blind and straining eye ("this planet of the soul/strains from the craving throat") and the actual mouth in which strains are expressed on the substitute organ, the mouth-*organ*, allows us to hear the blind eye's expression of its blindness. Thus the transaction between the speaker of the poem and the blind victim, which displaces sight onto hearing, is repeated in a doubled version of the same transaction but this time between the speaker and poem and between poem and addressee – the poem now speaking prosthetically for victims of the war, working as if it were an organ for readers to see what the blind have seen. And the breathing of the mouth organ manifests the dawning of a prosthetic expression both darker and more fundamental than anything either seen or heard. This is not, despite appearances, a simple displacement from sight to sound, the simple prosthetic supplement of a sound presentation substituting for an absent visual one. Rather the poem can be regarded as a singular example of Loy's poetics, in which she attempts to produce a peculiar mimesis – a writing that allows sound to evoke blindness

Figure 2.2   *The Blind Man* (New York, April 1917) Cover, with pieces by Loy with permission from Ryerson and Burnham Libraries, The Art Institute of Chicago

– a mimesis that draws attention to the possibility of mimesis in the otherwise unbridgeable gap between sensate phenomena.

The discovery that the visual range far exceeded that of the human eye resulted in the concept of "black light", an effective blinding in conceptualising the sensorium. But it also helped further the division in the visual field between the public and the private spheres. The black light beyond the biological organ, the seeing what we can not see, becomes the prerogative, as well as the *raison d'être*, of visual prosthetics propagated by state and industrial forces for combat and commerce. The limited visual field we can pick up with our flawed eye became the domain of the individual. And not even that was left to us, as the twentieth century became less the age of the image than the age of the optical effect.[31] The black light of the optical effect flickering in cinema houses, as well as from zoetropes, chronophotography, stereoscopes, anamorphic pictures, phenakistiscopes, kaleidoscopes, thaumatropes, praxinoscopes, photodromes, Pepper's ghosts and magic lanterns, was nineteenth-century prefiguration of the death of the image in the optical effect that marked a yearning and an anxiety in early twentieth-century avant-garde aesthetics and poetics. Showing the blindness as blindness emphasised the larger effects of the optical effect. At the same time, this gesture gave modernism a means of expression that revealed the threshold of what could not be expressed or represented. The science of optics, in essence, left the image in the dark, or in synesthetic terms it rendered the image mute.

If prosthetic technology produces an illusion of simultaneity, closing the gap between visible text and remote object, then some experimental poetics would seem to be increasing that gap. Such writing slows down the reading process, introducing an irreducible though unstable spatio-temporal dimension between text and referent. It also manifests a fascination with synesthetic qualities of verbal discourse, which can act like a threshold between sight and sound or, as Joyce has it, between the seeable and the hearable. It is possible to see in these diverse strategies attempts to make the threshold itself visible, with a concomitant loss in the visibility of the visible itself, as exemplified by the texts of Joyce and Loy. So while sections of Part IV of *Finnegans Wake* focus on the rising sun as it illuminates a stained-glass (and animated) triptych for observers inside the village church (or the cinema, "Obning shotly"), the language makes it difficult to avoid seeing that you cannot *see* through it. The layers of filtering and mediation operative in Joyce find resonance in the mimetic density of Loy's poem that renders the visible image all but invisible.

The parallel stories of either tightening or slackening the gap between visible text and remote object allow two mutually exclusive discourses of prosthetics to emerge as an integral aspect of the institutionalisation of aesthetics. On one hand, a prosthetics of origin is assumed according to which a text is subordinated as extension of, or refinement to, some extra-textual origin in perception. The ideal text in this case would be one that tightened up any slackness between origin and medium, thus reducing to the fullest extent any possibility of error or decision on the part of its interpreters. In this case the technology of prosthetics would improve on any presumed slackness of sensible perception (as Descartes puts it, "the weak foundation of the senses"). On the other hand, it is just this perceived slackness, or presumed weakness, that draws attention to the possibility, strongly suggested by modernist poetics, of a prosthetics *at* the origin, which disturbs not only the formal aspects of representation but also the relation between representation and the thing represented. Such a prosthetics appears not as an enhancement or addition to an original and deficient perception. Rather perception itself is regarded as originally prosthetic and thus excessive to any notion of immediate perception.

Prosthesis at the origin is, in fact, the topic of the 1924 Dudley Murphy and Fernand Léger experimental film *Ballet mécanique*, as well as the George Antheil composition of the same name. Murphy and Léger's examination of repetition partakes of the technological conditions that make the repetition possible. The famous opening shot of the woman on the swing repeatedly glancing upward toward the sky reveals the film's content and rhetoric. The repetition of daily life is extended to, projected onto, and intensified by various technological apparatuses, including the cinema camera. The motion of swinging toward and away from the camera, including reflections of the camera itself in a metallic pendulum, is repeated throughout the short film. The film's title suggests an erasure of the distinction between biological and technological, and this sequence fulfills that erasure. The remainder of the short film is essentially variations on this theme.[32]

Repeated images of fragmented portions of a female face, especially the eyes, but also the mouth, segment and isolate individual parts of the face from the remainder of the body. The very quick shots and quick cuts of the fragmented face that run throughout the film finally solidify in a relatively (for the film) long take of the actress's face whole, with the camera tracking around it in shocking solidity and integrity after its incessant and repeated dismantling. (The actress is Kiki, a famous Parisian model who appeared in a number of Man Ray photographs.) Immediately following this shot, we see an Uncle Sam puppet, swinging toward and away from the camera as the woman on the swing had done. The somatic "original" is juxtaposed with and made to repeat the prosthetic extension or mechanical replica throughout. Near the film's ending, Murphy and Léger have the disembodied legs of a mannequin perform, through stop-action photography common for clay and other forms of model animation, a dance. This particular mechanical ballet explicitly projects the relationship between prosthesis as simultaneously an extension of the organic *and* prosthesis at the origin, which runs throughout the examination of repetition in the film.

Antheil's score was intended to accompany the film but never was really used as such. Despite what seemed at the time to be little apparent overlap between the musical score and the film, in retrospect, the common ground is strikingly vivid. Both film and musical score work the doubled discourse of prosthetics that arrives back at the inescapable possibility of prosthetics at the origin with perception itself always having been an extension of the human. Continuing a particular strand of futurism in music, as pioneered by Luigi Russolo in 1913, Antheil's original score called for three xylophones, four bass drums, and a gong; two "live" pianists; seven electric bells, a siren, and three airplane propellors; and sixteen synchronised player pianos. The orchestration explicitly blends traditional acoustic instruments with those more overtly modified by mechanical or electric technologies, thus highlighting the inescapable technology operative in the canonical acoustic instruments. Therefore, claiming some instruments as technologically enhanced becomes a division predicated simply on the power to divide and define and without any solid material basis. Similarly the sounds they produce question the divisions drawn between "music" and "noise", an issue right at the heart of twentieth-century music production in Europe and the US.[33] The relationships between Antheil and Russolo, on the one hand, and Murphy/Léger and other futurist visual artists of the time, exposed a fundamental engagement with technology that argued a doubled, paradoxical relationship to technology: that mechanical and electrical technology might offer a "new" future for human expression but one that only returns us to the prosthesis that resides at the origin of perception that is, in fact, perception itself. The scandal surrounding Antheil's performance seems to be based more on the realisation of this relationship of original text (instrument, sound, and others) to prosthetic enhancement of it and what this means for human interaction with technology rather than on sirens wailing on a concert stage.[34]

The doubled discourse of prosthetics coincides with a pattern at work in the maintenance of institutions generally, but particularly those associated with teaching and academic research, in which text is relegated to the role of formal representation (as literary or visual media) and thus neutralised through institutional disciplinarity, while prosthetic technology is affirmed as capable of immediately presenting situations, events and environments to perceiving subjects independently of textual limitations. To maintain the illusion of prosthetic simultaneity, then, the institution must maintain a theoretical distinction between discrete texts, subjects and technologies. Given the striking correlation between developing military technologies and the institutionalisation of aesthetics, it is possible to draw attention to the discursive aspects of military technology, which enables a reduced responsibility in its prosthetically enhanced agents alongside an equivalent reduction of responsibility demanded by institutions.

Blind Eyes, Cut Eyes and The Unblindable Eye

Pulsating alongside, but arhythimically with, futurist technospasms were surrealist organic-spasms. With little patience for the fetishising of the new, the surrealists took their own blind turns, but ones that reinhabited the body in resistance to the machine and the budding cyborg discourse of futurists. For them, the "blinking of an animal eyelid" contained beauties and terrors untapped, as Luis Buñuel and Salvador Dali's *Un chien andalou* revealed. Blinking and blinding coalesced in this cinematic short in ways that resonate with other overt acts of modernist opacity. Turning a blind eye to the technological wonders the futurists fawned over, Buñuel and Dali allowed the cut of the editing table to signify the cut in the visual field, the cleave of public and private visual culture, and the incision of aesthetic expression that confined it increasingly, unremittingly and irrevocably to the individual psyche.

In what has become one of the most famous and shocking opening sequences in all of cinema history, Buñuel himself sharpens a barber's straight razor. He stands on a balcony contemplating the moon, the luminous orb that will be the first substitute for the soon-to-be sliced human eye. Quickly Buñuel steps behind a seated woman, and in a medium shot, he props open her left eye and holds the straight razor by it. The film cuts to a close-up of the eye, Buñuel's hand and the razor. Yet another cut returns us to the moon, which is symbolically sliced by a razor-thin cloud.

The film cuts to a close-up of an eye, and the razor lances the gelatinous organ.

This cut asserts the violent removal of visual possibilities allowed to the audience. All that can operate in their visual domain from now on are the individual, psychological dream images that follow in the remainder of the film. The cinematic "cut" between the symbolic and the biological eyes, the cinematic "cut" that leads to an act of blinding, also becomes the cut – the entryway, the incision – that leads to the individually aestheticised realm revealed in the body of the film. Only the ending takes us back to the public world invoked in the prologue, and it, too, involves blindness.

The cinematic and symbolic "cut" also is a cut with Eisenstein's montage school of cinema. The illusion of montage creates a continuity of images, even if it demands the audience provide more of the continuity than later "classic' Hollywood cinema" and its hidden editing did. Eschewing the Russian school, Buñuel and his cohorts, oddly enough, drew inspiration from the comedic shorts of Chaplin, Keaton and Harry Langdon (the latter, even more oddly, were directed by Frank Capra). Keaton's influence on various surrealist filmmakers and painters is well documented, but Buñuel seems less concerned with imagery per se than with the splicing together of various images. And it is this aspect of the early comedic short from which Buñuel drew inspiration. He writes in the late 1920s that "segmentation", the conceptual division and reconnection of images, is the most important aspect of filmmaking. By explicitly drawing attention to segmentation, especially in a film such as *Un chien andalou*, Buñuel makes visible what others blind audiences to. That is, he increases the gap between visible text and remote object, letting out the slack rather than tightening it up. In a prototypical modernist move, Buñuel shows viewers the conditions that make the representation possible while simultaneously showing them the failure of his ability to show them. He can only show them what he cannot show them.

Despite the fact that the surrealists can be understood as offering a set of aesthetic choices markedly different from those espoused by the futurists, Buñuel, at least, had some universalist, humanist hopes for the deployment of visual technology. Writing in *La Gaceta literaria* in 1928, he states that "The lens – that eye without tradition, without morals, without prejudice, but nonetheless able to interpret itself – sees the world. The filmmaker then commands it. Machine and man. The purest expression of our time, our art, the real art of every day."[35] Although this article barely predates *Un chien andalou*, Buñuel optimistically expresses his faith in technology to provide an expression and aesthetic for the quotidian. The eye he slices a year later is to be replaced by the cinema camera's "eye". Clearly, Buñuel's own view of the "*coup*" that is carving up the visual field does not forgo progressive possibilities, perhaps even in his first film. What is striking is not that Buñuel sounds a great deal like his Russian contemporary Vertov, but more hauntingly, that he sounds like a precursor of those who construct MANPRINT – a perfect blending of man and machine that has become "a pure expression of our time", of the "every day", which is no longer art but military and business technology. From the interwar period on, art must be relegated to the individual sphere abdicating visual culture to war and commerce.

An oblique cinematic allusion to *Un chien andalou*'s scandalous opening sequence, one that also leads us neatly back to the MANPRINT blending hinted at in Buñuel's 1928 article, can be found in the 1986 James Cameron film *The Terminator*. After Arnold Schwarzenegger's cyborg assassin is roughed up in an auto accident, he has to repair his damaged eye. Being a cyborg, only his outer layer is composed of human flesh and tissue, including the biological lens of the eye. In the shot that alludes to Buñuel and Dali, the monstrous machine wields a protractor to slice out the fleshy bit, and the audience's wince is akin to that provoked by *Un chien andalou*, this despite our knowledge that he feels no pain. Once the eye bit has been removed, we see the cyborg's "real" organ of vision: an infrared beam, for which the flesh cover was exactly that, only a cover. The damaged eye would have, in effect, blown his cover, so to restore his ability to "pass" as human, he dons dark sunglasses throughout the remainder of the film.

"What has gone? How it ends?" Two apparently disembodied questions from Part IV of *Finnegans Wake* are followed by a reminder: "Begin to forget it. It will remember itself from every sides, with all gestures, in each our word" (Joyce, *FW*, 614). What is forgotten returns obliquely, from every side, as displaced memory, as what cannot be seen of the visible.

When we awake with the dawn, when we emerge from cinematic night, when we snap off the TV or switch the PNAV from night to day, what is lost to forgetting? Partially, perhaps, it is the division of the visual field that has been commodified in the form of military technology. Perhaps it is the blindness of the quotidian articulated in modernist aesthetics. Perhaps it is the knowledge that the mythological position of pure perception is indeed mythological. Is it perhaps only a coincidence that the Apache's Longbow Radio Frequency guided Hellfire missile is called "the fire-and-forget" system?

Notes

1. Quoted in Paul Virilio, *The Vision Machine*, trans. Julie Rose (Bloomington: Indiana University Press, 1994) p. 29.
2. Quoted in Rey Chow, *The Age of the World Picture* (Durham: Duke University Press, 2006).
3. Paul Virilio, *War and Cinema*, trans. P. Camillier (London and New York: Verso, 1989).
4. Jonathan Crary, *Techniques of the Observer: On Vision and Modernity in the Nineteenth Century* (Cambridge, MA: MIT Press, 1990), p. 96.
5. National Advisory Committee on Aeronautics report 386, published in 1932 http://naca.larc.nasa.gov/digidoc/report/tr/86/NACA-TR-386.PDF

6. H. G. Wells, *The Complete Stories* (London: Phoenix, 1998).
7. The websites provided by various military organisations provide a productive source of information about current military technology, but, perhaps more importantly, also about the discursive military-state practices surrounding the technology and its application. While other resources offer more detailed technological information, the websites allow better access to the ways in which the different stakeholders in the technology position themselves in public discourse about it. Central to these sites, especially for North American military organisations, is the idea of "transparency" that the state espouses and the internet supposedly embodies. Citation: www-acala1.ria.army.mil/lc/cs/csa/aadesc.htm – (part of the US Army TACOM-RI homepage).
8. www.dmi.usma.edu/Milresources/weapons/ah64apac.htm
9. Australian Aviation-Technology Explained, www.ausaviation.com.au/TechnologyExplained/ApacheLongbow1.htm.
10. Paul Virilio, *Open Sky*, trans. Julie Rose (London: Verso, 1997) p. 93.
11. Aviation Encyclopedia, http://www.jolly-rogers.com/airpower/ah-64d/64d-av.htm
12. Jonathan Crary, *The Suspensions of Perception: Attention, Spectacle, and Modern Culture* (Cambridge, MA: MIT Press, 1999) pp. 134–8.
13. *Lumina 92*, quoted in Virilio, *Open Sky*, p. 94.
14. G. W. F. Hegel, *Phenomenology of Spirit*, trans. A. V. Miller (Oxford: OUP, 1977) pp. 6–7.
15. Ernest Hemingway manages to produce a similar effect in his (appropriately titled) *Fiesta: The Sun also Rises* (London: Random House, 1927). Two characters are drinking in a Spanish bar. One asks the other, "How did you go bankrupt?" The other replies, "two ways . . . Gradually and then suddenly" (Hemingway, *Fiesta*, 120). We are grateful to Henryk Jensen for bringing this quotation to our attention. For an account of post-World War I trauma as the consequence of a catastrophe that happened gradually and then suddenly, see his "Victimization and Technology", in *Approaching a New Millennium: Lessons from the Past – Prospects for the Future*, Proceedings of the Seventh Annual Conference of the International Society for the Study of European Ideas, 14–18 August (Bergen: HIT CDROM, 2000).
16. James Joyce, *Finnegans Wake* (Harmondsworth: Penguin, 1939) p. 593. For the earlier version, see *A First-Draft Version of* Finnegans Wake, ed. David Hayman (London: Faber and Faber, 1963) p. 270.
17. Ezra Pound, *The Spirit of Romance* (New York: New Directions, 1910).
18. William Carlos Williams, *The Collected Poems I*, ed. A. Walton Litz and Christopher MacGowan (New York: New Directions, 1986) pp. 14, 427. See also "At Dawn", p. 36 and "Dawn", p. 85.
19. William Carlos Williams, *The Collected Poems II*, ed. A. Walton Litz and Christopher MacGowan (New York: New Directions, 1986) pp. 250–2. The trope of a "nuclear dawn" was deployed early by the leading proponent of US air power during the Cold War, General Curtis LeMay, who said, "Between sunset tonight and sunrise tomorrow morning, the Soviet Union would likely cease to be a major power . . . Dawn might break over a nation infinitely poorer

than China – less populated than the US and condemned to an agrarian existence for generations to come" (quoted in Sven Lindquist, *A History of Bombing*,
trans. Linda Haverty Rugg (London: Granta Books, 2000) p. 294). One cannot
help noting that General LeMay's evocation of this dawn song lacks the elegiac
qualities found in Williams or the Provençal poets, though elegy would provide
the proper idiom for his utterance.

20. W. B. Yeats, *Collected Poems*, ed. Augustine Martin (London: Arena, 1990) p. 462.

21. Quoted in Dalia Judovitz, *Unpacking Duchamp* (Berkeley: University of California
Press, 1998) p. 5.

22. Mina Loy, *The Lost Lunar Baedeker: Poems*, ed. Roger L. Conover (New York:
Farrar, Straus and Giroux, 1996) p. 83. This poem has provoked both widespread
admiration and not a little bewilderment. Yvor Winters, a formidable critic of
modern poetry, considered it to be among her very best (see Conover's note 24
to *The Lost Lunar Baedeker*, p. 200). Carolyn Burke reminds us that it "challenged
readers in its time and is still difficult in ours, no doubt because satire and elegy
assume different emotions, yet here combine to suggest the extremity of the
period and the hope of some larger vision" (Carolyn Burke, *Becoming Modern:
The Life of Mina Loy* (New York: Farrar, Straus and Giroux, 1996) p. 318).

23. Burke finds an autobiographical strain running obliquely through the poem. For
her, the dam Bellona "hides the poet's own sense of deprivation in the figure of
war as a cruel mother" (*Becoming Modern*, p. 317).

24. F. T. Marinetti, letter to Severini, 20 November 1914, quoted in Caroline Tisdall
and Angelo Bozzolla, *Futurism* (London: Thames and Hudson, 1977) p. 177.

25. Thom Gunn provides an effective reading of the poem in his "Three Hard
Women", in *Shelf Life: Essays, Memoirs and an Interview* (Ann Arbor: University
of Michigan Press, 1993). He is concerned with her poetic expression of indignation and sees the word "eremite" as an ironic repetition of Keats (in "Bright
Star") used here as a way of "attacking the values of a culture through such
words, embedded as they are in the classics of our poetry".

26. Gunn, again, draws attention to the acoustic aspects of these lines: "reading them
aloud you realise that the greater sweep of their rhythm suggests the growing
scope of her indignation: in them she describes, by showing its termination, the
delicate mechanism of the sighted human being" (p. 49).

27. Tisdall and Bozzolla, *Futurism*, p. 75

28. F. T. Marinetti (ed.), *Manifesti del futurismo lanciati da Marinetti, Boccioni, Carrà,
Russolo, Balla, Severini, Pratella, Mme de Sainte-Pointe, Apollinaire, Palazzeschi*
(Florence: Edizioni di "Lacerba", 1914). An English translation appears in
Herschel Browning Chipp (ed.), *Theories of Modern Art; A Source Book by Artists
and Critics* (Berkeley: University of California Press, 1968) p. 303.

29. Albert Einstein, *The Principle of Relativity*, ed. A. Sommerfield, trans. W. Perrett
and J. H. Jefferey (London: Methuen, 1923).

30. Conover corrects Loy's spelling in his compilation. Loy's spelling is often eccen-
tric, and Conover puts it right here although one can argue that many of her
spelling "errors" are rather like those found in *Finnegans Wake*, that is intention-
ally blurry.

31. For a discussion of the twentieth century as the age of optical effects rather than images, see Paul Virilio, *The Information Bomb*, trans. Chris Turner (London: Verso, 2000).

32. George Antheil, having moved from the centre of avant-garde Paris and Berlin to Hollywood, met the actress Hedy Lamarr in 1940. Lamar had been married to the Austrian munitions manufacturer Fritz Mandal from 1933 to 1937. One of his major areas of interest was aviation and control systems. When in Hollywood during the bleaker period of World War II, Lamarr met Antheil, and they discussed weapons systems. She developed the idea of "frequency hopping" as a means of making guided torpedoes more accurate and less susceptible to radio frequency jamming. Antheil suggested that the frequency hopping could be obtained by the piano roll means he had used to synchronise the sixteen player pianos he deployed for "Ballet mécanique" some years past. Though encouraged by the head of the newly established National Inventors Council, Charles F. Kettering (also Chairman of the Board for General Motors), to patent the device, which they did, the Navy was reluctant to take it up. According to Antheil, the military brass did not like much the idea of placing a player piano in a torpedo. But the Cold War changed the military's position on this as the demands for both securing communications systems and helping with targeting of guided weapons became increasingly important. Shifting from the mechanical technology of the 1920s and 1930s to the electronic technology of the 1950s, Sylvania Electronics Division, working with the Department of Defense, developed a system based on the Lamarr-Antheil patent, deploying it first in the blockade of Cuba in 1962. It remains the central theoretical basis for the US Milstar defence communication satellite system. In this manner, Antheil's innovative use of player piano programming and technology for one of the most scandalous pieces of avant-garde music composed in the 1920s has become an integral dimension of current US military technology.

33. See Douglas Kahn, *Water Noise Meat* (Cambridge, MA: MIT Press, 1999) for a lengthy analysis of the arguments surrounding this division.

34. A wonderful anecdote exists about the US première of Antheil's piece, in which the performer who needed to crank the siren started doing so when the score indicated that the siren should enter at that moment. The performer did not realise the momentum required by sirens to get going and then their capacity for running on momentum. As a result, the end of the piece was drowned by the siren, which continued to whine long after the performance had ended. This unintended momentum of technology, which pertains to an essential part of its technicity, is taken up in our chapter "Manufacturing Emergencies".

35. Luis Buñuel, *An Unspeakable Betrayal: Selected Writings of Luis Buñuel*, trans. Garrett White (Berkeley: University of California Press, 2000) pp. 132–3.

Chapter 3

We Make It Beautiful

From certain angles Bell Helicopter's AH-1Z Super Cobra Attack helicopter presents an aspect that makes it seem oddly designed, for a military machine. It is as if the designers, in fulfilling their brief to create "the most capable and flexible multi-mission attack helicopter in the world", had wanted to make its appearance as striking as its capabilities. Its power, speed and agility, its "state-of-the-art" dynamics, its huge yet compact arsenal of weapons, and its avionics suites that "incorporate the most advanced survivability equipment available": all of this is somehow wrapped in a package designed as if its market was like that for the latest automobiles, with an eye for fashionable beauty. The marketing team at Bell Helicopter has noticed this too. The marketing text, of course, charts the full technological capabilities of this most advanced example of its ilk, but the images (in an admittedly hackneyed tradition of aircraft romanticism familiar in scenes, for instance, of Spitfires in the Battle of Britain or Apaches satirised to the sound of the "Ride of the Valkyries" in *Apocalypse Now*) indulge in silhouettes of the beast in flight against a setting sun or wide-angle poses of it lounging languorously like a beach bum jewel along the littorals where 70 per cent of the world population – friend and foe alike – resides.

So the hunting grounds of the AH-1Z are the littorals, the coastal regions that form the inhabited frontiers of the world's populations. The guidebook for the helicopter clearly states the needs to which the machine responds:

> The number one challenge facing armed forces on today's battlefields is the requirement to positively identify friend from foe and then be able to attack hostile targets with munitions so as to reduce or eliminate collateral damage to civilian personnel and property. To give our crews the best opportunity to survive on the battlefield, positive identification and target engagements must be done at ranges that keep aircraft well outside the effective range of enemy guns.[1]

Beneath the statement, obscurely supporting its common-sense efficacy, resides the history of a generalised sliding, a *glissement de sens* (English can offer at best only the weak "shift in meaning"), according to which the world's populations and its dwellings have merged with the battlefield itself, a field from which the armed forces must increasingly be distanced in ways that still allow them to fully engage in it. Battle is now waged remotely from outside the fields of battle, which are identified as densely populated civilian domains. Through these domains the battle lines are drawn suddenly, contingently, as if in mimicry of the fractal coastlines that constitute their edges. The armed forces can best survive on such battlefields by removing themselves as far from them as the technology allows.

The image that crops up most in the Bell Helicopter marketing campaign is the one called "Goodbye", a head-on view in battle that indicates why the marketing team has seized on the helicopter's potential for obsessive rhetorical (or at least aspectual) *prosopopoeia*. From this view the fearful symmetry of the beast of prey obscures the three-dimensional length of the mechanical helicopter, perhaps suggesting (and this is clearly the intention) flailing hair, bug eyes, a nose, wings, legs, feet and talons: the sole survivor materialised out of the smoke and flames of a dying world (rather crudely filled in behind the image). In fact, the helicopter's multi-faceted Cyclops eye resides dead centre. The Lockheed Martin Target Sighting System (TSS) provides target acquisition and designation in all weather conditions, day or night, allowing four fields of view: wide, medium, narrow, and narrow zoom for long-distance precision targeting. Because it is fully integrated with the AH-1Z Fire Control System, the delay between sighting and striking is reduced to a minimum ("See First, Strike First", as the guidebook explains). Furthermore, targeting and firing can be controlled remotely, thus transcending the limitations of pilot point of view and freeing him up for other activities. One remarkable aspect, then, of the AH-1Z would be the ways in which its mechanics, its ethics and its aesthetics interact, sometimes coinciding or folding over but sometimes too in contradiction. The mechanical dimension emphasises the following: precision and integration of sighting and striking; efficient remote capability; powerful arms capability; and dependable survival capability. These mechanical capabilities, which support the two functions of attack and defence, already overlap with an ethical dimension that distinguishes the civilian from the military with minimum risk of "collateral damage", also thus distinguishing the targets respectively of attack and defence.

So what, then, would be the role of its aesthetic aspect – of its beauty – as the marketing slogan would have it? An ad for the AH-1Z uses the "Goodbye" image with the following text:

> We made it beautiful. Because it's the last thing some people will ever see. The AH-1Z. First, it frustrates the enemy with a Target Sight System that detects, recognises and identifies them at extreme ranges. Then, it demonstrates the versatility of the widest array of ordnance available. Finally, if you wish, it permits the enemy to view a state-of-the-art helicopter like no other. The AH-1Z. Unbeatable proof that your mission is our mission. (Bell Textron Helicopter ad)

The text of the ad offers a virtual encyclopedia of the values of techno-science: agency, control, technological prowess, speed, intelligence (both human and machine), the power to render the invisible visible, and the

Figure 3.1　'We Make It Beautiful',
Apache Longbow advert. Image scanned
by Bishop and Phillips

intimate connections between aesthetics and technology. The division between the instrumental and the aesthetic is blurred in the advertising discourse, as well as in the helicopter itself. At the level of its performance, the helicopter and its technology of visual prosthesis, speed and firepower depends on rendering "the enemy" slow and blind. The power to do so – to make a killing machine beautiful, to have at one's disposal this massive array of ordnance, to allow the pilot the choice and agency to reveal the invisible object that will kill another at the speed it takes to make it visible, and to make that last moment an aesthetically pleasing and overwhelming one for the victim – hints at the divisionary (and visionary) power that rests at the heart of modern techno-science.

Following this hint, or at least following the trace of its outline, we will find that the source of this power can only be imagined ambivalently. The ad's message evokes enough glib humour to disguise the fact that its enunciative modality is deeply consonant with the performative modality of the helicopter itself. Glibness in idioms associated with military technology poses a procedural challenge, for the fluent plausibility of the advertising operates like a sophisticated decoy, at once distinguishing the discourse from the business of the technology's operation and at the same time contingently implanting the idea of operational fluency as a property of the machinery. The relation implicated between the ad's glib humor and the machine mobilises a certain glibberiness (from the Dutch *glibberig*, "slippery") that merges the operation of the machine with the end of the operation: the event, held in the gaze of its addressee (that of the machine and the ad) as it gazes back. The helicopter stands revealed at the point of the strike as the master of its own event, its well oiled operational complexity gathered up into this culminating and yet eternal moment.

The ad in fact provides in its disarming simplicity an awkward truth about the machines. The economic balance of space, time and visibility must be reduced to the calculable odds of 100/0 if the helicopter's promise is to be fulfilled. On the one hand, the claim implies an ability to eradicate altogether the spheres of space and time and to control visibility, when in fact it merely involves an advantage in the struggle between relative mastery over spatial and temporal relations in the destruction of an enemy. On the other hand, the glib reference to beauty unintentionally recalls a condition that under the complex nomination *aesthetics* poses a greater challenge than either man or machine can meet, in the irreducible interval that in fact always delays the prompt correspondence of a moment with itself (and between space and time).

The technology and the disingenuously banal aesthetics together manifest the divided root of military techno-science in its attempt to command the spatial and temporal fields of vision and calculation absolutely – as if in defiance of the decay that at once troubles and conditions its every advance. The attempt through technological means to overcome metaphysics, as the grounding condition of technology per se, is taken over by its own systematisation, which gathers a momentum that has from its beginning severed it from its origins. This momentum exceeds all agencies yet promises the agent the world, producing, reducing, mobilising or amplifying the supersensible through the techno-scientific repertoire of sensory enhancements and delights.

The helicopter thus belongs to an aesthetic sphere that, on one hand, can be reduced neither to the activities of artists nor to the artworks they produce, yet, on the other hand, can only be adequately addressed with reference to the operation of art in relation to the sphere within which its place and role has been appointed. There is much here to link the helicopter and its mode of address, satirised by its glibbery double in the advertisement, to the ambivalent aesthetics of the late eighteenth and early nineteenth centuries. Combining beauty, invisibility and death through melancholy – the missing link in fact and a concept that once perhaps seemed powerful enough to pose a form of resistance to the pragmatic and positivist economics of industry – the aesthetics of Romanticism adumbrates – and thus fails to resist – the onslaught that is the romance of the machine. What is recalled here would be the imagination of Keats (as opposed to Wordsworth or Coleridge for instance), for whom none of the drowsy escapisms of nature or narcotics could have matched the intense experience of capturing the beauty of cruelty in the production of a state of mourning.

Keats's "Ode on Melancholy" has a place in a series, which happens to develop in a chronological order, by outlining the kind of difficult performance that art exhibits with increasing ingenuity in the operations of the modernist avant-garde. We are challenged here by a kind of aesthetics of disappearance *avant la lettre*. The ode emerges as a kind of instruction manual on how to produce an ode: the creative source of the poem disappears so that the ode may be produced; yet the creative source already is nothing but its disappearance. The metaphors condensing images of beauty and misery serve to demonstrate that beneath the conventional sadness about the temporariness of existence lies a deeper, crueller logic of disappearance. You may intensify your misery by dwelling on something evanescent and visually beautiful, "a morning rose", or "the rainbow of the salt sand-wave". But, even better, if you do not have the mood yourself, borrow that of your mistress, fitting it like a prosthetic emotion attached to your own via the visual organs:

> If thy mistress some rich anger shows,
>   Emprison her soft hand, and let her rave,
>   And feed deep, deep upon her peerless eyes.[2]

The conventional metaphor identifies the "peerless eyes" of an angry woman (the *belle dame sans merci*) as a source of great creative (for which we must now read *prosthetic*) vitality, for those tough enough to withstand the intensity. The complexity of metaphors of sexual difference as they evolve during the century cannot be easily extricated from the many other spheres where issues of sexual difference operate at the battle lines of every kind of struggle (including social organisation, biology, and of course war). They function here in Keats to help produce the formal pattern of the mode of originary disappearance that the poem takes as its topic. The poem, no less than the helicopter, achieves its desired effect – its end – in the formal arrangement of a disappearance. This specific model of sexual difference, added to the rhetorical pattern that Keats outlines in the final stanza, forms the basis for the romance that will follow in repetitions of increasing frequency:

> She dwells with beauty – Beauty that must die;
>   And Joy, whose hand is ever at his lips
> Bidding adieu; and aching pleasure nigh,
>   Turning to poison as the bee mouth sips:
> Ay, in the very temple of delight
>   Veil'd Melancholy has her Sovran shrine,
>   Though seen of none save him whose strenuous tongue
>   Can burst Joy's grape against his palate fine;
> His soul shall taste the sadness of her might,
>   And be among her cloudy trophies hung. (Keats, *Poetic Works*, 220)

Here a classic prosopopoeia feminises melancholy as a source of agonistic (antagonistic and even sadistic) power that cannot lose: the best one can do in capturing her for even the few moments available is to give oneself up to her might, only to be hung alongside her other trophies. In other words, instant death awaits anyone capable of rendering her visible. In this sense, melancholy, in its aspect as immediate decay of the beautiful, would also be the personification of time. The ode thus fails to reproduce its object. The sexual relations operate as metaphors for the disappearance of the event that the ode takes as its topic. And so the ode replaces the impossible event with its own prosthetic and inadequate event, thus all the more clearly demonstrating the condition that aesthetics implies, as an alternative to technoscience.

The two modes of address, of the helicopter and its advertising (explicitly glossed in the banal dialectic "hello-goodbye"), can be recalled here. The helicopter itself addresses its victims, who indeed may feel for a moment – who would know? – the sadness of its might or the richness of its anger, while the ad addresses its potential master ("your mission is our mission"). The two aspects – malicious mistress and manageable beast – thus recall the power but displace the melancholy inherent in its Keatsian invocation (the helicopter probably just *is* the melancholy of its era). Technology promises more than it can provide in this sense, for time will not stand still even for a helicopter, but the intensification *of the attempt* to reduce absolutely the delay that temporality inevitably imposes has produced a forceful adversary. But the power has been won through the illusion of an absolute separation of (the helicopter's) victim and (its) master, a fake dichotomy that can only ever in fact be maintained temporarily. The helicopter attacks both with its powerful array of ordnance and with its rhetoric; and does so each time on the basis of a power that resides somehow in both ordnance and rhetoric at once. This power would be maintained only to the extent that a prior power can keep them (like victim and master) divided; the middle term, the hinge that at once divides and connects, would be melancholy itself, the mistress, the helicopter.

Keats in his own way belongs to the general condition of historical revolution that all over the globe, but especially in Europe and America during the early stages of the nineteenth century, and under the retrospective rubric of romanticism, begins to speculate on the conditions of life as fundamentally aesthetic, in the new sense of a new word that begins to emerge in the texts of Baumgarten, then Kant, and most radically Schiller. Aesthetics in some of these texts begins to take precedence over the logic and rationality of science. The artwork no longer answers to the classical demands of beauty and representation; and the sphere called aesthetic no longer can be maintained independently from increasingly technological spheres of social activity. Conventionally aesthetics tends to fall back into use in something like its early designation, as the branch of philosophical inquiry that takes as its object a theory of the beautiful (and sublime). It thus corresponds to the identification of art – the "artwork" – as the privileged, delimited site of treatment of the beautiful. The modernist revolution already beginning in romantic art, poetry and philosophy reveals, in and against aesthetics, that on the contrary beneath this designation lie several powerful strands of investigation, experimentation and production that cannot be reduced to the narrow view of aesthetics and in fact turn out to involve concerns closer to the operational functionality of technology itself.

As modernist aesthetics extends, revises, repeats and ultimately replaces the aesthetics of romanticism, some of the conditions of possibility for advancing technology – its powers – also emerge. Picking up on the economy of Poe's polyvalent arabesques, Baudelaire's prose poems – from *Le spleen de Paris: petits poèmes en prose* – celebrate the minor and temporary triumphs of the lyric poet over *le Temps*, which reigns sovereign (as it had for Keats). "La Chambre Double" particularly evokes the conditions according to which the realm where *le Temps a disparu* – where time has disappeared – always in fact coincides with the one where time continues to reign sovereign and must thus always re-impose itself violently, like *un coup de pioche dans l'estomac* (a chop in the stomach with a pick axe).[3] This mundane agent of the everyday is never ultimately defeated because it always outstrips the so called ideal, the "Idol", the sovereign of dreams, a familiar figure: "Yes, those are her eyes whose flames pierce the twilight, those subtle and terrible *mirettes*, which I recognise in their terrifying malice!" This is the choice that the "Double Room" presents: the ugly violence of time or the malice of timeless beauty. It is no choice, of course, for they imply the same thing: death, the ineluctable, which cannot be outstripped.

With Stéphane Mallarmé the power and appearance of advanced techno-science is explicitly connected with this emergent aesthetics, according to which the divided domain that Baudelaire's "Double Room" evokes must be regarded as having its basis essentially and primarily in incalculable division itself, not only dividing the ideal from the real but instituting them in their division. The division is itself double edged, a division in division: on one hand it suggests, yet in the same stroke prevents, completion and unity, it provokes a desire for, yet implants an interminable delay in our progress towards, the absolute; on the other hand, in the institution of these specific kinds of failure, it makes possible communication, community, prosthetic addition and, most crucially, poetry. Any perception that Mallarmé's poetics are pessimistic, the precursor of *Fin de siècle* decadence, may have been provoked by the fact that he seems to be foretelling the death of poetry (and thus of community and communication) as a consequence of the emergence of a techno-science that promises or threatens to erase division per se, to conquer time in at least some of its domains. In the early prose poem, "Le phénomène futur", Mallarmé outlines a vision of a world grown old: "A pale sky, hovering over a world that is dying of its own decrepitude, is perhaps going to depart with the clouds: the shreds of worn out purple sunsets fade in a river lying dormant on an horizon submerged in sunbeams and water."[4] Out of this landscape, whitened by the dust of time, rises the tent of the *Montreur de Choses Passées*: the Showman of Last Things (or Things Past). The poem cites the showman's sales pitch, his *boniment*:

Here is the gist of his claptrap: "No sign regales you to the spectacle inside, for there is now no painter capable of rendering even a sad semblance of its existence. I present, living (and preserved through all the ages by sovereign science) a woman of a former time. Some primordial and ingenuous madness, an ecstasy of gold, I don't know what! which she calls her hair, is folded with the grace of silk with her face lit up by the blood red nakedness of her lips. In lieu of vain apparel, she has a body; and her eyes, though they resemble precious stones are not equal to the expression that springs from her happy flesh: from breasts raised as if they were full of eternal milk, tipped towards the sky, to glistening legs that retain the salt of the primeval sea."[5]

The showman's spiel seems to describe, in Mallarmé's sad comedy, the *sublime* lost subject of Art, the subject for instance of Botticelli's *Birth of Venus*, but also (therefore) of a dominating tradition of sublime nudes transformed by *techne* into *objets d'art*. It promises the subject itself but without the awkward mediation of an artwork. In Mallarmé's perverse reconstruction – a version in this way not just of the late nineteenth century but a *per*-version also of the condition of art *per se* – art is no longer possible, yet its sublime object (previously always lost) is preserved by sovereign science, exhibited like a freak-show phenomenon for the sorrowful public of a dying world. This is Plato's ideal and invisible *agathon*, the type and genius of deep beauty manifested and preserved by science, or Immanuel Kant's transcendental subject impossibly preserved as an empirical object of human experience, the invisible made visible. In a world where neither art nor poetry is possible, the showman – the exhibitor or curator – claims that science has brought about the materialisation of the very thing that in its inexplicable absence previously allowed art and poetry to flourish.

"La phénomène futur" is at once deeply critical of the archiving values of the exhibition and the museum and scornful of the promises of modern techno-science, more or less equating them as a single tendency. The emphasis the showman puts on the flesh rather than the subject's eyes, which sparkle like jewels rather than gaze out, and the nutritional, alimentary power that he almost claims for the creature ("breasts raised as if they were full of eternal milk") fall foul of Mallarmé's poetics of the *blanc*, which affirms a beauty borne of (and haunted by) exactly *nothing*.[6] Here, on the contrary, the showman promises to make everything visible and material in a carnological (and carnival) revelation. Notably, the poem itself avoids any direct representation of the showman's exhibit but it does hypothesise a variety of responses from those who do gaze upon it:

When they have all gazed upon the noble creature, the vestige of an age already accursed, some, indifferent (for they will not have had the capacity to understand), but others, broken-hearted and with eyelids wet with resigned tears, will look at one another; while the poets of those times, feeling their dull eyes lighting up once again, will make their way toward their lamps, their brains momentarily drunk with an obscure glory, haunted by a Rhythm and forgetting that they exist in an age that has outlived beauty [*une époque qui survit à la beauté*]. (Mallarmé, *Collected Poems*, 88)

The play of contemplations (the voyeurs gaze upon the noble creature and then exchange glances with one another) focuses on the various states of the onlookers' eyes: eyelids wet with resigned tears or dull eyes lighting up with drunken hope, hinging in symptomatic form the thing seen and the emotional state it provokes. The states of their eyes correspond to the states of their souls (in Mallarmé's own phrase, perhaps, their *etates d'ame*), which are haunted by a rhythm and a forgetting. The only poetry possible in such a time will be born of the false promise – preserved by sovereign science – that a subject still exists for the poet.[7] But the irony here is double edged: on one hand, science threatens (or promises) to preserve what previously was evanescent, and so the sense of loss is thus to be replaced by a presentation of the object itself, miraculously not lost; but, on the other hand, this only serves to emphasise, to reinforce the sense of loss that was always anyway the provocation of the work (ghostly rhythms and forgetting). The disjunction between the empirical world and the invisible ideal (made grotesquely visible in Mallarmé's ironic prosopopoeia) remains and determines the various emotional states of the collective.

The sales pitch for the AH-1Z recalls Mallarmé's showman. It glorifies both the power and appearance of advanced techno-science, in an obviously revealing manner, for it too traffics in the trope of revelation. The power of the visible resides in the invisible, and the revelation of technological superiority operates as a sleight-of-hand that carries with it the aura of the invisible. But, as Mallarmé (in his skewed negative metaphysics) consistently demonstrates, *reductio ad absurdam*, the category *invisible* would not be reducible to a mere visible awaiting discovery or manifestation or release – as if it was just an as yet unseen visible. The invisible, rather would be related to the visible as that which cannot ever be seen – as the (for perhaps several reasons) absolutely un-seeable. It would be that which cannot be accessed by any kind of seeing at all; and it would be contrasted in this way to both the potentially and actually visible (visible things concealed but awaiting their potential revelation or already appearing in the field of vision).

The conceptual sleight-of-hand which promises to make the invisible visible repeats the claims of a techno-science that operates in the example (that we examined earlier) of the jumbo jet in slow-motion lift-off: the technological documentation of the miracle of technology. The technology of vision on display in the film clip and the ad for the AH-1Z reveals its intimate relation to speed and the closing of the gap of perception found in the technology itself. Both the slow-motion lift-off and the AH-1Z advert represent technology's celebrated harnessing of speed. Following a pattern already well established by the aesthetics of modernism, the film clip and the ad reveal that the power of modernity to divide the slow from the fast, the blind from the sighted, and the dead from the living is grounded in a deeper division which can be neither controlled nor appropriated without incalculable cost.

The interest in movement and speed is intrinsic to positivist forms of modernity, as is the claim that these interests are new to it. So it follows that the experimentation, observation and documentation of movement also become infected with a feeling of originality. The technology that provides access to movement in the form of experimentation, observation and documentation is also itself new, supporting the sense of the modern era's break with the past while simultaneously satisfying the interest in speed and movement and generating further interest. This interest in movement expressed by late nineteenth century experimenters such as E. J. Marey and Eadweard Muybridge coincides with increased mechanical speed of production, transportation and communication, as well as intensified exploration of the gap of perception that allows for the manipulation – the hinging and unhinging – of the senses. These three areas of interest are intimately related insofar as the inquiry into one necessarily involves the other two, as Marey's and Muybridge's experiments reveal. Marey's studies of wing movements by birds in flight (as in his photographic trajectory of a crow's wing), Muybridge's sequential photographic images of a horse's gait (that famous precursor of the cinema camera), and Ernst Mach's images of bullets travelling at the speed of sound show the problem of understanding movement as linked to the problems of documentation and observation. The failure of the visual sense to apprehend nature in its full complexity had become technology's opportunity. Once again, to understand speed, it has to be slowed down. All three visual experiments investigated perception, deception and speed. To understand and represent the speed of nature (and speed *in* nature), it needed to be slowed down to a point of stasis, to a frozen image (or time-space moment) of which an infinite number comprise the mechanics of speed made visible by mechanical modes of visual documentation. Thus, machinic speeds make accessible to sight velocities in nature not representable by unaided sensory perception. All the precursors of visual culture as we have come to know it emerge from this complex exploration of sensory perception, especially as it pertained to understanding and documenting speed in nature.

The extent to which the control of movement, the control of its observation, the control of its documentation and representation, and the control over the gap of sensible apprehension through the intensification of technologies of speed necessarily inform one another can be found in operations as diverse as the slow-motion lift-off footage and the AH-1Z helicopter ad. While Marey, Muybridge and, to some extent, Mach documented the speed of movement in nature not accessible by the raw, organic, biological eye, the slow-motion lift-off and the helicopter ad document the speed of movement in technology not apprehensible by the human organ, but which is accessible to the mechanical or electronic eye. As such, the film clip of the plane's dreamlike impossible lift-off and the ad about the helicopter's invisible speed document the development of technology itself – technology's intensified interest in speed at the level of performance of the object (for example, plane, helicopter, surveillance equipment, weaponry) and the level of enunciation

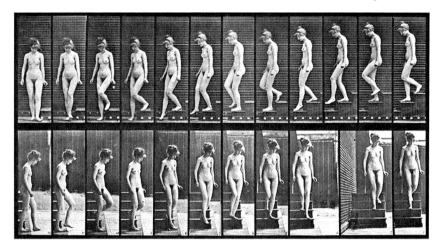

Figure 3.2   Eadweard Muybridge, *Nude Descending a Staircase*, Wikimedia
Commons

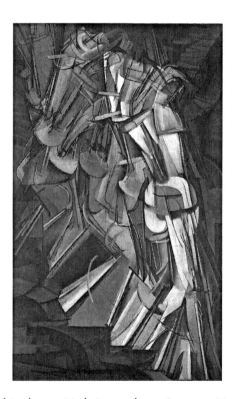

Figure 3.3   Marcel Duchamp, *Nude Descending a Staircase, No. 2* (1912).
Permission by Adagp, © Succession Marcel Duchamp/ADAGP, Paris 2010; image
provided by the Philadelphia Museum of Art

(for example, the camera, film, the machine image, the optoelectronic image). The two representations, then, tell us once again the tale of the impossible made possible by techno-science: we have made a harrowing weapon of war beautiful and a flying machine of enormous speed slow.

The connections between speed, vision, technology and aesthetics are made explicit in the motif of dynamism that unites the experimental writings, manifestos and artworks of the Italian futurists. Anton Giulio Bragaglia's photodynamism, which produced plenty of technical material for futurist artwork and sculpture, takes the innovations of Marey and Muybridge to another level. His aim, quite seriously, was the "almost infinitesimal calculation of movement".[8] It becomes a matter, once again, of rendering the invisible visible:

> with Photodynamism, remembering what took place between one stage and another, a work is presented that transcends the human condition, becoming a *transcendental photograph of movement*. For this end we have envisaged a machine that will render actions visible, more effectively than is now today possible with actions traced from one point, but at the same time keeping them related to the time in which they were made. (*Futurist Manifestos*, 43)

The interest is now no longer in the states that compose movement (like cinematography) but rather in the "inter-movemental states of the action". It is not so much an attempt to close the gap but to calculate it more completely. The implications of this attempt had been worked out as the response to a kind of need by the founder of futurism, F. T. Marinetti.

Deeply indebted to Mallarmé's poetics – but polemically opposed to the symbolist "static" ideal – Marinetti transforms Mallarmé's portrait of a debased world by hastening its logical consequences. His "Founding and Manifesto of Futurism" of 1909 celebrates the defeat of "Mythology and the Mystic Ideal", replacing the red lips of Botticelli's museum-bound *Venus* with the "torrid breasts" of a motor car: "we had no ideal Mistress raising her divine form to the clouds, nor any cruel Queen to whom to offer our bodies" (*Futurist Manifestos*, 20). The founding manifesto, only the first of a long series of such documents, events and works, seems always in danger of being underestimated in both its influence and its prophetic force, as if its rhetorical manner and polemic cannot fail to provoke an opposite and equal reaction.

Marinetti's explicit protestations of originality ("Look there . . . the very first dawn") and the gesture to the obscure dimension of the future seem systematically to provoke commentaries that painstakingly document precursors or that insist on the futurist preoccupation with *their* present. Peter Nicholls, for instance, charts with great care the intellectual origins and historical determinations of the movement before declaring that, "the content of futurism, then, was hardly original, but its extremism – formal and conceptual – certainly was".[9] The separation of content from extremist manner (one gets the sense inappropriately that this is perhaps a matter of taste) allows Nicholls, like so many others, to divorce what is forceful in the heritage of modernism – the ideas of dynamism and flux, the theories of action and energy, the concern with violence, the rejection of decadent poetics, the focus on the tension between cultural tradition and industrial innovation, the purging of sentiment and unfocused humanism – from what remains awkward, as if the futurists were like an important but somewhat embarrassing relative, scorning women, affirming lust and war in their actively fascist politics.

Nicholls is attentive to the rhetorical efficacy of this extremism, to be sure. "The rhetorical inflation," he points out, "which accompanies such fantasies [for example, the mock baptism by overturned car] carries us to the brink – and frequently over the brink – of total absurdity, thus undermining the marmoreal gravity of the decadent cult of death" (*Modernisms*, 86). And his discussion of the so-called "scorn for women" acknowledges the importance of the sustained futurist attack on the ideal embodied by the naked female body, an ideal which expresses in a complex way the inwardness of bourgeois subjectivity. The affirmation of futurism nonetheless serves a larger critical attempt that might be justified as a kind of defence against it. Evoking what he calls the "Nietzschean figure of 'discharge'", Nicholls identifies in Marinetti's attack on inwardness an attempt – in reaction to the kind of split subjectivity that Baudelaire's "Double Room" humorously evokes – to direct violence outwards, away from the self: "The literary manifestos thus urge an assault on all linguistic structures and the smashing of that 'jewelled' language of inwardness whose remnants must now be 'hurled in the reader's face.' The audience for the work becomes a target rather than a recipient" (*Modernisms*, 92). Nicholls's commentary aims to demonstrate why Marinetti's aesthetics must lead ultimately to utter annihilation and, more crucially, what ideological system his reduction to the brink of absurdity (and beyond it) supports. If art, as Marinetti's manifesto claims, is "a need to destroy and scatter oneself", then it remains for Nicholls to show that this is a need "which can only be met by the simultaneous annihilation of others" (*Modernisms*, 92). The analysis seems more than ever correct in light of the development of a technology that seems also to embody this need, which is why the rhetoric of the AH-1Z perhaps calls for a similar critical response. But in that case the designation *futurist* takes on a more prophetic force than Nicholls would like to allow.

These modernist attempts to subvert, or at least to rearrange, the confused idea of the sexual relation that lies at the heart of modern life are rendered transparent in what remains the most visible and celebrated of Marcel Duchamp's works, *The Bride Stripped Bare by Her Bachelors, Even*, or *The Large Glass*. On the one hand, the bride itself is evidently the result of a series of pictorial experiments that began with the deliberately caricaturist *Nude Descending a Staircase*, which performs an operation reminiscent (though apparently independently) of Bragaglia's photodynamism techniques on a famous Muybridge or Marey sequence (both Marey's *Woman Descending a Staircase* and Muybridge's *Descending and Turning Around* are

Figure 3.4   Marcel Duchamp, *The Bride* (1912). Permission by Adagp, ©
Succession Marcel Duchamp/ADAGP, Paris 2010; image provided by the
Philadelphia Museum of Art

evoked). Duchamp derived a more refined and increasingly abstract method
for depicting figures on the basis of *Nude*, which resulted in the final image
for the *Bride*. There are several immediately forceful aspects of *The Large
Glass*: the absurdist depiction of the relation between the bride (on the top
section) and her bachelors (the nine malic – male/phallic – moulds on the
bottom section) is mediated mechanically by a chocolate grinder and kind of
a double scissors contraption, supposed, according to Duchamp's notes, to
represent the incalculable mechanical effects of chance and delay. These are,
of course, exactly the effects that technologies like the Apache are designed
to reduce. *The Bride* thus demonstrates, in an image comically and absurdly
reminiscent of our helicopter before its time, that the very mechanisms that
a developing technology is designed to reduce can only exist by virtue of
those mechanisms. Once again, the end of technology can only be the end
of technology. Furthermore, the organic and the mechanical here achieve
no separation but, on the contrary, both are grounded on imperceptible,
a-material qualities (delay, chance) that make organic and technological
processes possible for us.

A second advertisement, this time for the Comanche helicopter, helps
to indicate the deeper determination of this consilience of aesthetics and

Figure 3.5   Apache Gunship on Tarmac. Permission and image, copyright © Boeing

speed. "It locates, disseminates, eliminates," runs the slogan, its brisk formalism thus supporting the brisk form of the machine itself, whose image hovers above the dust and flame sewn ground beneath it. "Whatever threat Comanche detects is history," claims the text, in a remarkable statement, which incidentally substantiates Paul Virilio's thesis about the relationship between speed and the aesthetics of disappearance. "With the invention of photography," he reminds us, "of the photogramme, that is of instant photography and of cinematography, from that moment onwards one enters into an aesthetics of disappearance".[10]

Virilio's distinction between the aesthetics of appearance and disappearance allows us to mark out a historical ground fairly exactly, but it also indicates a deeper problem in the *historicity* of that ground, demonstrated already in the reading of Keats. Virilio distinguishes between classical aesthetics, where the persistence of the visible (on canvas, in marble) has a material basis, and modern aesthetics, identified by him as the direct outcome of the electronic motorisation of images – where "persistence is no longer material but cognitive, it is in the eye of the beholder" (Armitage, *Virilio Live*, 33). The aesthetics of disappearance, then, corresponds to the impulse, which we are not alone in identifying at the performative level of modernity itself (especially in its technological manifestations), to close the gap of perception, to arrest the disseminative capacities of incalculable temporality, to render, each time in the modality of speed, the invisible wholly visible.

As our examination of modernist aesthetics demonstrates, there are at least two kinds of invisibility and thus two kinds of dis- or non- appearance. The invisibility of the visible would be invisible only contingently, but that contingency, as the accidental visibility of the empirical realm, should at the same time be understood as a kind of potential visibility. Affecting both material and cognitive conditions, and thus rendering them continuous, the invisible here gives itself up to uncountable possibilities of representation, which variously memorialise, represent, produce or destroy a previously or

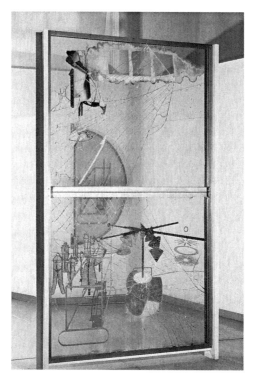

Figure 3.6   Marcel Duchamp, *The Bride Stripped Bare by Her Bachelors, Even (The Large Glass)* (1915–23). Permission by Adagp, © Succession Marcel Duchamp/ADAGP, Paris 2010; image provided by the Philadelphia Museum of Art

consequently visible. It is this potential that constitutes the visible and the invisible together as the field of vision and the horizon. The relationship between the disappearance implied by the electronic image and the elimination of the Comanche's enemies can be identified here in terms of *detection*. With the electronic image things owe their existence, as Virilio says, "to the fact that they disappear" (Armitage, *Virilio Live*, 33). With the Comanche the same rule applies except that things owe their non-existence to the fact that they *did* appear (and significantly, they appeared to an electronic eye, with "over the horizon" capability, rather than an organic one). The second kind of invisibility must be regarded as a condition of possibility for potential visibility (or contingent invisibility), which rests on a deeper ground in the potential *for* visibility – a potential that must now be thought outside the Aristotelian framework that subordinates potentiality to actuality. This would be not the invisibility of the visible but the invisibility of visibility, a potential for making visible but which cannot itself, as a structural condition, ever be made visible. Modern aesthetics, whether discovered in military technology or modern art and writing, responds to this deeper kind of invisible, despite Virilio's claims. In the case of military technology the design

Figure 3.7   Apache Longbow in Flight.
Permission and image, copyright ©
Boeing

seems to be to eliminate it. In the case of modernist aesthetics the aim would
seem to be to insist on it at all costs.

So, the Comanche and the Apache address their spectators no less than
any other discourse. The appeal of the helicopter is twofold – it literally
makes a double address, a radicalisation of the I-You relation that is the
foundation of all discourse. You must either want to adopt the enunciative
position of the helicopter (control it) or disappear in the face of its devastating beauty. The logical narcissism of military technology is thus revealed:
the obliteration of the *you* in the generalisation of the image of the *I*. The
aim of the technology of speed, then, is the obliteration of the enunciative
modality. Its aim is that of the power of modernity, its appropriation of the
capacity for division: to make the "you" slow, blind and therefore visible, and
the "I" fast, sighted and invisible. Success would thus be a matter of total
destruction.

The drive to make the invisible visible finds a particularly potent modern
form in weapons technology, as Virilio shows, where speed, vision, and
functionality merge into one another. The historical ground he demar-
cates as moving from the aesthetics of appearance to that of disappearance
coincides with the use of aerial reconnaissance, photography and weaponry
in warfare. The motorisation of images allows for invisible patterns of
troop movements to emerge as visible patterns for potential targets, and
the appearance of material military functions (or materiel) made possible
through optoelectronic technologies allows for their almost immediate
disappearance through ordnance. The distinction between the invisible and
the potentially visible is blurred by these technologies that seemingly can
make anything visible, eliminating the horizon for the enemy and securing
it for clandestine purposes by those with the technology (as the Comanche

illustrates). But the distinction that Virilio makes between the aesthetics of appearance and that of disappearance – an insight that we would not have wanted to do without – is possible only on the basis of the more fundamental invisibility that is the structure of visibility. So the conditions of visibility depend upon a blindness towards what, in the realm of the visible, cannot even *not* be seen. It is with this situation that Virilio's historical shift reveals the problem of historicity, insofar as Virilio wishes to limit his analysis to the conditions that render the *potentially* visible actually visible, rather than exploring those conditions of modernity that are less easy to analyse. These conditions emerge from the necessity of the absolutely invisible in the constitution of both the visible and the potentially visible for experience. The effects of this historicity need not be restricted to Virilio, for the implications will be felt whenever such a distinction is attempted: the conditions of historicity are what allow any historical shift or distinction to be made in the first place. An acute awareness of such conditions can be read in the modernist works we examine. Put in another way, then, certain modernist experiments give rise to and modify those attributes of modernity rather than vice versa. Following a similar logic, the aesthetic found in the slow-motion take-off becomes the means by which the technology expresses itself and reveals itself as technology.

Notes

1. Bell Textron Helicopter *AH-1Z Pocket Guide* 2. www.bellhelicopter.textron. com/en/aircraft/military/pdf/UH1Y_PG_04_web.pdf
2. John Keats, *Poetic Works* (Oxford: OUP, 1963) p. 220.
3. Charles Baudelaire, *The Flowers of Evil and Paris Spleen* (Rochester: BOA, 1991) p. 338.
4. Stéphane Mallarmé, *Oeuvres Completes* (Paris: Gallimard, 1998) vol. I, pp. 413–14.
5. Translation by Henry Weinfield in Stéphane Mallarmé, *Collected Poems* (Berkeley: University of California Press, 1996) pp. 87–8.
6. See "Correspondence choisie" and "Crise de vers", in Stéphane Mallarmé *Oeuvres Complètes* (Paris: Gallimard, 1998) vol. I, 632–821 and vol. II, 204–13 respectively.
7. Baudelaire's comment on the poem misreads it as a parable literally of the future yet also suggestively establishes the counter-aesthetic of ugliness that is inherent in it: "A young writer has recently had an ingenious conception, but one not absolutely justified. The world is coming to an end. Humanity is decrepit. A Barnum of the future shows the degraded men of his time a beautiful woman artificially preserved from a former age. "What!" they say. "Could humanity have been this beautiful?" I say this isn't true. *Degraded man would be astonished at the sight of beauty and would call it ugliness*" (quoted in Stéphane Mallarmé, *Collected Poems* (Berkeley: University of California Press, 1996), p. 242).

8. "Futurist Photodynamism", in *Futurist Manifestos*, ed. Umbro Apollonio (Boston: MFA, 1973) pp. 38–45.

9. Peter Nicholls, *Modernisms* (London: Macmillan, 1995) p. 84.

10. John Armitage (ed.), *Virilio Live: Selected Interviews*, ed. John Armitage (London: Sage, 2001) p. 33.

Chapter 4

We Don't Make it Beautiful

Have you, said the doctor, ever thought of the peculiar polarity of times and times; and of sleep? Sleep, the slain white bull? Well, I, Dr Matthew-Mighty-grain-of-salt-Dante-O'Connor, will tell you how the day and the night are related by their division. (Djuna Barnes *Nightwood*)[1]

The sclerosis of objectivity is the annihilation of existence (Karl Jaspers)[2]

It is worth examining those starker statements of modernism, the grimly hilarious works of Marcel Duchamp, Mina Loy and Djuna Barnes. While these stark worlds can be (and often are) related back to the experiences preceding and between the historical markers of two devastating wars, they also exhibit an awareness of and concern for an ethical ground which precedes those experiences, both logically and chronologically. In the confusion between automatism and life, in which both life and robotic activity turn up consistently as forms of imperfection, an ethical imperative is affirmed. This appearance in artworks of what has been called the *absurd* has a ground in the perceived need to affirm the uncompleted, the imperfect, the purely *potential* and always *undetermined* aspect of human relations, to slow down the effects of automation – including the automation of the senses by various military and artistic prostheses and technologies.

Commentators like Art Berman have underestimated the force of some aspects of modernist aesthetics in their resistance to the transcendental and universalising turns of romanticism in art, fascism in politics, and acceleration in technology (not to mention the generalizing trends of period criticism). In his *Preface to Modernism* Berman links what he calls the modernist's transcendentalism (which he argues remains deserving of praise) to a similar tendency in fascism (which, of course, does not):

While fascism shares the early modernist's transcendentalism, it does so not as an internationalized aesthetics but as a nationalized politics. Modernism is one of the glories of modern civilization, and fascism is one of its horrors. The universalization of spirit in art is not the same as the nationalization of spirit in culture, but the romantics themselves, at least in Germany, failed to make this discrimination.

That oversight has contributed to the stupendous havoc in the twentieth century, although the romantics hardly can be blamed for all that followed – nor can the modernists, who themselves did not clearly perceive this distinction before World War II taught everyone how essential it was.[3]

Modern writers, however, certainly seem to have developed a way of presenting the failure to universalise as a kind of ethical imperative. They do it under the sign of laughter – the comic, the absurd, the satirical – "Nothing is funnier than unhappiness," as Samuel Beckett wrote.[4] If modernism renders anything universal, we might be cautious of assuming, as so many have done, that the universal can be elaborated in terms of theme (as nationalism, for instance, always is). Themes identified with modernism have, significantly, been those of alienation, exile, loss and so on. Significantly, why? The divisions, transitions, scissions and splits that characterise so much of modernist art and writing might appear in some contexts to be symptoms of mourning or melancholia in response to the perceived disappearance of an always mythical or at least partisan (and thus already severely divided) milieu of untroubled relations, of communities and continuity, of governed bodies and spiritual certainties. Increasingly in these texts the human relation as such is presented in terms of its breakdown or at least its diminished possibility – if not of its outright impossibility.

The relationship of mourning to responsibility would undoubtedly have emerged as an intransigent element of these texts – a melancholic refusal to mourn, even, that might have been read as characteristic of mourning at its most intense – were it not for the fact that what disappears under the bland rubric of community, relation or continuity in these texts would hardly have been worth preserving in their terms. What remains fascinating, for its prescience, its delayed yet insistent effectiveness, and for its unremitting comic strangeness, is the production and maintenance, through various techniques, of the sense of division *itself*, with no reference to anything that division could once have been said to *divide*; it would be, rather, the sense of division that constitutes the *possibility* of spatial and temporal relations. The responsible imperative would be that which insists on the maintenance of the division as possibility as opposed to the widespread attempt to appropriate possibility, to mobilise its powers absolutely.

This peculiarly modernist aesthetic, which can be distinguished not only by a focus on division but also by its humour, emerges where artists and writers concern themselves with the work removed from its service as expressive or representational device, thus maximising what is already an irreconcilable division between the levels of enunciation and statement. In "Crisis in Poetry," Stéphane Mallarmé observes that:

> the pure work implies the disappearance of the poet as speaker, yielding his initiative to words, which are mobilised by the shock of their difference; they light up with reciprocal reflections like a virtual stream of fireworks over jewels, replacing the perceptible breath of the former lyric impulse, and replacing the poet's passionate personal directing of the sentence.[5]

So the poem or painting no longer *represents* the visible world, certainly, but it also no longer represents in any direct way the thoughts of the writer or artist. The writer is now concerned with mobilising the "shock of [a word's] difference", which means, to start with, its difference from itself – its division from itself in its repetition – and, thus, its capacity to signify *beyond* a writer's communicative intention. Mallarmé's poetry *evokes* rather than communicates, but in its insistence on blanks, emptiness, gaps, breaks, empty spaces, non-places and chance effects, what it evokes tends to be the potential of its language without any ties to a representational or expressive function: the virgin as blank. This does not, of course, imply an absence of intention. Quite the contrary, intense control is required for this mobilisation. But it does imply a removal of the communicating function of language in a milieu where language has *no* function *other than* communicating, the heritage of a world in which purpose and function subordinate everything else to the greater purpose of the intoxicating machine. Ironically, perhaps, the intoxication of the machine is also intoxication with the word become mechanical, inhuman, strange.

Once this liberation from the representational function is achieved, then several possibilities emerge: writers and artists *speak*, as it were (so some at least indirect effect is produced), by inhabiting, deforming, hybridising and revising existing *idioms*, inevitably putting into suspense anything that in art would once have been called *beauty*. Anything is fair game in this respect, like the widespread appropriation of new scientific and technological discoveries (photography, chronophotography, cinema, mechanics, cathode-rays and X-rays), or the adoption of elements of other cultural idioms (newspapers, commodities, objects). If the futurist sculptures and photodynamic experiments reveal a sustained enthusiasm for the aesthetic possibilities of an emergent technology, then Mina Loy, Marcel Duchamp and Djuna Barnes each engage directly with idioms of the new technologies and their still recently commoditised environment. But they also indulge in older – forgotten – idioms; again, anything is fair game. In this way the aesthetics of modernism not only inhabits but also preys upon and shadows the reproductive effects exploited by these emergent technologies of representation, especially broadcasting, cinema, photography and the gramophone. It also thus foreshadows the exploitation of these effects in military technology.

The Sensate Parasitism of the Avant-garde

Mina Loy's "Songs to Joannes" for thirty-four stanzas presents, it would seem (for these fragments do not cohere enough to form anything as homogeneous as a voice), a satirically euphemistic and for its time shocking address to a disappointing lover.[6] The sequence adopts and inhabits – and in the process darkles, or distorts beyond recognition – several of the categories of the Italian Renaissance love song, themselves refinements of troubadour idioms (the song at twilight, the aubade or dawn song, the midnight vigil, the lament, the May morning, and so on) while simultaneously satirising, by sewing them into her pastiche, several more contemporary idioms. Fragments of the languages of botany, zoology and husbandry, as well as phrases suggestive of sexual psychopathology, are embedded among echoes of the rather fruity and unashamedly romantic contemporary travelogues (or Baedekers), like those of the symbolist Edward Hutton, whose *Florence* from 1913 evokes the old world of Boccaccio, of rosy dawns over the Arno and peasant songs overheard from shaded or lamp-lit streets.[7] Loy's version exploits the latent pornography of the traditional dawn song:

> Licking the Arno
> The little rosy
> Tongue of Dawn
> Interferes with our eyelashes. (*Lunar*, 63)

Throughout Loy weaves the thinnest of diaphanous veils between euphemism and casual vulgarity, consistently evoking placid cocks, premature ejaculations, spatters of sweat, blood, semen, and the thick scent of detumescence.[8] Each stanza seems to address, more or less obscurely, the same emotional pattern: disappointment, the promise unfulfilled, the crumbling ruin of a rising hope deflated:

> The skin sack
> In which a wanton duality
> Packed
> All the completion of my infructuous impulses
> Something the shape of a man
> To the causal vulgarity of the merely observant
> More of a clock-work mechanism
> Running down against time
> To which I am not paced (*Lunar*, 53–4)

The several figures of manhood, intricately disconnected from the singular figure of aroused yet unfulfilled feminine desire, often fall from the promise of organic fecundity to the failed mechanics of clocks or clockwork toys wearing down, puppets dropped in heaps, he arriving home alone, she not knowing where to turn. The "skin sack" here is itself a duality, a Shakespearean quibble, literally describing the fruitful bag of the male organ yet figuring it as a corpse in the contemporary slang. At the heart of the emotion each time lies the irretrievable moment, the disjunction of time with time, of two incompatible temporalities running as if at different speeds.

Similarly, fragments of the scholarly discourse of neurology, which turn up in "Parturition," must compete with several other discourses in bizarre juxtaposition. Both these works signal as their minimal reference two basic functions with the same aim: conception (or its disappointing misfire) and childbirth (the experience filtered through aesthetic, medical and everyday discourses in bewildering juxtaposition). Both works rely consistently on procedures of repetition that each time foreground a division or a failure of connection. "Parturition" presents a dizzying text on giving birth that performs several discursive functions:

> I am the centre
> Of a circle of pain
> Exceeding its boundaries in every direction
> The business of the bland sun
> Has no affair with me
> In my congested agony
> From which there is no escape
> On infinitely prolonged nerve-vibrations (*Lunar*, 4)

The text includes a pagan hymn to the earth mother goddess ("I am the centre . . .") the faux-lyrical evocation of the prone mother-to-be, the trivial absurdity of the outside world, figured here by the sun and the bland world of business, later glimpsed in sound through an open window. The reference to "nerve-vibrations" recalls those neurological documents, but it also perhaps more significantly recalls Vasily Kandinsky's then recent quasi-mystical treatise on aesthetics.

Kandinsky, communicating with Arnold Schoenberg, had in 1911 established an argument for the purity of abstraction in art.[9] Modern music, he thought, "introduces us into a new realm, where musical experience is not acoustic but purely spiritual: the music of the future begins here." (*Concerning the Spiritual*, 17) Kandinsky's paintings from that time take yet another notorious step towards the non-objective, freeing the pictorial as if once and for all from its mimetic role, replacing it with a new parasitic one. And Schoenberg's compositions from the same period operate with an analogous move away from tonality to embrace principles of dissonance strictly opposed to current notions of beauty in art. Kandinsky's famous essay *Concerning the Spiritual in Art*, which acknowledges its debt to Schoenberg's *Theory of Harmony*, claims to offer an elementary manual on harmony for this new concept of painting in which the "interior sound" of colour and form has absolute value.

Loy's own experiments in poetic synaesthesia, the oscillations of the centripetal and centrifugal forces, her evocation of the nerve-vibrations, and the spatiality of inside and outside, which align her with several of the most experimental movements in modern art, music and writing, serve to mock the contemporary feminist (idealising the feminine) and physician (idealising science), while also inscribing a comic-ironic distance from potentially idealist pretensions in contemporary experimental art:

> I am the false quantity
> In the harmony of physiological potentiality
> To which

Gaining self control
I should be consonant
In time (Loy, *Lunar*, 4)

This mock-scientific equation again uses the ritual hymnal form ("I am . . ."), the Latinate metric doctrine of quantity (a pedantic joke by the end of the nineteenth century) and oblique terminology derived from neurological manuals. Loy's parasitical and satirical appropriation of an amalgam of discursive domains resembles both collage and the many kinds of talking machine (the dictaphones, graphophones, phonographs and gramophones) appearing in the first decade of the century. Broadcast and mechanical reproductive technologies behave in an inherently parasitical manner, and the effect of channelling effortlessly a virtually infinite number of discourses (as Loy does) anticipates the humans-as-talking-automata that we shall encounter in Djuna Barnes's *Nightwood*.

Loy's equation here reads uncannily (and perhaps satirically) like parts of Kandinsky's famous essay, which instructs the artist in filtering music, an immaterial element, through the technical means provided by his knowledge of the language and expression of the world of sound, thus evoking, through their displacement into visual media, the pure ideality of art. Loy's "Parturition" reveals that this ideality in fact masks a greater force: the possibility of a parasitism that both connects and disjoins, that connects through disjunction, demonstrating how the hinge supposedly connecting ideal and physical phenomena actually replaces the ideal *with this hinge*; and the physical now begins to dispose of itself in the artist's techniques as a kind of pure prosthetics, nothing other than, again, *the hinge itself* (between idioms, between senses, between temporal moments). Loy's later essay on "Modern Poetry" celebrates this possibility: "Poetry is prose bewitched, a music made of visual thoughts, the sound of an idea."[10] A further twist in these (what we might call corporeal function) poems, which merge the organic, the mechanical, the aesthetic and the verbal, lies in their powerful logic of temporal deceleration, which is not, despite it all, exhausted by the satire: the centre (of "a circle of pain") establishes the fugal and petal processes as departing from and returning to a point that gradually (and then suddenly) distinguishes itself from the normal rhythms of duration, as the outside world in its everyday measurable temporality leaves it behind and moves on . . .

Kandinsky's experiments towards establishing a calculable and determinate relationship between the invisible and the visible in art parallels and mirrors the simultaneous advances of visual technology into non-visible dimensions. While none of these experiments is without force in helping to over-determine its future, more powerful in that respect would be this decelerant logic of the avant-garde, which reverses those processes that gather momentum throughout the twentieth century. Instead of equating the power and aim of speed with *becoming faster*, the avant-garde slows things down and thus gains a surprisingly firmer hold on this future to which everyone else is racing (as if in parody of Duchamp's "swift nudes") than could have been rationally expected.

The Decelerating Logic of the Avant-garde

The modernist artwork does function like a kind of time machine, operating by a separation of the machine's temporality from the temporality of its starting environment. The separation is achieved by slowing down the temporal duration of the machine in relation to that of its environment. H. G. Wells describes the process in his ground-breaking novel *The Time Machine* (1894–5), which draws on much of the contemporary modern wisdom of time consciousness (specifically the teachings of Henri Bergson) as its key conceit:

> I took the starting lever in one hand and the stopping one in the other, pressed the first, and almost immediately the second. I seemed to reel; I felt a nightmare sensation of falling; and, looking round, I saw the laboratory exactly as before. Had anything happened? For a moment I suspected that my intellect had tricked me. Then I noted the clock. A moment before, as it had seemed, it had stood at a minute or so past ten; now it was half past three![11]

Wells's conceit thus lies in the possibility – in a fictional register – of separating the duration of the machine and its insides from that of the environment outside it. In a poetic register these paragraphs evoke the process of speeding up – of the age, of an individual, of the progress of the species, of the urban working day, of the destruction and rapid renewal of urban space – which in many other registers are the key concerns of modern life, night and day coming and going like the flapping of a bat's wings. They also evoke the technicalities of an environment increasingly governed by the flicking of switches. Yet an interesting contradiction also emerges and remains, not to be dislodged once the analysis of poetic and fictional techniques has been observed. The experience of speed – of *putting on pace* – can best be evoked, as we have already remarked – through the enunciative modality of slowness:

> As I put on pace, night followed day like the flapping of a black wing. The dim suggestion of the laboratory seemed presently to fall away from me, and I saw the sun hopping swiftly across the sky, leaping it every minute, and every minute marking a day. I suppose the laboratory had been destroyed and I had come into the open air. I had a dim impression of scaffolding, but I was already going too fast to be conscious of any moving things. The slowest snail that ever crawled dashed by too fast for me. (Wells, *Time*, 20–1)[12]

The time machine supposedly speeds up in its progress into the future, but in fact, through an ineluctable property of its own temporal-mechanical logic, it can only proceed in this way by *delaying* its progress, by forceful *deceleration*. The inevitable objection – that this is still nonetheless merely a fiction, evocative to be sure, entertaining without doubt, thought provoking, even poignant and not without philosophical merit, but a fiction nonetheless, so quite neutral and at best analogical when it comes to issues of technological practicality and scientific fact – would dissolve if this property emerged as operating at the very basis of modern life (and death).

Alfred Jarry's article from 1899, "Commentaire pour server à la construction pratique de la machine à explorer le temps" ["How to Construct a Time Machine"], harnesses the metaphysics of Bergson (his teacher), scientific discourse (particularly from Lord Kelvin), and the poetics of Wells, in the construction of a famous "imaginary solution" (of which in general pataphysics is the science).[13] Jarry's manual on the practical conditions required for the construction of a machine by which one can explore time deserves what belated reputation it has as a celebrated modern classic but it also deserves to be taken quite seriously as an analysis of the nature of the medium (time) itself. The treatise also commands attention as a theory of the machine and as a hypothetical account of how such a machine would work. Such a machine, Jarry observes, would need to be isolated from elapsing time:

> If we could *remain immobile in absolute space* while Time elapses, if we could lock ourselves inside a Machine that isolates us from Time (except for the small and normal "speed of duration" that will stay with us because of inertia), all future and past instants could be explored successively, just as the stationary spectator of a panorama has the illusion of a swift voyage through a series of landscapes. (Jarry, *Selected Works*, 115)

Jarry's time machine would be a framework containing gyroscopes that spin on their axes at such (controllable and variable) speeds that the machine's own duration in time could be slowed down at will. The external environment would thus be moving through *its* own duration at a greater (normal) rate, allowing the time traveller to proceed to future moments at great speed. Jarry performs a disturbing abduction of contemporary discourses of scientific discovery and visual tele-technology, rather like that performed by Loy (satirically) and Kandinsky (earnestly). For instance, the construction of the machine involves an ideal system of material particles that act on one another by means of springs: "The structure of the system of springs is analogous to the circulation without rotation of infinitely extensive liquids through infinitely small openings, or to a system consisting of rigid rods and rapidly rotating flywheels mounted on all or some of those rods." The mechanism that will allow such a system to be constructed is, Jarry claims, the gyrostat (a gyroscope fixed in a rigid case). The faster the gyrostats spin in space the slower will be the duration of time outside the machine.[14]

In harnessing the developing technology of communications and measurement for time travel, a possibility that runs counter to the modes of development that are designed to *reduce* distances of time and space in communication, Jarry reminds us of the non-existence of the *present*: "The Present is non-existent, a tiny fraction of a phenomenon, smaller than an atom . . . No one has yet measured the fraction of a solar second that is equal to the present" (*Selected Works*, 120). The present – as Immanuel Kant had taught – can only be analysed in terms of the division that it disguises through the subjective illusion of apperception (the always *quasi*-transcendental synthesis of past, present and future). The catachrestic analogy between spatial and temporal units thus allows Jarry to operate in the *gap* where this analogy breaks down – where the temporal unit of duration (the infinitesimally small *present*) cannot be located on the analogue of the smallest physical unit of space: not the atom but by then, amidst great excitement, the sub-atomic particle. Jarry's paper appeared two years after J. J. Thompson's "Cathode Rays", in which he presented his discovery of particles smaller than chemical atoms and demonstrated his new apparatus for measuring them. The infinitesimal that operates as the lynch-pin – or the pivot – of Jarry's text would thus be neither the *present* (at best a theoretical fiction) nor the sub-atomic particle, but the anti-analogical *hinge* that makes possible both experiments in measurement and tele-communications as well as in time travel.

Jarry bases his conclusion – a new definition of duration – on how time appears to one who sees it from the machine: "Duration is the transformation of a succession into a reversion. In other words: THE BECOMING OF A MEMORY" (*Selected Works*, 121). The trick in the tail, then, is that time travel in fact describes the normal state of the experience of duration but from a dimension ("4 dim") that is not accessible – cannot be made the object of an experience – from outside the machine. This "4 dim" and the breakdowns in analogical thought that allow it to be intuited form the basis of aesthetic experimentation in the first two decades of the twentieth century. It also emerges as the enemy – in a literal sense – when science and technology gather speed, under the aegis and sponsorship of state and military R&D programmes, in the drive towards breaking this division (a combination of visible and invisible hinges) down – paradoxically and catastrophically – into its constituent elements. The aim would be to leave nothing left unexposed.

The Non-Aspectable Power of Transition: Procedure Stripped Bare

Marcel Duchamp, who in this sense is exemplary amongst his contemporaries in the visual arts, recalls a Cartesian attitude not to be found in the philosophical legacy: a taste for the verbal, non-retinal, anti-analogical sphere of the *cogito intensif*, divided in itself and thus also from the extensive world, its swift (and sometimes slow) physical doppelgänger. This irreducible parasitism leaves no seat for any transcendental posturing, and it stubbornly resists coherent explanation. The effects of these works (beyond the incomprehension of their own contemporaries and the persistent befuddlement of an always residual critical conservatism) are, recalling Mallarmé, produced by mobilisations that immediately depart from their origins. So no univocal or certain content would be communicated by such works but, rather, their procedural basis would be, as it were, stripped bare, revealing an intention to inhabit parasitically, or reproduce mechanically, alien idioms for the production of unexpected effects.

It would be possible, for instance, to unravel in a provisional way several dimensions of the complex idiomatic confusion that gives rise to *Passage from Virgin to Bride* (1911): no longer to be referred to by the description "picture", this "delay" affectionately sends up the cubist experiments of Picasso and Braque but also reaches back to Picasso's *Les Demoiselles d'Avignon*, of 1907, which demonstrates an analytical design – the elastic yet rigid hinge between representation and art – that also reflects obliquely on the subject matter itself: the group of five nudes. Duchamp's delay also brings about the comic transformation of the three feminine stereotypes, reproduced throughout the nineteenth century and into the twentieth, of the virgin, bride and whore: the dichotomy virgin/whore supposedly sublimated in, or at least hinged by, the figure of the blushing bride.

Further contexts are evoked with the apparent motorisation of the bride (or what might, alternatively, be an insectification of the human figure) in its X-ray, chrono-photographic abstraction, and again it mocks the traditional notion of the blooming and blushing bride with what looks like the reproductive horned stigmata of a flower. Once again, it would be the *divisions* between these transformed idiomatic registers that emerge when we reflect on this work – the products of its perhaps ridiculous comedy. The focus would be on the notion of *passage* itself. In these works by Loy and Duchamp two ideals – the mimetic and the spiritual – are disabused of their pretensions, stripped almost (or beyond) bare, and revealing only the bold and authentic robberies that they manifest in singular yet irremediably parasitical statements.

In *Nightwood* (1936), looking back perhaps on more than twenty years of delayed action, Djuna Barnes includes in the chapter "The Squatter" a satire on the parasite in the figure of Jenny Petherbridge. Significantly, the parasite is quite unable to accomplish any of the normal expectations of a decorous aesthetic sensibility: "She writhed under the necessity of being unable to wear anything becoming" (Barnes, *Nightwood*, 285).

> Her walls, her cupboards, her bureaux, were teeming with second-hand dealings with life. It takes a bold and authentic robber to get first-hand plunder. Someone else's marriage ring was on her finger; the photograph taken of Robin for Nora sat upon her table. The books in her library were other people's selections. She lived among her own things like a visitor to a room kept "exactly as it was when –" (Barnes, *Nightwood*, 185)

The inauthenticity of her second-hand persona(e), combined with the inescapable relation to death, places the figure of Jenny Petherbridge alongside several what we might plausibly call *hinged* figures of the modernist avant-garde. The relation to death (she has been widowed four times, "each husband had wasted away and died") is at the same time a relation to the testamentary character of the language she speaks:

> She frequently talked about something being the "death of her," and certainly anything could have been had she been the first to suffer it. The words that fell from her mouth seemed to have been lent to her; had she been forced to invent a vocabulary for herself, it would have been a vocabulary of "ah" and "oh." Hovering, trembling, tiptoeing, she would unwind anecdote after anecdote in a light rapid lisping voice which one always expected to change, to drop and to become the "every day" voice; but it never did. (Barnes, *Nightwood*, 285)

This testamentary character – the emptiness of the repetitive, hollowed out, anecdotal delivery – is unmistakeably that of the contemporary environment of broadcasting and recording. Petherbridge is one of Barnes's "speaking machines" that, like automata, populate the novel as testamentary satires on the human as an extinct organic and spiritual life form. The name itself suggests a machine (the so-called spinning jenny). It is probably not by chance that her description can bring to mind another of the modernist avant-garde's notoriously *hinged* figures (not only the puppet Judy but) Duchamp's blushing bride stripped bare:

> She had a beaked head and the body, small, feeble, and ferocious, that somehow made one associate her with Judy; they did not go together. Only severed could any part of her have been called "right." There was a trembling ardour in her wrists and fingers as if she were suffering from some elaborate denial. She looked old yet expectant of age; she seemed to be steaming in the vapours of someone else about to die; still gave off an odour to the mind (for there are purely mental smells that have no reality) of a woman about to be *accouchée*. (Barnes, *Nightwood*, 284)

The key reference in this passage is to the mental smell, of course, which evokes a super-sensible-sensible dimension that is exactly that of the hinge, neither one nor the other but nothing else either. It also evokes the sensible super-sensible that various sensory prosthetic technologies seek to harness. The mental smell of someone else about to die would be the evocation not only of the sensible super-sensible but also of the parasite feeding off someone else's death: a chain of hinges replacing the super-sensible with a mortality at one remove, the parasite not quite alive enough to die her own death. Instead she is dependent, in Barnes's narrative logic, upon a figure that, with the motif of the *night*, would more clearly be identified with Duchamp's bride in its structural relations to the bachelors – the figure of the somnambulist Robin Vote.

The night is conventionally related to the day according to a series of fairly well established polarities or clichés: night and day, invisible and visible, forgetting and memory, indeterminacy and calculation. What Barnes consistently draws attention to, on the contrary, would be better described as the power of the transitional. Dr Matthew O'Connor promises to "tell you how the day and the night are related by their division" (Barnes, *Nightwood*,

296). Every figure in the text is related by a division or divided by a relation. The apparent oxymoron becomes the key pattern of the text – going into the night is like entering the darkness of an unknown tomorrow and it is significant that the figure associated with the night itself, Robin Vote, the somnambulist automaton and ambiguous figure par excellence, is regarded by each of the others in turn (except maybe Matthew, who awakens her) as a pure potential – the undetermined through whom they might determine themselves, or (even) the bride stripped bare by her bachelors. In this sense she does reveal them in their absurdity – the frauds, plagiarists, parasites and obsessives that they are – while remaining all the time undetermined, manifesting only the obscurity of potential (as opposed to the purity of the master race in the full automated throes of preparation as Barnes was writing). The point about the power of transition – that is, its potential – is that it can only be grasped as *power* in its undetermined or perpetually as-yet-un-determined aspects and so not as an aspect at all – as strictly not *aspectable*. The power of transition – the power of relation – cannot be presented except as non-relation.

The realisation of the non-aspectable power of transition, then, takes place as a paradoxical exchange between incompatibles, suggesting a milieu of possibility only in its absence or withdrawal, a milieu that could not appear except in the form of the impossible. *Nightwood* builds its sense of the obscure by gesturing consistently to both the disruptive emptiness of the trope of the night and the disorienting vacuity of a several specific contemporary discursive phenomena, most strikingly the incessant chattering of the Doctor, whose interminable switching of discourses resembles the ubiquitous sound of broadcasting technology, taking Loy's rhetorical and satirical strategy one step further. *Nightwood* introduces the Doctor during a scene that might have opened any number of contemporary operettas: "Standing about a table at the end of the immense room, looking as if they were deciding the fate of a nation, were grouped ten men, all in parliamentary attitudes, and one young woman" (Barnes, *Nightwood*, 29). The Doctor speaks and the others listen; interruption is "quite useless", as he gets "his audience by the simple device of pronouncing at the top of his voice (at such moments as irritable and possessive as a maddened woman's) some of the more boggish and biting of the shorter early Saxon verbs – nothing could stop him" (Barnes, *Nightwood*, 31). So it is appropriate that, in the key chapter of the book, "Watchman, What of the Night?", this figuratively disembodied voice presents a philosophy affirming the power of vacuity. The chapter is a discourse on possibility, always figured in terms of the night as the unreadable locus of change, and illustrating through a series of exemplifications that this power must elude all calculation and design (as traditionally) figured by the day. The passages require careful analysis.

First of all it is a matter of grasping *the division* between the tropes of night and day, to the extent that this is possible, as figured by only one of the two tropes: the night. The night stands in for the division between night and day. We focus then, literally, on an un-presentable by making one side of an apparent division the principle of the division per se. On the one hand this is a fairly straightforward reversal – the world of calculation and design finds its deeper determination in its negation, the indeterminate night. But it is not quite that simple, because if, on the other hand, the division is also inevitably a relation – the relation between the determined and the undetermined in their division – then it would be a matter of grasping *division* as the possibility of any and of all determinations. And it would be *that principle* (a kind of principle without principle) which determines the relationship between the determined decision and the undetermined future of its possibilities. The ground of decision would be the ungrounded power of decision itself. This will take us to the ethics of decision and determination, grounding us only in the ungrounded principle of potential change, which cannot fail to disrupt the thought of the calculable decision. Beyond even the complex scene of "overdetermination" that characterises the Freudian unconscious, then, *Nightwood* rests on the radical absence of ethical grounds, and it is on this radical absence – figured paradoxically by the catachresis of night – that its profound ethical *affirmation* is made. Barnes sails – in the mode of the most acute irony – close to contemporary discourses of existentialism and psychoanalysis, of death, the unconscious and love. The night, as the Doctor argues, is constituted from two kinds of act – that of the dead and that of sleep and love:

> For what is not the sleeper responsible? What converse does he hold and with whom? He lies down with his Nelly and drops off into the arms of his Gretchen. Thousands unbidden come to his bed. Yet how can one tell truth when it's never in the company? Girls that the dreamer has not fashioned himself to want scatter their legs about him to the blows of Morpheus. So used is he to sleep that the dream that eats away its boundaries finds even what is dreamed an easier custom with the years, and at the banquet the voices blend and battle without pitch. The sleeper is the proprietor of an unknown land. He goes about another business in the dark – and we, his partners, who go to the opera, who listen to gossip of café friends, who walk along boulevards, or sew a quilt seam, cannot afford an inch of it; because, though we would purchase it with blood, it has no counter and no till. She who stands looking down upon her who lies sleeping knows the horizontal fear, the fear unbearable. For man goes only perpendicularly against his fate. He is neither formed to know that other nor compiled of its conspiracy. (Barnes, *Nightwood*, 127)

Our attempts to purchase with blood this "other business", conducted "in the dark", are doomed to fail, for this other business is outside calculation and therefore absolutely heterogeneous to the lived experience that is simultaneously enchanted and disenchanted by it. *Nightwood's* characters are not characters as such but seem to combine the sub-human with the mechanised super-human as if they were entirely guided by instinct (as in a conventional image of the animal) operating as the automata of a mechanised rationality.

In this case Barnes seems to be gesturing with the trope of the night to the invisibility of a condition that is outside the instrumental rationality of modern urbanism. As the figures suffer in turn the (dis)-enchantments of their affairs with Robin Vote, a series of scenes characterise the vacuity of the opera, the gossip of café friends, walks along boulevards, and so on, that is, the business of modern urban life. The attempts, however, as the metaphor of blood indicates, harness a destructive kind of power. If *relation* is indeed conditioned by division, and the unavoidable caprices it generates – dissemination in an actual sense – then we find here another presentation of the impossible conditions of possibility, which the discourses of technology and modern science seem designed perpetually to attempt to master. Again, this mastery does not simply fail. But it is *produced* through its inevitable failure.

Nightwood subtly pits Europe against America as tropes for the vapid and inauthentic histories of a European mock-aristocracy against the unwritten "blank slate" on which further historical signs may be inscribed:

> The Baron admitted that he . . . wished a son who would feel as he felt about the "great past." The doctor then inquired, with feigned indifference, of what nation he would choose the boy's mother.
>
> "The American," the baron answered instantly. "With an American anything can be done." (Barnes, *Nightwood*, 61)

In this sense Barnes's text provides as powerful an account of the catastrophic political conditions of her time as many contemporary philosophical discourses do. The invention of the baron – the son of a "Jew of Italian descent" and "a Viennese woman of great strength and military beauty" – mocks Europe's pretensions to being the rightful heir of a great historical and metaphysical tradition. Europe, rather, is presented as this site of confusion between automatism and life, in which instead of characters we find a collage of poorly functioning speaking machines.

Existential Ambiguity

Loy, Duchamp and Barnes in different ways locate the horizon traditionally domesticated as that between the masculine and the feminine no longer as a natural and eternal division between essentially opposed organic or spiritual forms of life, but as the paradoxical and incalculable *division* that would seem to characterise modern human experience generally. It is as if the traditionally gendered marking of this division manifests a concerted unconscious attempt to cope with the abyssal quality of anxiety, always in relation to the cluster of terms that surrounds it – secret, invisible, future, unknowable, immeasurable, incalculable, and so on – that add up to an un-aesthetical and absent realm of terrifying possibility.

Once we acknowledge that this relationship between anxiety and the unknowable reproduces, in the shadowy metamorphic ways of modern art, the relationship between military-driven technology and its several yet unconquered domains (darkness, slowness, failure and the other vulnerabilities), then an interesting pattern once more emerges. As is well known, modern domains of knowledge, through their own drive to conquer the unknown, regularly stumble over key terms that cannot be explicated, for they designate the condition that drives the system itself. Anxiety, for instance, has played this role in both psychoanalysis and philosophy.[15] According to this strange – estranging – figure of knowledge production, the object of a contemplation turns out to have been the inexplicable source of contemplation itself.

A related pattern occurs with military technology, which harnesses a force that increases the power and speed of mechanical and electronic processes only by dividing domains into slow and fast, blind and sighted, more vulnerable and less vulnerable, with the inevitably implied aim of producing a capacity for absolute division between the obliterated and invulnerable. The radical reduction, as we have shown, cannot succeed absolutely for the domain which cannot be obliterated (nor even made visible) is the source of technological power itself: division. Under such conditions, the greater the degree of success, the more catastrophic would be the consequences.

The catalogue of modernist motifs when gathered together suggests a strong sense of the wretched tenacity of this *division* that has nothing particular to divide: it reorganises the sense of time passing, dividing time itself into a past that has never been present and a future that never will be, and achieving an evanescence of the present moment too, which disappears leaving behind ghostly images like Salvador Dali's *Invisible Man* (1929). More precisely, it implants a sense of delay into human experience that is not necessarily related to anything that one could say has been delayed – but the delay itself – in its paradoxically pure state. Dali's invisible man emerges as the spectral figure of a seated man, which covers the length of the canvas but is constructed entirely from the lines of a landscape of lifeless arcades, statues and ruined structures. The first of his paranoid double images, *The Invisible Man*, connects the peculiar polarity of times and times paradoxically in a play of presence and absence, figure and ground, that evokes only what disappears in its evocation.

In this and other paintings and drawings of Dali's period of so-called paranoid-critical experimentation, he borrows from two rather different idioms of psychology: studies of emotional states and studies of mental perception. In the clinical sense, paranoia describes the chronic emotional disturbance according to which aspects of external reality furnish delusional proofs for a more or less systematic (and delusional) idea. Dali's paranoid-critical activity exploits the possibilities of paranoia to create what he calls an "irrational knowledge" based on "the systematic objectification of delirious associations and interpretations".[16] The technique, however, that produces the doubling effects of these paintings belongs to the phenomena of ambiguous figures. An illustration of one of these ambiguous figures, the so-called duck-rabbit, had appeared in the German humorous magazine *Fliegende Blätter* in 1892. It provoked a strand of scientific research on mental perception, piqued by the question of how the brain switches back and forth between seeing, in this case, a rabbit and a duck in the same image. The duck-rabbit was observed in 1899 by American psychologist Joseph Jastrow, who used it, together with other such figures, to show that perception is not just a product of the stimulus, but also of mental activity.[17]

For mainstream psychology, ambiguous images like these perform an unambiguous function; that is, they illustrate the role of knowledge or expectations (at Easter children tend to see the bunny; in October they see the duck), or just the direction of attention (left to right or right to left). But Ludwig Wittgenstein, in his celebrated discussion of the figure in *Philosophical Investigations*, notes that the capacity to perceive an object as playing different roles at different times – or more than one role at the same time, so that it acts as two different objects in the same image – cannot be reduced to visual perception alone: the phenomenon is widespread.[18] In the realm of art experimentation the device when linked to the paranoid-critical method, subjects perceptual space to what André Breton affirmed as the "omnipotence of desire" removed from all political opportunism. What Breton affirms in Dali's method is the property of "uninterrupted becoming", which could be mobilised in anything that is made the object of the "ultra-confusing activity of the obsessing idea":

> This uninterrupted becoming allows the paranoiac who is their witness to consider the images of the exterior world as unstable and transitory, or suspect; and what is so disturbing is that he is able to make other people believe in the reality of his impressions.[19]

These two distinct properties of the paranoiac – the destabilisation of the image of the external world and the power to convince others of his delirium – can be used effectively in the field of aesthetics, to be sure, but in the field of military experimentation the potential has been yet more fully developed. In his claims for the uses of "reframing perception" as a powerful weapon in war, Colonel Michael McKim points out that:

> Generating the firm belief that your base is at visibility zero for miles in every direction, can be just as effective an air defense against a visibility-based opponent as if you had perfect Patriot missiles ringing you.[20]

Experimentation in visual technology has played a powerful role in the development of twentieth-century military technology, notably in navigation, deception and targeting, and experimentation on the joints and frames of perceptual space – the labile hinges between perception and what is perceived – can be regarded as powerful weapons. The military definition of p-space (perceptual space) is as follows: "the whole thing: every thought, opinion, belief, sensory input, mental model, mental organization, relationship set, logic rule set, psychological 'baggage,' act of awareness, etc". The aim of a "reframing" would be to alter the p-space of some individual or group. McKim's example reveals his psychological source:

> A simple example would be turning over the picture used in psychology classes, which looks like a happy person one way, but a sad person when inverted. The orientation you use when presenting it to others would be an example of reframing their p-space. You physically altered nothing, but you completely altered their perception of the picture.

Anything that can have an impact on p-space is regarded as a reframing element (an RE) and, like everything else in perceptual space, REs are distinguished according to their relation to chronological or temporal domains: a T- RE [a time negative reframing element] alters the past; a T0 RE impacts on the continual present; and a T+ RE alters the future. There would also be P-time, which in relation to real time can be slowed down or sped up (for example, "making things seem more recent than they really are"). So the military logic of perception, without which the rich history of military deception, decoy, disinformation and so on would have had no purchase, shares its grounds with the paranoid method of modernist experimentation. The target of p-space reframing would always be a "notus" [that is, not us]: "the p-space of the ones who control or influence the country, forces, economy, situation, or other entity you want changed".

The perceptual ambiguity delineated by McKim (the latest version of a traditional technics) has always been the domain of the military, which harnesses without anxiety or concern whatever technologies suit its requirements. The perceptual ambiguity also points toward the ways in which the aesthetic elements of modernism we have been charting resonate with, and are at odds with, the contemporary emerging existential philosophy. In his philosophical novel *La Nausée*, published shortly after *Nightwood*, Jean-Paul Sartre suggests an aspect of existence that stubbornly resists all attempts either to conceptualise it or to fit it into the conventions of sensible perception. The gnarled root of an ageing chestnut tree remains for Sartre's narrator, Antoine Roquentin, invulnerable to any kind of explanation:

> That root, with its colour, its shape, its frozen movement, was . . . beneath all explanation. Each of its qualities escaped from it a little, flowed out of it, half solidified, almost became a thing; each one was *superfluous* in the root, and the whole stump now gave me the impression of rolling a little outside itself, denying itself, losing itself in a strange excess.[21]

This strange excess, a somewhat canonical early performance of the experience of the *absurd*, renders this invulnerable superfluity as a kind of stubborn material persistence. In Sartre's text, however, the excess itself is ambiguous. The root is either excessive in itself – excessive to the conceptual frames that otherwise explain it – or the conceptual frames, the active projection of mental perceptions, are, as Heidegger had taught, excessive to the mere existence of the root. This oscillation of these two kinds of excess in the perception of an existing thing, Roquentin's nauseous fascination with the inexplicable absurdity of it, has its precise philosophical complement in the insoluble problem of other minds. In *Being and Nothingness*, with a sly reference to Descartes's second meditation and introducing the celebrated section on "The Existence of Others", Sartre observes that we cannot know whether the Other is anything other than a machine:

> It remains possible that the Other is no more than a body. If animals are machines, why shouldn't the man whom I see pass in the street be one? What I apprehend on the face is nothing but the effect of certain muscular contractions, and they in turn are only the effect of a nervous impulse of which I know the course.[22]

Again, the mind of the Other cannot be reduced to a system of connected representations amounting to knowledge but must be regarded as a non-objectifiable "I think" analogous to my own, but only insofar as my own is objectified through the Other as a freedom of choice: "the intimate discovery of myself is at the same time the revelation of the other as a freedom that confronts mine, and which cannot think or will without doing so either for or against me".[23] My knowledge of the Other is dependent on the twin possibilities of my acting on the Other and the Other acting on me. We do not need to risk becoming mired in the other minds debate to recognise that what is at stake in the issue – which is undoubtedly a question of action and ethical if not political relations – is the inessential gap of perception. Philip Mairet, introducing Sartre's *Existentialism and Humanism* to an English reading public in 1948, makes the case as plainly as possible:

> If we draw, for example, a black maltese cross upon a white square, we can perceive either the cross itself, or the spaces between its limbs, as the statement that is being made, but we cannot perceive it both ways at once. In the latter case – taking the black as spaces between – we see the figure as a conventionalized four petalled flower in white upon a black background. A gardener would perhaps be more likely to see it as the flower and a military man as the cross. Perception depends on the pre-existent element of choice, which determines the form in which we perceive not only all the varieties of geometrical figures but every phenomenon of which we become aware. (*Existentialism and Humanism*, 13)

The oscillation between the *en-soi* (the existing thing in itself) and the *pour-soi* (consciousness of it) represents the existentialist interpretation of ambiguous figures as exemplary of any phenomenon capable of being perceived. The phenomenon of ambiguous figures is itself ambiguous. Existentialism traces the inexistent gap to a pre-existing element of choice; surrealist experiment opens it up to the uninterrupted becoming; constructivist psychology fills it with pre-existing knowledge and expectations; and military technology either eradicates it or colonises it for the manufacture of deceptions. What these idioms share in their diverse interpretations is a sense of the relation to the other (the Other, the *notus*, the enemy, the friend), the target of diverse persuasions.

The decade or so following World War II is marked in Europe, America and the Soviet Union by a further oscillations between the claims of rationality and those of the irrational. William Barrett's *Irrational Man*, which is generally acknowledged as a key influence in introducing existentialism to America, makes a remarkable observation, in this respect, regarding the disparity he sees between "the enormous power which our age has concentrated in its external life and the inner poverty which our art seeks to expose to view".[24] Recalling Karl Jaspers's worry that there was now nothing left to prevent the logic of technology from leading to the destruction of human existence on earth, Barrett both deliberately overestimates (with a wry reference to over-reachers like Icarus) the competence of technological power and underestimates the resilient wit of the modern artist. The age that has discovered and harnessed atomic energy has "made airplanes that fly faster than the sun, and that will, in a few years have atomic-powered planes which can fly through outer space and need not return to mother earth for weeks". Against this, he poses the grim worlds of modern art:

> But if an observer from Mars were to turn his attention from these external appurtenances of power to the shape of man as revealed in our novels, plays, painting, and sculpture, he would find there a creature full of holes and gaps, faceless, riddled with doubts and negations, starkly finite. (Barrett, *Irrational Man*, 65)

The disparity that Barrett observes here would seem to repeat exactly the division imposed by technological thinking itself, as if it had produced a paranoid delusion about itself that, by the time that Barrett is writing this, fulfills a Cold War logic at its most intense: "this violent contrast is frightening," he admits, "for it represents a dangerous lagging of man behind his own works; and in this lag lies the terror of the atomic bomb which hangs over us like impending night" (*Irrational Man*, 65). The night here is not of course the night of *Nightwood*, but rather the dawn of 1,000 suns, or the final day: another strange moiré effect? In any event, and despite Art Berman's confidence in World War II's pedagogical lucidity (which we examined at the beginning of this chapter), any philosophical failure after that war to grasp the intricate connections between a starkly secular modernism (Mairet calls it a "pitiless atheism") and the intensification of military technicity would probably signal the corresponding success of that technicity's power to maintain the opposition.

Caught in the Pincers

A passage from Martin Heidegger's *Introduction to Metaphysics*, from the summer of 1935, shortly after his resignation from the rectorship he held under the Nazis, connects in both profound and disturbing ways to the issues we have been pursuing, and reveals beneath Heidegger's compromising adherence to a spurious kind of geopolitical propriety a degree of insight that will ultimately make his political position untenable:

This Europe, in its unholy blindness always on the point of cutting its own throat, lies today in the pincers between Russia on the one side and America on the other. Russia and America, seen metaphysically, are both the same: the same hopeless frenzy of unchained technology and of the rootless organization of the average man. When the farthest corner of the globe has been conquered technologically and can be exploited economically; when any incident you like, in any place you like, at any time you like, becomes accessible as fast as you like; when you can simultaneously "experience" an assassination attempt against a King in France and a symphony concert in Tokyo; when time is nothing but speed, instantaneity, simultaneity, and time as history has vanished from all Dasein of all peoples; when a boxer counts as a great man of a people; when the tallies of millions at mass meetings are a triumph; then, yes then, there still looms like a specter over all this uproar the question: what for? – where to? – and what then?[25]

Heidegger's characterisation of Europe – with Germany at its core – is quite complex. Europe would always have been the heir of the historicity of metaphysics which, as Heidegger teaches, completes itself in technology. Europe's "unholy blindness" would therefore be the inability of the modern subject to see its own essence. The "darkening of the world" thus described by *Introduction to Metaphysics* implies a fulfillment of Europe's metaphysics in Stalin's Russia and in capitalist America, now returning as the ends of the pincers and surrounding their own source. Thus Europe would be at once the hinge and the ends of the pincers. What Heidegger is most concerned about here is the instrumentalisation of what he calls *spirit*. The tripartite geographical distinction represents three types of reduction of spirit to the mere instrument of intelligence: the arranging of material relations (in Stalinism); the ordering and explanation of the present to hand (of positivism); and management of vital resources and race (not mentioned but thinly disguised as National Socialism). So *spirit* relates to the dimension in which the gods (definitively none of the gods currently worshipped in the world) might again become thinkable: that is, to the holy. The realm of the holy [*das Heiligen*] and its cognate *Heilen* or "healing" (resonating at once with notions of salvation, well-being and wholeness) signal both Heidegger's theological heritage and his absorption of ethics into his fundamental ontology. But we can avoid reading this as a kind of theology.

We might note that the questioning, which this passage enacts, embodies a mode of thinking through which, as Heidegger explains elsewhere, the truth of Being "becomes a distress".[26] The "what for? – where to? – and what then?" represents the echo of Heidegger's question of being, insisting beneath circumstances which by the mid 1930s had become commonplace as the systematic global urbanism of modernity spearheaded by mass communications and the rapid expansion of military powers. The mantric recitation is more powerful in its rhythmic pulse than in its statements, and foreshadows Heidegger's great unpublished work, translated now as *Contributions to Philosophy (From Enowning)*, which contains his most effective account of the abandonment of Being in modernity. Being is not anything that *is*. So Being withdraws in granting to beings their presence. Everything that exists does so because we as Dasein stand in a relation to Being. But Being will be discovered in its most essential form, time and time again – and in this repetition – as *nothing*. "There is nothing to being." The statement is enacted in the enunciation of increasingly empty phrases and achieved through this recitative mode, which springs from the various "moods" – deep awe, wonder, boredom, and so on – that disclose beings in relation to their Being. Heidegger's lifelong philosophical project – to empty all ontic statements of their content in order to open up the relationship between the proposition and its enunciation (beneath which there is nothing) – can now be seen as sharing a profoundly similar impulse to the aesthetics of modernism that we have been examining. The imperceptible yet irreducible space between enunciation and statement provides the clue to what we have called the gap of perception which, in Heidegger's terms, brings beings to presence by withdrawing from the (resulting) present.

The fact that this withdrawing can only be experienced as a lack is what allows Heidegger, especially in his *Überwidung der Metaphysik* (published in 1954 but based on notes made during the 1936–40 Nietzsche lectures), to characterise technology as the perpetual organisation of this lack – where technology "is related to the emptiness of Being contrary to its knowledge".[27] Just as in Barnes's novel, the animal (or sub-human) instinct is indistinguishable from calculating rationality (or "the conditionless empowering of super-humanity", that is, the *ratio*). Heidegger's reflections here turn to the phenomenon, which for him fulfils technology, of armament, as the inevitable consequence of "the ordered use of beings which become the opportunity and the material [and materiel] for feats and their escalation" (Overcoming, 106). What remains concealed by the escalating consumption of beings is that the aim of technicity is pure aimlessness: "in the unconditionality of escalation and of self guaranteeing armament runs out and in truth has aimlessness as its aim, the using is a using up" (Overcoming, 106). To put it succinctly, the end of armament is the *end* of man. In this way the groundlessness of an ethical ground – unconditionality as the power of an incalculable division – shows that self-guaranteeing armament seems designed to remove the power of decision and responsibility entirely from the human sphere – a point made startlingly vivid in the semi-autonomous and fully autonomous weapons systems created to manage and control nuclear arsenals and their delivery systems. The rationale for the implementation of these systems that remove "the human factor" from the decision-making and operational loop has always been, of course, speed. The crucial effect of this is the removal of the ethical ground:

> What does machination mean? Machination and constant presence: *poiesis – techne*. Where does machination lead? To *lived experience*. How does this happen (*ens creatum* – modern nature and history – technicity)? By disenchanting beings, as it

makes room for the power of an enchantment that is enacted by the disenchant-ment itself. Enchantment and lived experience. (Heidegger, *Contributions*, 10).

If Heidegger's distress points to the way "the average citizen" has been entirely captured by the machination of a technicity that he fails to grasp in the slowness of historical time, and so is in this way enchanted by his disen-chantment, then the emergence of this distress would nevertheless still be found as symptomatic first of all in the technicity itself. Heidegger's mantric recitative maintains a close relationship to those talking machines: the dicta-phones, graphophones, phonographs and gramophones that were rapidly developed and produced throughout the first half of the twentieth century, first in order to reproduce speech and then to reproduce music. A profound and disturbing truth beyond truth emerges, which inevitably imposes a powerful deconstruction on Heidegger's simultaneous adherence to the *spirit* of the German *Volk*, still inherent in his arguments of the mid to late 1930s. That is, this technicity is not only the disenchantment of man but it is also what maintains and saves him. Once again Sartre's *La Nausée* helps to underline this fact. A passage at the end describes how a gramophone record supplies another existential breakthrough for Roquentin:

> The Voice sings:
> > Some of these days
> > You'll miss me honey
> Somebody must have scratched the record at that spot, because it makes a pecu-liar noise. And there is something that wrings the heart: it is that the melody is absolutely untouched by this little stuttering of the needle on the record. It is so far away – so far behind. I understand that too: the record is getting scratched and worn, the singer may be dead; I myself am going to leave, I am going to catch my train (Sartre, *Nausea*, 249).

The scratch on the record alerts the listener to an, in principle, infinite dis-tance between the performance (and later the writing) and its playback but only in so far as the performance survives by virtue of this technical distance. It is an example of the way in which a medium designed to *close* the gap can sometimes reveal its irreducibility: recording technology – like military sur-veillance technology – is designed to reduce the evidence of the technology itself, bringing the performance into your living room or bar, replacing "live" music, perhaps to the detriment of live performers. However in this case we must acknowledge that survival resides in the possibility of repetition:

> Behind existence which falls from one present to the next, without a past, without a future, behind these sounds which compose from day to day, peels away and slips towards death, the melody stays the same, young and firm, like a pitiless witness (*Nausea*, 249).

But what survives is not the melody – young and firm, like a pitiless witness – but the record, which gets worn and scratched, reversing the normal order according to which the organic origin is supplemented by a prosthetic extension. In a remarkable insight Sartre provides us with a trope of existence according to which the existent is indistinguishable from the prosthesis but located in and as the gap – the milieu itself – between production and performance. Here lies the undesirable milieu of decision.

Notes

1. Djuna Barnes, *Nightwood* (London: Faber, 1936) p. 296.
2. Karl Jaspers, *Existentialism and Humanism*, ed. E. B. Ashton, trans. Hans E. Fischer (New York: Russell F. Moore, 1952) p. 11.
3. Art Berman, *A Preface to Modernism* (Chicago: University of Illinois, 1994) p. 250.
4. Samuel Beckett, *Endgame* (NY: Grove Press, 1958) p. 18.
5. Stéphane Mallarmé, *Oeuvres Complete* (Paris: Editions Flammarion, 1998) p. 204.
6. Mina Loy, *The Lost Lunar Baedeker: Poems*, ed. Roger Conover (New York: Farrar, Straus and Giroux, 1996). Biographies tell us that the titular Joannes was Giovanni (Joannes) Papini, Loy's lover between 1914 and 1915, at which point the first of the thirty-four songs was composed. Loy's autobiographical "third-person" notebooks record the following: "Raw from her enforced intimacy with mollycod-dles & her aborted love for Joannes, she felt the salutary jar of being lifted up & let down" (Burke 164). Originally called "Love Songs" (a reference, perhaps, via ordinary translation to *The Kama Sutra*) this remains Loy's most celebrated work.
7. A sample of Hutton's Florentine prose: "Then very early in the morning I will rise from my bed under the holy branch of olive, I will walk in my garden before the sun is high, I will look on my beloved city. Yes, I shall look over the near olives across the valley to the hill of cypresses, to the poplars beside Arno that tremble with joy; and first I shall see Torre del Gallo and then S. Miniato, that strange and beautiful place, and at last my eyes will rest on the city herself, beautiful in the mist of morning: first the tower of S. Croce, like a tufted spear; then the tower of liberty, and that was built for pride; and at last, like a mysterious rose lifted above the city, I shall see the dome, the rosy dome of Brunellesco, beside which, like a slim lily, pale, immaculate as a pure virgin, rises the inviolate Tower of the Lowly, that Giotto built for God."
8. The veil between euphemism and casual vulgarity is sown at the level of the clause, for instance, with the sly anagrammatical restructuring of the derogatory "casual" as "causal", thus producing as if by accident a critical point in the lines that follow.
9. The birth of atonality proceeds from the Schoenberg-Kandinsky exchange *Arnold Schoenberg/Wassily Kandinsky: Letters, Pictures and Documents*, ed. Jelena Hahl-Koch (London: Faber and Faber, 1984); Wassily Kandinsky, *Concerning the Spiritual in Art*, trans. M. T. H. Sadler (New York: Dover, 1977).
10. Mina Loy, "Modern Poetry", *The Last Lunar Baedeker*, ed. Roger Conover (New York: Farrar, Strans and Giroux, 1966) p. 157.

11. H. G. Wells, *The Time Machine* (London: Penguin, 2005) p. 20.

12. Another tale, "The New Accelerator" from 1901, reverses the process, speeding up elapsing time relative to normal duration: "He pointed, and there at the tip of his finger and sliding down the air with wings flapping slowly and at the speed of an exceptionally languid snail – was a bee" H. G. Wells, *Collected Tales* (Harmondsworth: Penguin, 1958) p. 493.

13. Translated in *The Selected Works of Alfred Jarry*, ed. Roger Shattuck (London: Methuen, 1965) pp. 114–21. On pataphysics, see especially page 144. Further references in text.

14. Jarry's ideal system of material springs might serve to remind us that Ferdinand de Saussure and his system of differences with no positive terms develop out of the same experimental scientific environment.

15. On the foundations and limits of psychoanalytic knowledge, see, especially, J.-B. Pontalis, "The Question Child", Trans. Catherine and Philip Cullen, in John Phillips and Lindsey Stonebridge (eds), *Reading Melanie Klein* (London: Routledge, 1998) pp. 81–90; and Jean Laplanche, *New Foundations of Psychoanalysis*, trans. David Macey (London: Blackwell, 1989). On the concept of *Angst* in existentialist thought, see David Cooper, *Existentialism* (London: Blackwell, 1990), in which he is concerned to demonstrate that a main strand of thought common to a wide range of what he calls mainstream existentialist philosophers concerns a kind of anxiety that is rendered absurd and that this absurdity is not something that could be overcome: "It would be an essential, ineradicable aspect of the human condition" (144).

16. Salvadore Dali, "Philosophic Provocations," *Documents* 34 (Brussels, 1934) p. 414.

17. Joseph Jastrow, 'The Mind's Eye', *Popular Science Monthly*, 54 (1899) 299–312.

18. Duchamp's *Fountain-Urinal* is the perhaps most effective example of a double object in art, Duchamp-Mutt (if not Duchamp-Sélavy) perhaps the most famous example of a double artist.

19. André Breton, 'What is Surrealism?', in *What is Surrealism? Selected Writings*, ed. Franklin Rosemont (London: Pluto, 1978) pp. 112–141, 137.

20. http://www.au.af.mil/au/awc/awcgate/awc/reframing-p-space.htm

21. Jean-Paul Sartre, *Nausea*, trans. Robert Baldick (Harmondsworth: Penguin, 1965) p. 186.

22. Jean-Paul Sartre, *Being and Nothingness*, trans. Hazel E. Barnes (London: Routledge, 1958) p. 334.

23. Jean-Paul Sartre, *Existentialism and Humanism*, trans. Philip Mairet (London: Methuen, 1948) p. 45.

24. William Barrett, *Irrational Man* (New York: Random House, 1958) p. 64.

25. Martin Heidegger, *Introduction to Metaphysics*, trans. Gregory Fried and Richard Polt (New Haven: Yale University Press, 2000) p. 40.

26. Martin Heidegger, *Contributions to Philosophy*, trans. Parris Emad and Kenneth Maley (Bloomington: Indiana University Press, 1999) p. 10.

27. Martin Heidegger, "Overcoming Metaphysics", in *The End of Philosophy*, ed. Joan Stambough (New York: Harper and Row, 1973) p. 107.

Part II

Broadcast, Hinge, Emergency

Chapter 5

Ventriloquism, Broadcast and Technologies of Narrative

It darkles, (tinct, tint) all this our funnaminal world. (James Joyce, *Finnegans Wake*)[1]

In this chapter, we analyse the links between three distinct but interrelated kinds of technology: ventriloquism, broadcast and narrative. The skill of ventriloquism allows performers to act so that their voice speaks as another, which is dissociated from its source through cunning illusion. This other voice is produced not from the throat as normal but from the belly, and yet the spectator hears it as if from some other unlikely site, for instance, from a puppet or model or the inside of a closed casket or, as was sometimes the case, from a coffin, thus providing the canonically eerie effect. The skill exploits the differences between hidden techniques and evident effects. Pre-modern instances of ventriloquism have been documented but the modern forms generally exploit the exhibition of skill in the maintenance of the illusion, so spectators marvel at the illusion as an illusion rather than believe that a puppet talks or that a voice comes from the dead. While the *technē* remains hidden, what is on display is its ability to hide itself. As in previous chapters, we retain the Ancient Greek term, which benefits from a fecund yet narrow and thus well focused frame of definition: a *technē* is a skill, a kind of a know-how that capitalises on knowledge and well honed techniques in the service of some practical and intentional end.

The two-way radio might seem perhaps to involve a *technē* of a quite different quality, with different historical contexts of development, motives for use, and technological specifications. The two-way radio is capable of both transmitting and receiving signals. The face-to-face discussion thus appears to be the model – the hypothetical *origo* as linguistics would have it – where the senses of hearing and sight supplement each other in reception and transmission. The two-way radio thus allows an audio and wireless supplement of the face-to-face encounter at a distance. One speaks to another and the other replies, just as in telephony and then all kinds of real-time electronic communications.

The main complication philosophically when considering both ventriloquism and radio technology is that the face-to-face relation is already constituted in the distance, and the potential for bridging it, that grounds all communication whatsoever: the medium of a language and, at any given moment, its always as yet undetermined uses among unimagined interlocutors. The face-to-face is constituted in relation to an always potential other. This is what the ventriloquial act exploits in its simulation and in clever parody of actual face-to-face encounters (or belly-to-face in the classic instances). So while ventriloquism presents the illusion of two or more speakers addressing each other and replying, it does so by capitalising on the distance between two or more interlocutors, which implies a kind of a priori interruption as the possibility of a further encounter. The ventriloquist's dialogue with him/herself satirises the actual dialogues between two or more that constitute societies, and does so by invisibly exploiting the insistence of the gap – the interval – in the form of its phoney polyphony.

The explicit connection then between ventriloquism and the two-way radio emerges in the development of broadcast, for which the model is a one-way address. The ubiquity of sirens in urban space adds to an assortment of one-way communication systems linking industrialised labour with civilians under natural or military threat.[2] The increasing number of uses to which sirens were put over the early part of the twentieth century was coincident with the emergence of broadcast technologies, creating a host of unidirectional communications systems. In the one-way address we discover the ideal form of technical militarisation, which is increasingly concerned with attempting to minimise the actually irreducible spaces and thus the chances of social interaction. It might seem that logically speaking a two-way address would be ideal for military purposes (for instance, for the exploitation of remote transmission of command and reception of intelligence from the field). This is not the case, however, grounded as it is on the ancient model of the courier.[3] Military technology increasingly exploits the resources of one-way transmission and does so by distinguishing between the powers of making the other visible and those of making oneself audible (though otherwise hidden). In this way the two roles of intelligence (the demands of which can be reduced to rendering visible what is otherwise hidden) and command (as the key modality of address) follow relatively distinct and autonomous mechanical procedures. The reply from the field can thus be reduced to an audiovisual blip on the monitor and the command can be reduced to the guided missile.

The increased prevalence of broadcast technologies in the first few decades of the twentieth century saw them become the fundamental building block for conceptualising communications technologies generally, superseding the face-to-face dialogue of which telephony is its supposed mechanical avatar.[4] The face-to-face model, as we have noted, already possesses spatial gaps to be overcome but which are somehow elided in the communications theories for which it is a model, and the technology of the telephone is just as likely to complicate the gap it is meant to overcome. A familiar procedure in modernist writing dramatises a situation that can be read in two ways: both as the failure of communications technologies to achieve their aims; and as the hyperbolic continuation by these technologies of an already more original hindrance to the aims of communication in general. For instance, the celebrated telephone passage in Kafka's *The Castle* implicates technology in its maintenance of an already unbridgeable gap. K faces a one-way telephone exchange that adds further interference to many situations of failed or foiled dialogue, including canonical face-to-face discussions that serve both to exasperate the protagonist and to confound the sense or direction of the narrative. Even one-way communications of messengers and letters are sent on interminable delays in Kafka's novel. When calling the castle by phone, K is confronted by aural information more reminiscent of a radio gone wrong than a telephone, reinforcing the unidirectional tendency of a technology nonetheless modelled on a two-way situation.

> From the mouthpiece came a humming, the likes of which K had never heard before. It was as though the humming of countless childlike voices – but it wasn't humming either, it was singing, the singing of the most distant, of the most utterly distant, voices – as though a single, high pitched yet strong voice had emerged out of this humming in some quite impossible way and now drummed against one's ears as if demanding to penetrate more deeply into something other than one's wretched hearing. K listened without telephoning . . . against the telephone he was defenceless.[5]

This sad and funny passage builds its situation on, first, the identification of a humming familiar from the noisy state of telephonic technology, and, second, an attempt by the hyper-sensitive K to account for the aural effect of this humming, deriving from it the image of singing from "countless childlike voices". From humming to polyphonic song to the idea of the One ("a single high pitched yet strong voice"), the passage describes a parodic operation in which (and "in some impossible way") the longing inscribed in medieval religious devotion achieves its end in a nonetheless incomprehensible response that surpasses the feeble senses: as if the history of Renaissance music (from plainsong chant to polyphonic rapture) has been recaptured in the buzzing of an out-of-order phone call.

The parody gathers a malevolent dimension and a further sinister note when the voice of the incomprehensible One, now a kind of tympanic thunder, threatens penetration through the ear drum into something of the self beyond the senses. Not only does this passage refer us to the techno-scientific assumption of the fallibility of organic senses in need of prosthetic extension, but it also shows how the promise of dialogue-at-a-distance offered by telephony can fall prey to the distance it ostensibly seeks to resolve. And so the promise of dialogue can be easily superseded by incomprehensibly oppressive monologues. Communications technologies if anything help to colonise this promise, replacing the tyranny of monotheistic structures with that of techno-scientific ones, which turn out to be more or less the same thing.

The relationship between broadcast technologies and hierarchically arranged systems and institutions, which are predisposed to perpetuate monologue, is evident enough, but the fact that the aesthetic effects of these technologies on their audiences anticipate and magnify military goals is a bit more obscure. The futurists, though, were able to discern these connections quite clearly. Marinetti and Pino Masnata's manifesto for "La Radia" (1933) glorifies radio's many accomplishments (including those of radio-television, or broadcast writ large) and what they might signal for the future. Amongst these was the abolishment of time. La Radia was "an art without time or space without yesterday or tomorrow The possibility of receiving broadcast stations situated in various time zones and the lack of light will destroy the hours of the day and night The reception and amplification of the light and the voices of the past with thermoionic valves will destroy time."[6] Marinetti and Masnata clearly realise the import of "real-time" technologies for shaping and altering time-space relationships, as well as for providing simulated or virtual communication communities. The powers of "real-time" technologies, and the powers resultant from their manipulation, became a predominant element of the C^{3}I (containment, control, communications and information) strategy of US Cold War policy insofar as the Cold War demanded twenty-four-hour surveillance of the globe with "real-time" response demands. Information was conveyed and acted on by another broadcast technology: satellite – with satellite becoming the next phase in the intensification of broadcast's influences. The ability to obliterate distance and time lags, as we have noted, remains a key goal of US military technology. So, too, is the ability to make the enemy experience time and space in ways different from those experienced by the military command wielding the technology. For military technology, making the enemy slow and temporally removed from the targets they wish to strike is just as essential as making them visible, audible and traceable. The aesthetics of broadcast technologies have just these potential effects on the audience, and it is these aesthetics that create the grounds of possibility realised in contemporary military technology.

So again aesthetics conceals – in its domesticated state – a far more powerful knowledge than is usually recognised outside or, as often as not, inside literature and art departments. Military technology and modernist aesthetics can be understood as two phenomena within modernity that would appear to have little in common. A careful reading can reveal that the distinction is constitutive of modern techno-science.

To take a privileged and singular instance, James Joyce's *Finnegans Wake* (henceforth *FW*), which appeared in 1939 after seventeen years of work during the traumatic period between the world wars, confronts readers with what is often described as a frustrating experience. The text has been deliberately and systematically *darkled* (that is, it has been rendered obscure)[7] through the deformation of nearly every word so that, as one of its earliest expert commentators remarks, "if almost every word of the first eight chapters of 'the book of Doublends Jined' (two ends joined, two ends *jinn*-ed (magically modified by a genie or a *jinn*) and Dublin's giant) carries three or four meanings, almost every word of which carries 'three score and ten toptypsical' meanings or more".[8] The common strategy of quoting from the text in order to help out with the commentary reveals a key factor about the novel's aesthetics: *FW* nearly always can be read as a commentary on itself. However, there is considerably more to it than that. For instance, it can in fact be read as a kind of complex and timely sequel to one of the formative texts in social thought, Giambattista Vico's *New Science* (1744).[9]

Vico, and his heritage in Hegel, Marx and others, offers an alternative to the more standard Cartesian version of modernity, by opposing to Descartes's assertion of a transcendental reason an evolutionary version, which derives the lowly and ignominious beginnings of humanity as a darkness that tortuously approaches the light of modern civilisation. Vico summarises his work as follows: "The darkness in the background of the picture represents the uncertain, formless, and the obscure material of this science" (*New Science*, 28). Vico saw his science as illuminating the passage from darkness to light that civilisation had for him taken. Two hundred years later Joyce seems to have seen a need for something like a reversal of the process ("the Doublends Jined" (20.14)), a possibility that Vico dreads and warns against: the spiral structure of history imploding on itself in the chaos of diffuse cultural energies. But as always with Joyce, his is an ironic appropriation of Vico, and he lends the New Science a teleology and determinism not necessarily found in Vico's work; hence, the spiral structure of *FW* itself.

Supplementing and extending the Vichian critique of the narrative of Cartesian reason – both metanarrative and critique signal inherently modernist strategies – *FW* challenges some of most sacrosanct ideals of modern philosophy: "Like *The New Science*," John Bishop argues,

> *Finnegans Wake* generates a vision of human consciousness in which individual personality can be spoken of only as the summed collection of all persons who have collided with it, made its existence in history possible, and even vaguely helped to shape it; paradoxically set entirely within an individual body, the book devastates as completely as the condition of sleep the whole notion of discrete individuality.[10]

Interesting though these assaults might be, it is the intentional darkening and obfuscation of light and clarity found in the novel that is essential to our argument. *Finnegans Wake* provides a retrograde movement to the arc of modernity's narrative that allows us to discover links between modernist aesthetics and contemporary military technology. The multilingual punning frustrates the forward narrative movement. It obscures the sense of closure and ending, promising these while forcing readers to go off on innumerable tangents and encouraging them instead to revel in its infinite digressions. What Joyce calls his "root language" (*FW*, 424.17) – by which he means a penchant for obscure etymological play – reveals the layered histories embedded in words.

Joyce, "using Vico for all he is worth",[11] darkles Vico's project not only by foregrounding the murky background out of which it emerged but also showing that this murky darkness remains also to come (that is, morning comes but night will come again). Joyce addresses those strands of modernist thought that argue the era's new dawn and explicit teleological break by foregrounding that narrative's own past and by condensing then current technologies with archaic knowledge. In this manner, *FW* looks forward to what unfolds today in the form of military technology. For instance, the techniques of military stealth and penetration rely on the capabilities of illusion.[12] Following the dominant trends of nineteenth-century inquiry into the empirical nature of knowledge and the senses themselves, the aesthetic strategies of *FW* deploy various technologies with the power to dupe the senses, in an explicit examination of their conditions. To render the invisible visible, and vice versa, is an essential component of military technology, just as it is for Joyce's "Book of the Night".

"From the earliest days of biplane fighters that attacked with the sun at their backs," writes General "Buster" Glosson, architect of the Gulf War's air campaign, "one adage has always held true for the combat pilot: you cannot destroy what you cannot see. With the advent of radar and 'fire and forget' missiles, however, fighter pilots could no longer rely on the fallacies of the human eye to avoid detection."[13] This is the prelude to so called "penetration" technology, which degrades the effects of radars and other sensors used by air defence systems. Penetration technologies, therefore, make aircraft "invisible", to use military jargon, to radar. The military metaphor of "invisibility" with regard to radar sight requires a type of technological synaesthesia, as the mechanised vision of the radar system depends, of course, on sound waves. Thus, if radar vision makes sound visible, then penetration technologies must attempt to render sound (produced by aircraft) invisible, thereby blinding the radar. *Finnegans Wake* performs through its darkling procedures this aesthetic confusion of the sensorium. The rhetorical effects that produce the illusion of synaesthesia provide an essential strategy for modernist aesthetics, from Rimbaud to Baudelaire to Kandinsky to various Italian futurists. Because of explicit blurring in synaesthesia of sensory information, during a time of "rational" separation of the senses and inquiry into their operation, it has long held a provocative, perhaps even subversive, position in relation to scientific inquiry (though various psychologists and neurologists, most importantly A. R. Luria, have explored the varied forms of this phenomenon). Similarly, as Douglas Kahn has argued, various mystical, anti-Enlightenment movements, such as that led by Swedenborg, used synaesthesia to articulate an underground anti-biomedical explanation of the senses, one that corresponded nicely with surrealist and dadaist agendas.[14]

Joyce's novel evokes, amongst other things, how sensory information permeates the dark and blind dream world of sleep that commingles with the still functioning sensate world (this commingling is accessed largely through the ear, which, as Joyce notes, cannot be closed as can the eye). Much as radar technology allows sound waves to see, Joyce's dreamer sees with his ears in the sleeping state for the eyes, largely covered in the dream world, are stimulated by the unplugged ears and sound shapes the images of dreams. This stands in marked contrast to Joyce's major rhetorical device, the multilingual pun, which depends on the ear far more than on the eye, and it is the eye that must learn how to hear if one is to read the novel. But the ways in which the eye tricks the ear and vice versa are as much a part of *FW* and its aesthetics as any specific instance of synesthesia. The trickery inherent in the synesthetic text destabilises the solidity of the sphere of so-called empirical experience, the closure of the senses, which techno-science attempts to rationalise and control.

Ventriloquism: The Dissociated Voice

The burden of Dumah.
He calleth to me out of Se'r, Watchman, what of the night? Watchman, what of the night?
The watchman said, The morning cometh, and also the night: if ye will inquire, inquire ye: return, come. (Isaiah 21: 11–12)
Witchman, watch of your night? Es voes, ez noes, nott voes, ges, noun. It goes. It does not go. Darkpark's acoo with sucking loves. (James Joyce, *FW*, 245)

Ventriloquism, or *engastrimythos*, which means *speaking as if from the belly*, is a technology of illusion that uses and confuses the two senses of sight and sound in the following ways: through polyphony (the ventriloquist must know polyphony in that he must be able to speak in many voices including simulations of voices at varying distances, but he must be able to do so without moving his face or lips) and distraction (the watcher can be distracted by movements or imagined movements at a distance from the actual source of the sounds). The key strategy, however, is substitution, which really involves six techniques: substitution of some specific sounds (or combinations thereof) by others that sound similar, but need no lip or chin movement; avoidance of sounds that cannot easily be substituted (the text to be spoken can be known in advance, and one can choose synonyms for difficult words); keeping one's mouth almost closed, which serves to hide movements of the tongue; hiding the movements of the chest while breathing; distraction of the audience (for example, with the dummy); and manipulating the fact that people tend to understand what they want to understand, and not what their ears are actually receiving. These techniques seem to have been known for millennia, as numerous documents attest. Their effects have been associated with prophets, who seemed capable of making the dead talk, and with witches, for whom ventriloquism was just one of a repertoire of conjuring tricks and illusions. By the mid-nineteenth century the apparently supernatural mystery of dissociated voices had dissolved, only to be replaced by a mystique far more powerful in the evolution of the human race, that of *explanation*. The reduction of knowledge to *technē* perhaps reaches its apex at this time, when the personal libraries of the bourgeoisie were filled with growing volumes of encyclopedias, personal education manuals, readers and dictionaries of all kinds. The modern information explosion is little more than a blank parody of this, as the technicity of knowledge production and explanations for the millions gains momentum. Chambers's classic twenty-volume *Miscellany of Useful and Entertaining Tracts* (1844–7) devotes thirty-one pages to ventriloquism and in doing so exposes the techniques of several well known entertainers of the time:

> Ventriloquism (or stomach-speaking) is a vocal mimicry of sounds, by which an illusion is produced on the hearer that the sound comes not from the mimic, but from some other appropriate source. When these imitations are made without moving the lips, features, or body, the illusive effect of the mimicry is perfectly magical. Of course the art depends upon a knowledge of the principles of acoustics – such as relate to distance, loudness of sound, pitch of voice, and the like – and also upon great command of features, coupled with long-continued practice. Another extraneous aid of great importance, is the direction of the auditors' attention, either by word, gesture, or look, to the quarter whence the sound is supposed to come. If any individual in company turn his head, with an air of attention, to any particular quarter, we involuntarily do the same, and upon the skilful management of this particular much of the ventriloquist's illusion in reality depends.[15]

The fascination with conjuring in the nineteenth century owes less to credulity in the face of the supernatural and more to the entertainment value of the likes of jugglers and ventriloquists. The power of these forms of entertainment is that they have a practical explanation, no matter how improbable or diabolical.[16] Steven Connor's book on the cultural history of ventriloquism seems credulous to the power of its illusions:

> The dissociated voice is always closer to the condition of a cry than of an articulate utterance. A cry is not pure sound, but rather pure utterance, which is to say, the force of speech without, or in excess of, its recognizable and regularizing forms. A cry always seems in excess of the one from whom it issues, and in excess of the semantic content which it may have in the cry, something else speaks apart from the person. In the cry, and its associated forms, we near, not so much the voice of the feelings, or even of the body, as in certain accounts of hysterical speech, but rather the uttering of utterance itself.[17]

Connor's book is an important contribution to the study of this relatively neglected phenomenon in cultural history but we have some reservations. His most important point needs to be underlined. If the dissociated voice emerges, in his words, "as a category of excess, a figure of nonfigurability", then this is related to the tendency to privilege the voice in human experience, and it also plays a specifically and paradoxically technical role throughout the history of modern philosophy.[18] Phonocentrism, privileging the phonic element of language, designates the condition according to which the voice acts as guarantor and even seat of the singular experience of individual human beings. The covert phonocentric message in Descartes' principal idea (*cogito ergo sum*) would be "I speak, therefore I am". Phonocentrism, then, involves the essentially mistaken assumption of the promptness of voice to intended meaning, the assumption and illusion of a perfect present-tense relation between addresser and addressee. Much as telephony and two-way radio seek to eliminate the effects of distance, ventriloquism, once exposed as a *technē*, only reveals all the more that speaking is always anyway just a *technē* – the insertion of an a priori distance that in fact joins dissociated beings, as for instance Kafka's *The Castle* shows in its albeit negative dialectic. The excess of ventriloquism is the excess of speaking rendered uncanny. But at this stage we must distinguish between the three kinds of excess.

Three Kinds of Excess

The first kind would be that which troubles the ideal, waste naively construed as unnecessary fall-out to be sublimated, contained, expelled or destroyed. Excess 1 comes up as the inessential body and its predicates against the eternal essence of the human soul and its natural intelligence (Plato, Descartes, Kant, Husserl). The body's status as excess is somehow given support by the fact that the body itself distinguishes between its essence and its excess by the endless production of waste products; it shits, cries, bleeds and sweats, wastefully ejaculating unnecessary amounts of the seed and passing of the unfertilised ovum it uses to reproduce itself. Less naïve accounts of Excess 1 acknowledge the technical efficacy of waste (redundancy in language, white noise) but still distinguish between the usable and unusable, thus still retaining the primitive notion of unnecessary waste that Excess 1 designates. There is no doubt that we need such a designation. A tidy home, a clean body and the delete option on one's inbox are essential components of one's practical life. However, in its rhetorical form it comes to stand for that from which a subject in its idealised transcendental form can be distinguished, hovering over and above the finite mortal world, which, throughout modernity, has stood as the goal of human endeavour (often through the aid of technological efficiency compensating for and improving upon diagnosed human limitations).

The second kind (Excess 2) is affirmed by accounts that refuse to accept the distinction between necessary and unnecessary. In a Hegelian universe Excess 2 would be the negative or negation of Excess 1. But – as would always have been the case – this is a strange reversal that fails to escape the onto-theological structure it purportedly opposes. Instead of an eternal and transcendental divinity, it is the non-logical, non-negatable waste that is hypostatised as sacred, and excess is championed as the superfluity over practical life that defines the human in these accounts. Excess 2 emerges in all kinds of materialist accounts of human evolution, not least Vico's, for whom the primitive men, left alone by their mothers to wallow in their own waste, grew strong on it and developed into the giants of so many legends that fascinated Vico in his reconstruction of prehistory. Excess 2 thus also reappears in rhetorical form as a messy multiplicity (language, the chain of the signifier, the bad infinity of endless culturally specific particulars). From this point of view language, along with its myriad excesses, becomes the seat of the human subject.

The third kind (Excess 3) is even less easy to pin down than are the other two. In fact it is impossible to do so: this is the character of its excess. Aristotle gestures to it in Book 5 of the *Nicomachean Ethics* (on social justice) without analysing or exploring it as such. His term is *achresis*, which translates as "without need" or "without demand" (depending on the context of the discussion).[19] It is better characterised as the future possibility of a relation where no such relation at present actually exists. But all relations are in fact predicated upon it as their possibility. In the context of language we can see this operating as a kind of *reserve* according to which events of address and events of reference remain *in potentia* owing to the structure of enunciation – that is, the inherently repeatable and a priori dissociated function of the statement in relation to the ability to make it by marking it (and, as *FW* inexhaustibly demonstrates, remake it in remarking it). The *indeterminate* thus comes up as that which remains to be determined (remarked, remade) – *the as yet undetermined* – in connection with a determinate meaning and its essential repeatability. From the point of view of Excess 3, then, the human subject is actually *not there*, insofar as it is dependent upon an excess that allows for the subject to be posited as subject, but which at the same time removes a subject from their subjectivity. Joyce hides this revelation, appropriately enough, in an acrostic in the first seven words of the opening sentence of *FW*, II. iii: "It may not or maybe a no concern of the Guinnesses but. [I'm no man . . .]" (309.1).

This schematic distinction of the three kinds of excess at once repeats and parodies Vico's "three kinds" arguments, according to which he is able to identify three distinct stages of human evolution. Vico claims to have discovered in the three ages of mythology the stages that nations pass through on their way to rationality, and further, three distinct kinds of human nature: "in all their various and diverse customs," he argues, "nations proceed with constant uniformity through the three distinct ages which the Egyptians noted in their earliest history: the ages of the *gods*, *heroes*, and *men*" (*New Science*, 395). Our own three stages of excess do not exactly correspond with the stages that Vico identifies but with the help of *FW* dig beneath them as if in excavation. They can be seen as an attempt to dig beneath *all* notions of human nature. In this way, modernist aesthetics allows us to put modernity into a new perspective. Many of the modernist texts we examine in this book reach back to modernity's prehistory but at the same time they reach forward towards what cannot be calculated in advance of its future. This incalculable space includes as one of its possibilities technical procedures that operate within a sphere governed by the wish to render all phenomena calculable. The reserve, otherwise known as the ethical relation to the other, before and beyond any actual relation, can also be understood as the ground of history, which is related to it as its historicity. In terms of its relation to what always remains to come history is oriented not *towards* but *from* the future.

Finnegans Wake also gestures to the ethical relation to the other by excavating a kind of irreducible *achresis* that insists against and within the nineteenth-century European master narratives of history. The novel loosens the grip that plagues Stephen Dedalus in *Ulysses*, when he famously claims, "History is a nightmare from which I am trying to awaken". Rather than awaken from it, Joyce re-dreams it through a gathering together of the voices of the marginalised, vanquished and disempowered and self-reflexively demonstrates the conditions that make history possible but which are excluded from its narrative (*histoire*). As these are the conditions that are domesticated and then degraded as Excess 1 by mainstream modern historiography, Joyce deploys the various devalued linguistic forms that Vico argued were the archives of history's cannon fodder: puns, jokes, popular songs, folk tales, and so on. Especially in the "Shaun" chapters, Joyce provides an extended supplement to the triumphalist history of Europe, the teleological dimensions of which were sorely tested by World War I. So, "Shaun the Penman" says that he will "giv[e] unsolicited testimony on behalf of those absent . . . to those present" (*FW*, 173.31–2) touching on both the *achresis* that gives rise to his endeavour and the unsettling relation between the absent and the present. The upshot is this oblique examination of the conditions that make the experience of presence possible.

From this perspective the economic conditions of production and reproduction that are too often said to characterise modernity – an intensification of commoditisation and commodity diversification – can be regarded as a specific kind of action on and attitude towards what we are now calling the ethical yet strictly impossible ground of social relations. It is this reactive dimension of historical development that we have designated by the term *technicity*, which implies several things: first, in the ordinary sense, it implies a condition in which practical results or methods are privileged; secondly, it implies an intensification of active technicisation in which all aspects of life are increasingly dominated by technicism (evoked nicely by Aldous Huxley's post-WWII forecast that "the world will become even more completely technicized, even more elaborately regimented, than it is at present"); thirdly, it implies a condition that develops its own momentum (this is technicity, strictly speaking) with the potential of its current condition only reaching activation in all kinds of consequences beyond the control of human agents and chronologically much later. This last implication involves an irreducible time lag between conditions and their realisation. However, it also implies a further intensification as new technical innovations are introduced to deal with the unforeseen consequences of the previous ones, thus producing yet further problems and solutions down the line (as in the series of rapid advancements in military detection-avoidance technologies and, in response, yet more sophisticated long-range target acquisition and missile guidance systems). What happens is that a surplus of usable technologies can be distributed as consumer hardware (for example, digital computers, digital telecommunications systems, real-time broadcasting and wireless telephony) yet it always remains available for military re-appropriation as and when required.

As we have argued, the essence of modern technicity can be regarded as the response at a fundamental level (a "funnaminal" level) to the insuperable challenge of the excess implied by the ethical relation: the relation to the other, *always yet to come*. Whether in language or in economic exchange, the desire to close the gap between individuals in the social sphere finds its technicist correlative in the various attempts to enhance the supposedly impoverished capacities of human action and perception: especially power, speed, hearing and sight. A distinction arises, then, between the organic and the technological, with paradoxical effects: the organic is regarded as inherently flawed, as black light and ultra-sound "prove", an object from the seventeenth century onwards of considerable distrust; and the technological is increasingly privileged in selected spheres. What we continually discover in our readings of the modern artists and writers in this book is a sphere of operations in which the distinction between an organic base and its technological prosthesis cannot be seriously maintained. It is this same sphere that exercises the R&D of military experimentation.

The aesthetics of modernism entails operations of darkling (again appropriating this self-exemplifying term from *FW*). Specifically, the modernist text *darkles* the presiding distinctions inscribed within modern techno-science. One powerful strand of this darkling – a strategy consistently applied in *FW* – involves a paradoxical rendering of the relationship between the text and other technologies of telecommunication. The operation consistently imposes on readers an experience that places them in the midst of a confusion of sensorial and technological stimuli. The paradox involves a confusion between what ought to be a two-way communications model (an addressor and a receiver) and a one-way polyphonic broadcast, where the receiver turns out to be caught within an endless relay or loop, and where the communication always returns to its source darkled. This aesthetic strategy does not solve the contradiction between dialogue (two-way) and polyphonic broadcast (one-way) but rather it deepens the confusion.

And perhaps the most darkled passage of all modernist works is *FW*, II. iii (or Chapter XI). Here the three technologies we have discussed are joined: the polyphony that disguises a single voice and thus reveals the singular voice as already irreducibly multiple; a setting that includes several kinds of simultaneous broadcast (a two-way ham radio, a broadcast wireless, and a new-fangled mechanical, possibly even an early electronic, television); and the placing *en abyme* of several narratives and narratives of narrative, all speaking across each other and struggling against the odds to be heard above the rest. So great is the degree of condensation in this long chapter that it takes considerable study to unravel the numerous simultaneously unfolding narratives-that-are-not-narratives that compose it. With help from voluminous secondary sources (the explication of this text has occupied entire scholarly careers) one ought to be able to identify at least nine often-simultaneous narrative strands. What interests us here is a description of a two-way radio, the "field" radio developed by the military, which operates as a condensation of the workings of the ear:

> Whyfor had they, it is Hiberio-Miletians and Argloe-Noremen, donated him, birth of an otion that was breeder to sweatoslaves, as mysterbolder, forced in their waste, and as for Ibdullin what of Himana, that their tolvtubular high fidelity daildialler, as modern as tomorrow afternoon and in appearance up to the minute (hearing that anybody in that ruad duchy of Wollinstown schemed to halve the wrong type of date) equipped with supershielded umbrella antennas for distance getting and connected by the magnetic links of a Bellini-Tosti coupling system with a vitaltone speaker, capable of capturing skybuddies, harbour craft emit-tences, key clickings, vaticum cleaners, due to woman formed mobile or man made static and bawling the whowle hamshack and wobble down in an eliminium sounds pound so as to serve him up a melegoturny marygoraumd, eclectrically filtered for allirish earths and ohmes. (*FW*, 309.11–310.1)

This exceptionally darkled passage effectively confounds attempts to find an entirely coherent narrative logic, working as it does with the dream-logic of conflation and analogue. The semantic field in which these are at play is that of hearing as prosthetically extended by very particular wireless technolo-gies, amongst which we find a twelve-tube high-fidelity wireless transmitter with umbrella antennas: "as modern as tomorrow afternoon". The operation of darkling merges some contemporary technical material on radio signals at Very Low Frequency (VLF) with the other aspects of the text already in play. Much of this material Joyce recorded or referred to in his notebooks, but a little reverse engineering in our reading strategies would allow us to recon-struct parts of several such documents. The umbrella antenna (so called for the shape of the spokes at the top of its long mast, like an umbrella without the cloth) is used to send LF and VLF signals, especially to submarines (now as then). Richard Compton-Hall, in his *Submarines at War 1939–45*, explains:

> Signals were sent *to* submarines but submarines were only exceptionally expected to send messages to shore . . . Traffic was therefore usually passed from shore on Very Low Frequencies (VLF), typically around 16 kilocycles (16 Khz), whose ground-waves followed the curvature of the earth and enabled submarines to listen at periscope depth virtually worldwide. The wavelengths for such low fre-quencies required proportionally long transmitting aerials ashore as well as very powerful transmitters.[20]

This pattern of operations, according to which a remote signal can direct a submarine to its target at vast distances, forms the current situation enhanced somewhat by digital and satellite technology. Communication must be reduced to the simplest signals on this frequency range (3 Khz to 16 Khz) since not much bandwidth is available and all kinds of electromagnetic interference is likely. The kinds of "traffic" capable of emitting LF and VLF signals include not only sundry air, land and sea craft, even vacuum cleaners ("capturing skybuddies, harbour craft emittences, key clickings, vaticum cleaners"), but also lightning and other mundane or natural kinds of electromagnetic interference that cause the so-called (and self-explanatory) "whistlers". We are returned, perhaps, to the apparition of Kafka's single tympanic voice in the form of this now wireless technology (in Marinetti's words, communication "without strings").

This cacophonic soup, the celebrated "melegoturny marygoraumd", which for the filter of the ear may be a simple mulligatawny merry-go-round, marries, for the patient reader, several interfering supplementary senses: both the beauty of the melody (*melos*) and the spinning in space (*Raum*) of the words themselves (each formed around a "go"), merging the visible and the audible in self-exemplifying ways. We read of mulligatawny, in the 1886 edition of *Hobson-Jobson*, that "the name of this well-known soup is simply a corruption of the Tamil *milagu-tannir*, 'pepper-water'".[21] And so *FW* reveals, beneath the obscured array of telephonic disturbances, what we might justifiably call the formal possibilities of communicative transaction: disturbance a priori, or *achresis*. The sphere of the disturbance, a "coupling system", returns us again to one of the chief motifs of modernist aesthetics, the failed coupling of man and woman. Here this is rendered in an amusing way, the woman "formed mobile" and the "man made static" (also, of course, "man-made static") in a pattern that repeats the relation of Duchamp's bachelors (the "malic moulds") to his bride in the *Large Glass*. Duchamp's retinal static is here, however, echoed by an audio static of bawling and howling from the ham radio, mingled with the vatic pronouncements of the "vaticum cleaner".

If the viaticum designates the Eucharist for a dying person, then perhaps the entire system addresses, via the medium of the failed sexual relation, a testament to a dying subject. The one to whom the various broadcasts are directed, now dispersed through the sub-aquatic world of dream, fails to amount to much. The dreamer, as Bishop notes, is an "Absent Subject" converted into a plethora of devices capable of capturing invisible frequencies (Bishop, *Joyce's Book*, 273–86). The section provides a meditation on the sleeper's ears as models for all antennae that punctured the ether in a rapidly expanding "otological life" (*FW*, 310.21). Just as HCE's sensory receptions continue to seep into his dream world, so had all human senses seeped into the larger domains of techno-science's desire to collapse time-space distances. The description of the dreamer's ear documents both biomedical knowledge of how sound works *and* its prosthetic appropriation by techno-science to convert the corporeal body into an increasingly targeted site of broadcast bombardment.[22] Joyce delivers this reframing of the subject towards neither the first nor the second mode of excess but rather towards the impossible third mode, towards a subject that is simply not there. The disappearing subject functions as an essential ground for the emergence of a communication event but what Joyce's text perhaps reveals is how broadcast technologies aim towards an ultimately catastrophic erasing of the singularity of an addressee. Aimed at individuals en masse, broadcast technologies deployed sensory information purloined from the body and modified in monological addresses to a mass that was only present in the form of the broadcast itself. Not even an absent subject remains (no absence in total presence). So the overwhelming overflow of acoustical information and muddled terminology (both biological and electronic) in this two-page section thus leans towards Excess 3, an *achresis* that animates Joyce's aesthetic and ethical project as if from beyond its reach. Once again, failure is essential.

Finnegans Wake and Modernism's Darkled Modernity

> Do he not know that the walleds had wars. Harring men, is neow king. This is modeln times. (James Joyce, *FW*, 289.fn6)

If we consider that the technology of prostheses, especially that found in broadcast media, figures so explicitly and obscurely in the novel, then *FW* is often, even if obliquely, about military technology and the powers of division it exploits and attempts to control. Joyce claimed that this novel expresses "the aesthetic of a dream", which stands in necessary structural relation to the wide-awake world of instrumental reason, even if it is the very negation of this fundamental dimension of modernity. "I want to describe the night," he wrote in a letter, for "here is the unknown".[23] Joyce directly and darkly works the terrain of the necessary condition of invisibility for visibility, as well as the unknown for the known, and does so through extensively blurring the senses and language, those being the dimensions of human experience that divide up the world into sensible components – how we make sense. But Joyce shows that nonsense is the condition out of which sense can be made and for sense to be made. An irreducible power resident within modern history, that of division itself, appears at the origin – where the senses and language help each of us, collectively and individually, to make sense of the senses. These senses had been examined thoroughly by biomedical science, manipulated by them for entertainment and other purposes, and converted into commodities of broadcast and other technologies for at least seventy years when *FW* appeared, and Joyce used this situation to his advantage. Two assumptions had been operative since at least *Portrait of an Artist*: that our senses are blurred and synaesthetic at birth and only become focused as one ages; and that language helps to sort them out and divide them from one another.

Joyce's weighty final novel undermines consistently and systematically (that is, with the consistency and systematicity of a dream) any attempts to control the power of division while simultaneously revealing division's stark power.

The aesthetic of the dream reminds us that Morpheus is the Greek god of dreams, and that he is a shape shifter. His elasticity is his signature. The obscured language of *FW* makes the most of chirographic play, as well as cross-linguistic punning, and perhaps most so when the topic at hand is the senses. Synaesthesia keeps the senses from being too neatly divided in the dark aesthetic of "eyedulls and earwakers" (*FW*, 351.25). The synthesis of synaesthesia that Joyce's text slurringly celebrates reveals the slippery ground of the modalities of enunciation being decisively demarcated by an increasingly technological power of division operative in an array of social domains. He hit upon this power's own paradox: its capacity to delete the very elements it requires for its existence. So synaesthesia in *FW* plays several roles. Joyce's sad message concerning sensory modelling in our model modern times ("modeln" (*FW*, 289.36)) would seem to be that the senses become more muddled the further they are extended technologically and separated out empirically.

Joyce figures the centrality of his various *topoi*, including the stirring together of senses and technologies, from the outset. Consider the following line from early in the novel: "Hear? . . .' Tis optophon which otophanes" (*FW*, 13:14, 16). The dream-like synaesthetic apparatus that allows the blind to read by converting signs into musical noises in the treble region, which was called "the optophone", is also the apparatus that profanes the optic-as-ontic as it brings things (Gk: *onta*) to light (Gk: *phaino*, to appear). In the reign of his "aural eyeness" (*FW*, 623.18) that emerged in the late nineteenth century, and which was industrialised, institutionalised, codified and militarised (the last providing the hinge connecting and generating the others), and which continues in our pixelled-present, the eye cannot be separated from the ear despite the all-powerful divisions that the technology affords. "Our ears," Joyce's dreamer reminds us, are our "eyes of the darkness" (*FW*, 14.29). And all the senses "leak" – as it were – when asleep, none completely impervious to external stimulation. None is closed airtight; none is contained or containable.

No matter how tightly we close our eyes, light plays through the lids. And that which does not come from without, comes from within. The light in *FW* lies below that which is sensible and beyond the organically visible spectrum. The black light of science and visual prosthesis (especially productive in and for military purposes) finds natural correspondence in our night-time "vidual"(*FW*, 79.26). The book's language offers us "invision" (*FW*, 626.28) and "meoptics." (*FW*, 139.16). "Nighthood's unseen violet render all animated greatbritish and Irish objects nonviewable to human watchers" (*FW*, 403.34–6). Not only is the night's hood a dark nightwood (pace Barnes) but its "irmages" (*FW*, 486.33) (images, mirages, iris-images) are those lit by ultraviolet light, a light that erases all objects for human viewers: being

Figure 5.1 IHADSS Helmet. Image provided by NASA Images Archive, NASA/ courtesy of nasaimages.org

visible perhaps only to machines, visual prosthesis and dreamers. The division between visible and invisible light became the signature of the military as it developed penetration technology, as we have discussed, and it furthered the assault on empiricism's reign as technology revealed, again, the "flaw" of the organic essential to technology's technicity.

As was the wake's author, the wake's dreamer is "a bland old Issac" (*FW*, 3.11). In fact, he has all of his senses sealed up in nocturnal insensibility, which means only partially sealed up. In this state, the dreamer is like the pilot in an Apache helicopter or in a fighter plane, but without the optoelectronic and telephonic supplements to enhance what has been removed. The pilot becomes techno-science's dream of the dreamer, equipped with night vision, multiple perspectival potential, precision targeting capacity, detachable enhancements of sight and hearing – complete control over the expanded sensorium, which allows for complete control over time-space domains. The pilot's senses have been initially erased and then strategically targeted so that only the information necessary for completion of the mission is allowed to penetrate the armoured body.

The IHADSS (Integrated Helmet and Display Sighting System, pronounced "eye-hads") discussed in Chapter 2 can suggest dreamlike reversals of sensory perception familiar to all readers of *FW*. The helmet includes as part of its miniature, mobile display unit – cocked in salute at the right eye – a projecting device called "the exit pupil",[24] a term reminiscent of Buñuel and Dali, even Aristotle. The technological appropriation of the eye's capacity for visual reception is here dreamily inverted as the eye's capacity to project. In this manner, the darkled language of military technology displays the enunciating subject as controlling both input to the senses and the object from whence the sensory information comes. When the visor of the helmet is lowered and only the Helmet Mounted Display with its exit pupil can be seen, the inverted world of the camera obscura and its visual omnipotence emerges. Such dream desires are blind, perhaps, to their own materiality and enunciative postion, but Joyce was not, as the wake painstakingly evokes.

Sleep and dream-states strip layers of conscious sensory perception, just as the cockpit does, but the latter, as we have noted, replaces them with the most current technologically enhanced versions of such receptions. The military has intervened and imposed a camera obscura, of sorts, over the pilot's senses in order to divide them to its own ends, with direct digital and laser inputs while screening out all undesired information. Just as we learn from birth to separate and target important information for our corporeal senses, the pilot learns to alter them according to the demands of the machine he flies. A new techno-scientific synaesthesia occurs. Sound waves become visible, and the tactile heat of incoming weapons yields a visible "signature."[25] And with all the power to divide and invert (as with "the exit pupil") that resides in techno-science, the IHADSS can convert the heat signature to a "cool" one if the terrain the helicopter is operating within is itself hot. To avoid tactile-visual confusion, the pilot's helmet can divide and parse every sense in synaesthetic mode as needed. The pilot entombed in the cockpit finds analogy with the sleeper, both tracing the vague horizon between states of sensory consciousness, thus revealing how the early twentieth century urban citizen anticipates the pilot in the cockpit.

For the wake's dreamer, a large amount of sensory input comes from within as a transformed "traumscript" (German: *traum*: dream, transcript, dreamscript, trauma, trauma-script) of sensory perception, all muddled in synaesthesia. In an altered but anologic manner, stereoscopes, gramophones, radios, movies, and so on, materialise externally these same sensory imprints in mechanically reproducible form, which were the results of extended nineteenth century scientific inquiry into the senses, perceiving subjects and distortions of both. Bishop argues that much of the novel is devoted to having the evidence presented by the senses put on trial. The passage 86.32–87.12, for example, literally has the senses provide evidence in a trial. "Remarkable evidence was given, anon, by an eye, ear, nose and throat witness . . . he was patrified to see, hear, taste and smell, as his time of night." Working his way through the sensorium and technology's alterations, extensions, magnifications, detachments, appropriations and diminishments of it, Joyce darkles the very evidence upon which the rise of empiricism was largely predicated. In so doing, he finds an aesthetics derived from what we have designated by the term *achresis* residing at the heart of the future of the novel, if it were to have a future, as well as at the heart of the military-industrial complex amassing itself globally for confrontation, which was certainly to have a future.

FW, Ventriloquism, Broadcast: Technologies of Iteration

HCE, the dreamer, does thousands of voices, via ventriloquism and broadcast technology. "Playing on the least change of his manjester's voice." (*FW*,

173.13–14) HCE's dream voice offers us the least change of "his master's voice", which is the mechanical replication of voice and sound the Victor Talking Machine promised its gramophone listeners. HMV/Victor/RCA's "nipper" sits on the lid of his master's coffin with head cocked in wonder over the conjuring power of the magical machine and its ability to produce the voice of the dead. The metaphysics of technology's capability to overcome time and space occurs nightly, of course, in our dream-space that is regularly populated by the dead as well as the living. The technology of dreams, and the dream of technology, allows the dead to speak, weapons to see and hear and make decisions, over-the-horizon weapons to strike invisible targets, and the complete erasure of space through real-time technologies and detection systems. "As we there are where are we are we are there from tomittot to teetootomtotototalitarian" (*FW*, 260.1–2); the space-time stereoscopy provided by technology and dreamed of in dreams has totalising and totalitarian effects.

Broadcast media as a forerunner of other real-time technologies was not only or even primarily entertainment or diversionary technology, which are not as easily separable from military technology as it might seem. Broadcast media, as did outdoor amplification technology and cinema, also held terrific appeal for state regimes in the interwar period of the novel's composition and provided some of the most interesting aesthetic moves on the part of different modernist experimenters. Joyce, though, reminds us incessantly that the prosthesis of broadcast media, as with all technologies related to the senses, reveals a prosthesis-at-the-origin. As such, the prosthesis returns us to the organic senses but in such a way that neither rationality (taking priority over the senses) nor empiricism (grounding the senses as originary) reigns over the sphere of experience. A prosthetics at the origin implies something like an a priori condition of possibility in the Kantian sense but only to the extent that it designates a functional and yet inexistent sphere of operation (approximate, then, to Aristotle's *achresis*). HCE's head best embodies this in the passage of monumental obtuseness running from 309.1 to 311.4, discussed above. A staggering range of broadcast and military acoustical technology can be found residing in and composed of HCE's head: radar, radio, telegraph, sonar and even television. Bishop argues that the media evoked in *FW* are all "sensing devices that have in common the ability to elicit inaudible signs streaming out of the dark ether from invisible sources, and to make them audible and interpretable to human ears" (Bishop, *Joyce's Book*, 276).

What HCE's optophonic dream-sense provides is most powerfully realised now (and even then) in military technology's capacity to render the inaudible audible (and visible), the invisible visible (and audible), the dark ether light, and the light of day dark (via decoys and camouflage). This passage that follows the acrostic "I'm no man" manifests the reserve that simultaneously makes the human subject possible and *not there*. The aesthetics of sleep that underlies broadcast and military technology resides in the confusion of senses, electronics jargon, advertising and waves filling the air on the eve of

World War II. The passage takes on the narratives of modern positivity, revealing the conditions that make the narratives possible, the play between the foreground and the murky background that allows the foreground to stand out. These are also the conditions of sensory manipulation at play in broadcast media, electronics, and other technologies that arrived through the military or in conjunction with it. Their future is found in the present on the electronic, computerised battlefield and in the attack helicopter cockpit.

The book thus returns us to the very problems of face-to-face communication that broadcast technologies seek to obscure or overcome: the space between interlocutors and the time lag of perception. The conditions wrought by distance are, however, what necessitate communication to begin with and make its existence possible. Thus, to overcome them is to do away with communication (individual, collective, corporeal, technological) altogether. The cry "Hear, O world without!" (*FW*, 244.1) signals the desire to enunciate to a world outside the self (that of the addressee) but from within and to a world increasingly "without" the modalities for enunciation or the conditions to hear. "Our ears, eyes of the darkness" (*FW*, 14.29), as apt a description of radar technology as one will find, are clogged with "static babble" (*FW*, 499.34) and the incessant rants of "uncontrollable nighttalkers" such as HCE and Barnes's Dr O'Connor.

Finnegans Wake exercises and exorcises the technologies of narrative, broadcast and ventriloquism as conditions of positivist modernity at its level of performance. The accidental relationships between these technologies prove essential to Joyce's aesthetics but they underlie techno-science, and the technicities it manifests, as causal relationships. The "closed world" of the dreamer recreates the solipsistic and omnipotent dream that one finds in the helicopter/fighter pilot, as well as in the Cold War's operating goal of C^3I (containment, control, communications and information). The fantasy of complete control of the terrain, including time and the seasons, operates in each. But in each case, the outside, the beyond, the uncontainable – that is, the logic upon which the hinge and *achresis* operates – always reinserts itself, or better, it removes itself from its removal. The false division between aesthetics and technology shows that techno-science's power can be found in virtually every darkling word of the novel. The aesthetics of high modernism articulated here is the technology of modernity itself.

Notes

1. James Joyce, *Finnegans Wake* (London: Faber, 1939) p. 244. Further references will use the standard pagination and line number referencing system for *FW*.
2. See Chapter 7 for our analysis of the siren.
3. For the aporias of the military courier see Geoff Bennington's "Postal Politics and the Institution of the Nation", in Homi Bhabha (ed.), *Nation and Narration* (London: Routledge, 1990) pp. 121–37

4. For an extended examination of broadcast media on urban planning in relation to the military, as well as futurist architecture, see Ryan Bishop's "'The Vertical Order has Come to an End': The Insignia of the Military C3I and Urbanism in Global Networks" in Bishop, Phillips and Yeo (eds), *Beyond Description: Singapore Space Historicity* (London and NY: Routledge, 2004) pp. 60–78.

5. Franz Kafka, *The Castle*, trans. Mark Harman (NY: Schocken Books, 1998) p. 20.

6. Filippo Tommaso Marinetti and Pino Masnata, "La Radia", in Douglas Kahn (ed.), *Wireless Imagination*, trans. Stephen Sartarelli (Cambridge, MA: MIT Press, 1994) p. 267. Missing punctuation in original.

7. *Darkle*: 1. *intr.* To lie darkling; to show itself darkly. b. To lie in the dark, conceal oneself. 2. To grow dark. b. Of the countenance, etc.: To become dark with anger, scorn, etc. 3. *trans.* To render dark or obscure (OED).

8. William Tindall, *A Reader's Guide to Finnegans Wake* (Syracuse, NY: Syracuse University Press, 1996) p. 153.

9. Giambattista Vico, *New Science*, trans. David Marsh (Harmondsworth: Penguin, [1744] 1999).

10. John Bishop, *Joyce's Book of the Dark: Finnegans Wake* (Madison: University of Wisconsin Press, 1986) p. 214.

11. James Joyce in a letter to Harriet Shaw, May 1926.

12. We will discuss this in more detail in Chapter 9.

13. "Foreword", in Paul F. Crickmore and Alison J. Crickmore, *F-117 Nighthawk* (Osceola: MBI, 1999) p. 7.

14. Douglas Kahn, *Water Meat Noise* (Cambridge: MIT Press, 1999) pp. 116–21.

15. "Natural Magic", *Chambers's Miscellany of Useful and Entertaining Tracts*, 20 vols (Edinburgh: William and Robert Chambers, 1844–7), vol 9 (1846), p. 22 [article separately paginated, 1–32].

16. Edgar Allan Poe's satires of roughly the same period, especially his Dupin detective stories, expose the absurd components of the desire for explanation. Yet, as often happens in literary history, his satires provide the basis for a fully fledged and still thriving detective fiction market.

17. Steven Connor, *Dumbstruck: A Cultural History of Ventriloquism* (Oxford: Oxford University Press, 2000) p. 33.

18. One key strand of Jacques Derrida's *Of Grammatology* involves the systematic disclosure of a phonocentrism that underlies the western concept of language: "in terms of what . . . attaches it *in general* to phonematic or glossematic production, to language, to voice, to hearing, to sound and breath, to speech" (trans. Gayatri Chakravorty Spivak (Baltimore: Johns Hopkins Press, [1967] 1974) p. 7).

19. Aristotle, *Nicomachean Ethics*, ed. I. Bywater (Oxford: Oxford Classical Texts, 1864) 1133a 26–30. For more on *achresis* see John Phillips, "Just Sentences: The Incalculable in Postmodern Justice" in Steven Earnshaw (ed.), *Just Postmodernism* (Amsterdam: Rodopi, 1998) pp. 29–50. For more on the "logic of three kinds", see John Phillips, "Failures: The Deconstruction of the Teaching body", *Parallax* 40 (July–September 2006) 27-42.

20. Richard Compton-Hall, *Submarines at War 1939–1945* (Penzance: Periscope Publishing, 2004) p. 42.

21. Yule, Henry Sir, *Hobson-Jobson: A Glossary of colloquial Anglo-Indian words and phrases, and Kindred Terms, Etymological, Historical, Geographical and Discursive.* New edn, ed. William Gooke (London: J. Murray, 1903).

22. See Bishop, *Joyce's Book*, 278, for a lucid diagram detailing the complex connections between parts of the ear and broadcast technology.

23. Qtd. in Bishop pp. 6–7.

24. http://www.globalsecurity.org/military/systems/aircraft/ah-64.htm

25. Ibid.

Chapter 6

The Military Body and the Curious Logic of the Hinge

Detachments

To detach: (*Military* and *Naval*) to separate and send off (a part from a main body) for a special purpose; to draw off (a regiment, a ship, or the like) for some special mission. *Detachment*: A portion of an army or navy taken from the main body and employed on some separate service or expedition; any party similarly separated from a main body. (*OED*)

The minimal unit of the military body would be not the *milēs*, the soldier, but the *tack* or the *tache* (a contrivance for fastening two parts together like a clasp, a buckle, a hook and eye). There would be no military body without (such) joints. Thus the military body would always have been conceivable in terms of its attachments and detachments. And in terms of its attacks, as it fastens on or falls upon other bodies with force or arms, joining battle. The *tack* or the *tache* provides the hinge upon which an important element of our overall argument turns: the military body as corpus of infinitely assemblable parts. Without the *tack* or joint or hinge, the military body is an inert mass, incapable of mobilisation, rigid, and static. Without the joint, of which the *tache* is but a prosthetic device, the military loses its capacity to select, add and shed as it needs in its acts of incorporation and exclusion.

The imperial military body was always formed out of an act simultaneously of attachment (union) and detachment (dividing to conquer and to rule). The British Empire begins with the conquest and simultaneous incorporation of Scotland. This pattern of attaching a territory and then detaching armies from it to secure other territories (for example, the Scottish army in India) performs the dual function of foundation and extension. The *tache* is elemental to this pattern.

The capacity of the military body to appropriate various modes of power, personnel and materiel, as well as its capacity to release anything that impedes its mobility or its capability as a military body, proceeds on the logic of the *tache*, combining the attachment to with detachment from. Not merely the core element (the linguistic lemma) of both attachment and detachment, the *tache* is actually implicated in all material and immaterial military technicity – from global strategy to the tack on a ship. It allows the military body infinite flexibility, mobility and metamorphoses. Because it is at the same time so large (potentially infinite) and so minute (possibly a strap or a toggle switch), operating at so many levels and in such fundamental ways, the *tache* cannot be seen easily, theorised or represented, yet it remains the hinge upon which every dimension of the military body depends for its survival, operation, application and transformation. We remain blind to its power and its capacity because this is also one of its most salient and potent capabilities: the power to render the visible invisible and vice versa.

The logic of the *tache* can be analysed to an extent wherever the military operates, most evidently as the various branches of the armed forces: army, navy, marines, air force, and not much less evidently as covert operations, intelligence agencies and security services, which already covers a wider range of interests than either those directly attached to the state or those governed by the armed forces. Security services not directly attached to the state include those for corporations, institutions and private property. The intelligence agencies and security services manifest in alarm systems, gated communities, CCTV and a plethora of well documented surveillance technologies and strategic deployments. The logic of the *tache*, which connects these elements of military operation, also allows the relative detachment of the elements from one another as well as the state from the military. Thus we see that the logic of the *tache* operates in the civic, fiscal, economic and private domains as well as the military and connects them all, while allowing their evident and operational detachment as a constituent function of attachment. The increasing tendency of military strategy made possible through military technology to place the centre of command further away from the field of action while maintaining control is a function of the *tache* in its power of simultaneous attachment and detachment. However, it is also the logic of this empowering connectivity that imposes intractable limits on the desire for ultimate control, as the *tache* always indicates something beyond the corpus, something outside the locus of control.

Postcolonial Blindness I: The End of the Tether

In a remarkable passage from *The End of the Tether*, Conrad attaches two bodies – the body of Captain Whalley with its fading senses and that of his serang, the Malay steersman (a native captain). Between them, the colonial and the native add up to a single yet divided body, mind detached from senses, a literal designation of the divided Cartesian subject. The serang operates almost exactly as a prosthetic device. The focus throughout the passage is on eyes and their adjuncts, a series of metonyms amounting to a sketch of the colonial subject itself (substance and adjuncts), an apparently mutual dependence. The following passage begins by literally looking into the serang's eyes and then moves in mid sentence to loosely focalise on the serang's own point of view in a brief analepsis:

> His peering eyes, set aslant in a face of the Chinese type, a little old face, immovable, as if carved in old brown oak, had informed him long before that the ship was not headed at the bar properly. Paid off from the Fair Maid, together with the rest of the crew, after the completion of the sale, he had hung, in his faded blue suit and floppy gray hat, about the doors of the Harbor Office, till one day, seeing Captain Whalley coming along to get a crew for the Sofala, he had put himself quietly in the way, with his bare feet in the dust and an upward mute glance. The eyes of his old commander had fallen on him favorably – It must have been an auspicious day – and in less than half an hour the white men in the "Ofiss" had written his name on a document as Serang of the fire-ship Sofala. Since that time he had repeatedly looked at that estuary, upon that coast, from this bridge and from this side of the bar.[1]

The ironic reference to the captain's eyes falling favourably (at once signalling the serang's customary superstition and the commander's role in relations of economic power) emphasises the captain's *loss* of sensible power. The union is fragile because the captain is dependent on the serang only so long as the serang remains ignorant of that dependence, an at least displayed ignorance that allows him to function mechanically as a visual prosthesis:

> The record of the visual world fell through his eyes upon his unspeculating mind as on a sensitized plate through the lens of a camera. His knowledge was absolute and precise; nevertheless, had he been asked his opinion, and especially if questioned in the downright, alarming manner of white men, he would have displayed the hesitation of ignorance. He was certain of his facts – but such a certitude counted for little against the doubt what answer would be pleasing. (Conrad, *Tether*, 164)

Conrad's characteristic irony is suggestive here of the peculiar relationship that constitutes colonial subjects (heads without sense and senses unable to question the head) but *The End of the Tether*, as the title implies, looks to the end(s) of colonialism and the stark conditions of a coming postcolonial situation already governed by global capital. Problems of economics get tangled with the fading senses.

As Captain Whalley stands blindly next to his sighted and knowledgeable serang, he stands not only at a hinge in the transformation of the colonial world to the postcolonial world, he also stands on the deck of a ship that reveals the *techne* through which this transformation will be realised: the military body. Whalley, as a captain who made his name on wind-powered ships, has had to adjust his nautical skills late in his career to iron-sided vessels with steam-driven engines. The materials and means of transformation signal a significant shift in the role of the navy, as steam makes ships more amenable to strategy, order and other military *techne*. The inextricable economic dimensions and applications of military logistics in both colonial and postcolonial contexts play pivotal roles in the tale, as they did in the situations of which he writes. But as Conrad makes clear, the transition from colonial power to postcolonial power is not a simple hand-off from the ageing, fading colonial figure of Whalley to the intelligent postcolonial native, but rather a complicated relationship that makes the shift less a transition than a transformation, with fundamental elements of colonialism remaining in play. Colonialism might be at the end of its tether, but the two bodies will remain intimately tethered to one another.

On the surface Conrad's tale concerns the dying days of the colonial merchant, formerly "Daredevil Harry Whalley", hero among "the white-winged flock of clippers that lived in the boisterous uncertain life of the winds, skimming big fortunes out of the foam of the sea" (*Tether*, 119). But indications of the military role in this conspicuously colonial heroism litter the narrative. Whalley himself, we learn, "would have entered the navy if his father [Colonel Whalley] had not died before he was fourteen" (*Tether*, 123). His notoriety rests on an episode connected in a significant way with the military: "His fame remained writ; not very large but plain enough, on the Admiralty charts. Was there not somewhere between Australia and China a Whalley Island and a Condor Reef?" After being stranded for days in his clipper *The Condor*, "throwing her cargo overboard with one hand and with the other, as it were, keeping off her a flotilla of savage war canoes" (*Tether*, 111), he earns this distinctly military honour: "the officers of Her Majesty's steam vessel *Fusilier*, dispatched to make a survey of the route, recognized in these two names the enterprise of the man and the solidity of the ship" (*Tether*, 111). Apart from the existence of the "flotilla of savage war canoes" indicating that what is to become "Whalley's Island" probably already has a name, what Conrad's economic narrative irony suggests is that the haphazard exploits of merchants and ship owners across hitherto uncharted territories, like "the unsurveyed tracts of the South Seas", operate as a kind of avant-garde for military cartography. Military operations inevitably fold out into the commercial realm, which remains available for military access and appropriation, in a pattern that once again exemplifies the logic of attachments and detachments. The merchant ships serve a decidedly military interest here. The opposition between wind and steam that structures much of Whalley's self-consciousness supports the point. After losing his invested savings in "the crash of the notorious Travancore and Deccan Banking Corporation, whose downfall had shaken the East like an earthquake" (*Tether*, 112), the necessity of working hard to maintain his living, "opened his eyes to the fundamental changes of the world" (*Tether*, 118). The central irony of the tale is signalled by this metaphor of the eyes, which while open to the changes of the world are in fact blind to the deeper forces beneath the changes, just as Whalley's open eyes straining against the light are actually failing with his age. He notices the changes in the ships, which "now had yellow funnels with black tops, and a timetable of appointed routes like a confounded service of tramways" (*Tether*, 118). The replacement of sail by steam echoes the Navy's belated charting by steam of Whalley's hazardous route by sail. And while steam is now associated by Whalley with certainty, calculability and death – charting routes as if they were tramways – sail remains the nostalgic siglum of uncertain fortune and life, now gone, along with Whalley's financial speculation.

Conrad has set things out such that the difference between sail and steam, which is undoubtedly clear in the focalised consciousness of his main character, provides a source of ambiguity. The difference behaves like a kind of hinge yoking commercial and military operations together to the extent that it is now impossible to distinguish them, despite the fact that they are evidently quite distinct. Forced to sell his clipper, Whalley becomes the reluctant owner and captain of one of the new steam ships, apparently provoked by a typically chiasmatic reflection: "if a ship without a man was like a body without a soul, a sailor without a ship was of not much more account in this world than an aimless log adrift upon the sea" (*Tether*, 131). The connection between rhetorical and optical chiasmus can be seen as an especially effective hinge in *The End of the Tether*, which operates in a manner not unlike that of the camera obscura, manifested brilliantly by this chiasmatic analogy, which equates the sailor with the ship on the model, again, of the Cartesian duality, despite affirming the man as head (*psyche*, *nous* or *pneuma*) of the ship's body. The second part of the analogy turns it into an antimetabole: a shipless man is as an unmanned ship, an aimless log as much in need of a soul as is the ship without a man. The soul is figured, then, as the connection itself, which puts man and ship together. To complicate matters further, Whalley's reverie on the difference between steamers and sailing ships seems to suggest that the animating forces for these vessels has more to do with the wind or steam that fills the sails or drives the engines. Here we are reminded of the tramway simile from earlier:

> A laid-up steamer was a dead thing and no mistake; a sailing ship somehow seems always ready to spring into life with the breath of incorruptible heaven; but a steamer, thought Captain Whalley, with her fires out, without the warm whiffs from below meeting you on her decks, without the hiss of steam, the clangs of iron in her breast – lies there as cold and still and pulseless as a corpse" (*Tether*, 151).

As Whalley's associations turn to the thought of death, the "pulseless corpse" of the steamer now acts as a form of identification for his own "solid carcass" (*Tether*, 151). As captain of the steamer *Sofala*, Whalley has become little more than a postman, a connection between stations, repeating a single route in the manner of a tram driver, bringing post to customers like Mr. Van Wyk, "the white man of Batu Berau, an ex-naval officer who, for reasons best known to himself, had thrown away the promise of a brilliant career to become the pioneer of tobacco-planting on that remote part of the coast" (*Tether*, 207). Another hinge, then, between military and merchant practices, Van Wyk represents the isolated and discretely singular face of the colonial itself, though his role in the plot is as Whalley's confessor. Discrete and singular, isolated and detached, the Van Wyks of South East Asia will ultimately, of course, give up their role to newly independent and naturalised citizens of the region's (post)colonial nations, whose own independence will therefore have been another version of detachment from, and thus attachment to, the colonial powers whose fire and steam animates the military body itself.

So Conrad's dense novella provides a complex evocation of the metaphysical, material and geo-political intricacies of the shift from colonial to postcolonial South East Asia, and it offers a hinge on which our argument hinges, a way into a series of homologous relations related to the *tache* and its import for the (post)colonial military body. If the defining element of the (post)colonial military body involves the capability of attaching and detaching at will, then a series of related and homologous attachments and detachments flow from this capability: the power of sovereignty to create diasporas (attaching some to the civic body while detaching others), the generation and circulation of capital (both clean and "dirty" along with the power to define it as such), the detachment of the colonial state from the colonial body and its attachment to the global regime of the Cold War (often camouflaged under the rubrics of nationalism and postcolonialism), and the transformation of the colonial military body into the postcolonial body.

Each of these concerns can be found in the figures provided by Conrad and manifest themselves through tropes of the visible and invisible, which themselves reveal the power of the (post)colonial military body in visual terms; that is, by making visible the visible and rendering invisible the invisible, the (post)colonial military body shows its capacity to enact patterns of organisation. Need we note that the end of the tether is a type of *tache* seeking an anchor, a hook looking for an eye?

Body Politic and Mobile Sovereignty

In South East Asia today, a specific type of military body exists: the covert influences of the Cold War hidden behind the camouflage of nation building in a postcolonial environment. From Indonesia to Thailand to the Philippines to Vietnam to Cambodia to Malaysia to Burma, the story of postcolonial nation-building in the post World War II world provides cover for the varied and nefarious manipulations by different powers and their ideological and economic designs. The postcolonial military body replicates the colonial military body, but the camouflage of the triumph of the autonomous nation-state hides from global view the imperial activities of the superpowers in the region.

With an absolute monarchy, as Foucault has pointed out, the body politic is incorporated in the corporeal manifestation of the monarch, and this concreteness lends a substantive quality to otherwise metaphorical language.[2] With the rise of nation-states lacking such a singly defined entity as a monarch, the body politic is abstracted from the collective of the populace and is, in theory if not in practice, to be found in every body of everybody under the nation-state's rule – a situation realised in the birth [*nascita*] of the native [*natio*] citizen of the nation. The onset of the Cold War posed yet another crisis of increased abstraction for the body politic. When the body politic, along with the corporate body, went global, it was no longer bounded in the same geographical manner, nor was it as easily recognisable as a political entity. Nonetheless few citizens in most nations had a difficult time conceptualising what the body politic was, even if they could not easily put their finger on it.

The crisis of the body politic is that it has grown increasingly attenuated and abstracted from the body of the sovereign. Through representative government, the head of state merely enacts via the synecdoche of democracy the will of the people. One body stands for the other. Concomitant with the loss of the sovereign body is a loss of the sovereignty of the state per se, in the wake of World War II and the Cold War. But a disembodied sovereignty allows for a mobile sovereignty, which materialises during the Cold War and is equivalent to it. If there is no territorial boundary for the nation-state in a global environment, then anywhere, any place, *in potentia*, is a sight for enacting sovereignty. The globalisation we live with today is an inheritance from the C³I (containment, control, communications and information) of the Cold War, and this very globalisation, as has been well documented, displaces the politico-juridical concepts of sovereignty.

In South East Asia, the postcolonial moment is inextricable from the Cold War. The emergence of postcolonial nation-states in the South East Asian region is but the ghost of sovereignty, a sovereignty on loan from the Cold War superpowers. And the fact that this sovereignty will exercise its mobility and leave the scene is ever present, as Cambodia and Burma, among others, have brutally learned. The conflicts in the region were central to US foreign policy during the Cold War but in the post Cold War era, now that new nodal networks of interest have been drawn, some of the nations that had warranted policy attention have been allowed to slip from view because they did not matter to the bottom line. They now occupy a spot below the bottom line.

Postcolonial Blindness II: The Cold War

The notion of the postcolonial most often taken up in various ways by Postcolonial Studies has led to a profound blindness about the role of the Cold War in the formation of postcolonial nation-states, especially in South East Asia. Speaking of Sukarno or Suharto as postcolonial political figures of differing nationalist stripes blinds us to the myriad ways in which US, Chinese, British and Japanese policies in the region have kept corrupt regimes in power from the moment of autonomous statehood. Although

Sukarno's rhetoric is that of postcolonialism, and perhaps he even truly envisioned his anti-western enterprise as such, he was viewed by the US, China and the Soviet Union in distinctly Cold War ideological terms that were completely indifferent to colonial relations. The struggles most Indonesians faced were not ones of forming a national identity in the sun of independent sovereignty once the Dutch had left, but rather ones of how to make ends meet under the shadow of dictatorial administrations that waged direct and indirect war on their populations. The struggles were not over conceptions of autonomy and self-rule but how to get rice on the plate and shelter over one's head. Postcolonial Studies tends to focus on another side of the situation, however, generating an anaesthetising and distracting anxiety about self-determination, such that national identity as an equal among the global family of nations begins to occupy the consciousness of citizens.

Similarly the Philippines under the Marcos regime manifested a logic of the Cold War much more than it did that of postcoloniality. The US sponsored the oppressive regime because it was amenable to US desires, allowed it the base at Subic Bay, and was staunchly anti-communist (even if embarrassingly also anti-democratic). The locus of postcolonial inquiry often resides in a postcolonial anxiety unrelated to the geo-political machinations of the Cold War, despite its being the chief cause presiding over the births of nations during this era. As such, it ignores many of the larger issues that went into nation-state formation and perpetuation in the postcolonial era, concentrating a narrow, myopic vision on the position of intellectuals who had long yearned for independence. In fact, the postcolonial blindness manifest in Postcolonial Studies often turns its blind eye to the entire South East Asian region, rarely granting it postcolonial status or status worthy of postcolonial inquiry.

The transformation from the Cold War era to the post Cold War era also removes a number of South East Asian nations from global sight. Cambodia is a cruel exemplar of this invisibility. Cambodia, it is worth noting, is the most mined nation in the world and, as a result, it is the greatest importer of prosthetic limbs in the world. All of its citizens are daily and constantly under attack although the direct military aggression has been gone for decades. In a palpable manner, the mines are a prosthetic extension of the military bodies that once inhabited the territory. Their sovereignty over mobility remains in place although the military bodies and the *nous* that rationalised their presence there no longer have Cambodian citizens in mind. The *tache* by which the prosthetic limb is attached to the truncated biological one provides an insignia of the military. As a ruin overlaps with a monument and reveals the abbreviation essential to the power of the military's insignia, the prosthetic limb's overlap with the abbreviated corporeal one sends the same signal of sovereignty. That many landmines implanted during the 1970s take the leg off just at the knee is an intellectual and historical irony. The civilians of Cambodia have been hobbled by Cold War warriors, reminding them of mobile sovereignty's wrath and the power of abbreviation. The *tache* of the body politic operative in the abbreviation replaces and repeats the knee of the civilian body. Like diasporas whose enforced wandering reveals land-tethered sovereignty, those maimed by landmines show the harness of a mobile sovereign rei(g)n lost to the annals of postcolonial inquiry.

Trucks and Transformers: The Chassis of (Post) Colonialism, Mobile Sovereignty and Nomadic Militaries

The term "military bodies" also includes trucks to which various types of armaments and equipment can be attached and detached. The major point of description for marketing and explaining these military bodies is their compatibility with and deployment of an array of detachable and attachable parts. They can be used as mobile platforms for launching weapons or flatbeds for moving troops. They move and can be made to perform a number of functions related to the *tache*. As with so many other elements of the larger military body, these military bodies themselves can be attached to the larger military body when needed or detached if required (fitted out with various other prosthetic attachments, themselves detachable from the trucks) to dispatch the enemy. For instance on Marion's vehicles for Theater High Altitude Area Defense (THAAD), the electronics to power and control a Patriot missile system rides on a military platform body.[3] Other military bodies include features like folding walkramps, bench seating, removable sidewalls, missile launching pods, heavy-duty winches, and welding and repair equipment compartmentation.

The logic of mobility and the *tache* that we have argued is essential to understanding the military body manifests itself in the 1980s Japanese (Takara) and US-produced (Hasbro) toys known as "Transformers". The toys appeared with advertising taglines that evoke many of our themes, such as "More than Meets the Eye" and "Robots in Disguise". Initially a series of toys launched in Japan that did not perform well in the US market, Transformers saturated the North American market in 1984 in the midst of the Reagan reheating of the Cold War with both an animated television series and a comic book line. Displaying the starkly binaristic discursive practices of the Cold War begun in the 1950s, Tranformers joined a host of other animated series that marked the world as a Manichean division of good versus evil, a welcome relief after the vague nature of the enemy during the Vietnam War. The good "autobots" waged endless war with the evil "decepticons" over sources of energy required to keep their civilisations (here reduced to the military bodies of the machines) alive and literally running. The TV series, comic books and toy lines also introduced the future of warfare as envisioned by Nikokai Tesla as far back as 1901 in which machine battled machine, whether with autonomous agency or not.[4] Following the simplistic equation of these shows, technological superiority equated with moral and ideological superiority, or merely disappeared (as should all technology) in the light of its usage for good or ill.

The primary element of the transformer, however, is its hinge, its joint, its *tache*, which allows each individual transformer to be a fighting robot soldier, a weapons-delivery system and a mode of transportation. That is, a given transformer can, for example, be one minute an upright mechanical soldier ready for battle and the next minute a tank or helicopter by means of origami-like folding and unfolding. Weapons system, transport system, communications system and soldier combine in the transformer, making the manifestation of the military body explicit in a single machinic corpus capable of multiple transformations. The transformer is the quintessential synecdoche for the military body because not only does each part stand for the whole, it *is* the whole hidden in parts. As with the military body and its actions, this whole or any of its constituent parts is made visible or invisible with the turn of hinges to carry out a specific mission or task. Similarly, all of these tasks – whether targeting, transporting, communicating or embodying – perform an attachment to and/or separation from the military body.

But the logic of the military body we have been invoking does not end there, for each transformer is controlled by a leader – a head, or sovereign, or *nous/pneuma* – that is *composed of* the transformers under its control. The various transformers in the Decepticon series operate under a given leader and can attach to one another to form a giant transformer, called Devastator, from which they can detach to act individually. Similarly they can attach to each other and attack as a single military body. The transformer embodies the logic of the many and the one (*omnes et singulatim* as complementary) that has dictated the structure of military body from its inception. The transformer toys are not some futural vision of military engagement but a repository of historical and present-day logics that govern the military body. This can be seen in the cyborg-qualities of the soldier of the future on the drawing boards of the US military now and being field tested in stages. The qualities possessed by the transformer are increasingly being attached to the human body of soldiers in the military now and for future use, outfitted as they are or will be with prosthetic means of enhanced mobility, sighting, hearing, engaging the enemy and endurance.

The logics of transformation turn out to be central when considering the role of the militarised body in a *post*-colonial setting. A transformation, whether considered as the action of transforming or as the fact of having been transformed, implies a relationship between two conditions – the condition before transformation and the condition after. Even in the case of the appearance of a total transformation (in many cases, of course, aspects of the prior condition remain recognisable in the subsequent one) there will be invariants.[5] In the case of the transformer (and, as we have already established, the military body) the invariants would be the joints, the hinges

Figure 6.1   Transformer Toy as Soldier and Transport. Permission and image by Wong May Ee

Figure 6.2   Soldier of the Future. Permission and image by RangerMade Associates, http://www.rangermade.us/store/catalog/Army_Technology.php

(and in the case of origami, the folds) the pliable or flexible moving parts of the organism. By focusing on the *tache*, then, we ought to be able to identify those aspects according to which what looks like a revolution or transformation would turn out to be in fact a conservation or mere repetition of the same. However the *tache* as the manipulable locus of control remains extremely ambivalent and uncertain.

The notion of the locus of control opens onto the question – partially worked out by Michel Foucault – of capabilities (and for us, of course, the question of how military capabilities are established). By the term *capabilities* Foucault gestures towards something rather more general than either knowledge or power but that nonetheless combines those notions. A capability would be anything that makes a body more "able" (skills, disciplines, physical prowess, strength and so academic as well as martial arts, anything a body can be trained to do, and so on). The increase in discourses of "autonomy" – the free individual able to make choices in a free society, and so on – coincides with an increase in the levels of "capability" people actually have, though not in the simple way encouraged by the high pitched claims of a global media. We do not simply become freer and more skilled. Rather, the technologies that constitute our capabilities also at the same time constitute the power relations according to which bodies function in the system. So a capability can easily be the opposite of what it seems. Foucault's point is that an increase in personal power is normally not separable from an intensification of power structures, despite appearances.

To take this insight further we would locate the hinge at the point that constitutes for Foucault the "relation of power". The locus of power (which can also define who has power over whom) tends to shift. Such shifts, however, can take relatively systematic forms in terms of what Foucault calls "mechanisms of power". A mechanism has its own history, its own trajectory, its own techniques and tactics. To quote Foucault, "one must . . . see how these mechanisms of power have been – and continue to be – invested, colonized, involuted, transformed, displaced, extended etc, by ever more general mechanisms and by global domination" (*Power/Knowledge*, 152). If the legal system and fiscal bureaucracy in Malaysia or Singapore were once British but now function in the service of independent postcolonial republics, whose governmentality involves cautious transformations of these mechanisms, then what function does the republic's military capability play? We can easily analyse how a kind of quasi-legal system operates in global media discourse (one is raging right now) that is supported by and that supports "actual" legal procedures and specific types of legislation. What is perhaps not so easy to *see* (with the emphasis on the empirical senses) would be how the relatively localised and thus restrictively mobile military bodies of postcolonial states constitute a collectivity of capabilities that increase the overall capability of powerful global forces. What we have would be a kind of overlap of transformations as colonial fiscal and military rule passes into the discrete hands of newly independent nations (with all manner of strictly localised effects – for example, Burma/Myanmar) contiguous with and fundamentally in support of the transformation of colonial imperial forces as they pass into the hands of the great superpowers of the latter half of the twentieth century.

Foucault's famous question, "how can the growth of capabilities be disconnected from the intensification of power relations?", now points to a question about how these capabilities can be used without subordinating them to the existing power relations (global domination).[6] It is out of this kind of question that we hear talk of counter-colonisation (or postcolonialism as it has become), critical transformation, involution, displacement, counter-hegemony, counter-discourse, even deconstruction, as kinds of putting to use of capabilities inherited from our histories, systems and traditions (and nations) in ways that go against the perpetuation of global, totalising forces.

However, it becomes clear that the active transformer of any transformation would always be located at the level of its joints.

Money Laundering/Dirty Money

"No; there was not much real harm in men: and all the time a shadow marched on his left hand – which in the East is a presage of evil." (Joseph Conrad, *Tether*, ch.6)

As decades of deregulation and globalisation have softened the stance of the nation-state on the world economy, production and trade of illegal goods and services have become part of the daily life of most postcolonial countries, despite conspicuous severity of the punishments for those charged with such offences. The income stream resulting from this type of economic activity, together with the monies from crime, corruption, tax fraud and tax evasion, has created a new macroeconomic category: dirty money. Even if tax fraud and tax evasion are excluded, as some economists suggest they should be, dirty money accounts for a conservative estimate of at least 6 per cent of global economic activity, involving relatively autonomous economies of drugs, sex, corruption, illegal arms trade and the so-called shadow economy, in the economic foundations of all global capital. The profits from production and trade of illegal goods and services are considerable. In the United States, official estimates of the amount of drug profits moving through the financial system have been no higher than a conservative $100 billion, though it is accepted that actual figures (for obvious reasons incalculable) must be much higher. While governments acknowledge that they must deal firmly and effectively with increasingly elusive, well financed, and technologically adept criminal organisations, they seldom acknowledge the extent to which the legitimate flow of capital and free enterprise now depends on them. These organisations do not simply *subvert* the financial systems that are thought to be the cornerstone of legitimate international commerce but they significantly contribute to them. As organised crime develops economic power, it becomes increasingly indistinguishable from state and business institutions and the "free enterprise" it is thought to be undermining. It is well known, for instance, that in Europe a massive percentage of Italy's wealth is the consequence of the circulation of dirty money. What remains to be analysed is the extent to which postcolonial currencies are grounded on it, and the extent to which these currencies depend on and emulate the military body.

The circulation of dirty money operates in a homologous way to the organisation of the military body itself. The largest source of illegal capital is the international drugs trade, which has as its head (*pneuma*) the drug dealer – not by chance the iconic villain of scores of contemporary cinema thrillers. The dealer is the chief executive officer whose main problem is to render invisible the conspicuous bulk, usually hundreds of pounds of small bills earned through the sale of heroin and cocaine. The dealer needs the currency to enter into the mainstream economy. He therefore employs a number of lieutenants, whose role is to clean this dirty money. They in turn hire couriers called "smurfs" (named by investigators because the couriers move so fast they seem like the little blue-skinned creatures of the TV show) to deposit funds, divided into small amounts, in multiple accounts under different names at branches of banks in cities around the world (most nations require banks to report large deposits of cash). These accounts can be merged (for example, in Thailand, Hong Kong or Singapore) and returned to the United States or Europe as clean, legal money.[7] The anonymous dealer now has access to huge amounts of legitimate electronic cash. These "smurfs" (which now include not simply the human illegal banking couriers but anything that can be described as a minimal unit of money laundering) combine to create (or corrupt) an entire bank, which can act as a massive institutional smurf (like the transformer combiners – robots in disguise). In Asia, South East Asia, China and the Middle East, "alternative remittance systems" – *hawala* in India, *hundi* in Pakistan and Afghanistan and *chop* in China – are used. These centuries-old systems allow assets to be transferred from place to place, with little or no paperwork. No money changes hands at all with the Chinese *chop* system. Instead "tokens" (or passwords sent by email) are used as the equivalent of letters of credit for gold or diamonds deposited with trusted third parties.

Special Agent Harold D. Wankel (Chief of Operations, Drug Enforcement Administration) has observed that,

> Money laundering in [South East Asia] is conducted through a complicated maze of trusted confidantes who have done business together for generations. These underground banking systems go back years and years to a time when family members worked away from home and needed to get their wages back to their families in other provinces. That same system exists today and is used to launder millions of dollars in drug money for Southeast Asian traffickers.[8]

The special role of migrant and diasporic communities in the perpetuation of postcolonial currencies is brought into focus here but what the special agent fails to acknowledge is that the exploitation of these underground banking systems must be grasped as a sophisticated development of the basic strategies of colonialism. Colonialism involves two simultaneous and mutually supportive processes: the military expansion of territory and the commercial exploitation of resources for the production of capital. In what we know as the postcolonial era, the military expansion of territory proceeds covertly and in terms of its attachments and detachments. The identification of global urban hubs like Singapore as sites of legitimate business yet as vulnerable to exploitation as effective venues for money laundering reveals the consequences, especially in postcolonial territories, of separating the good from the bad, the clean from the dirty and the legitimate from the illegal. It is Singapore's legitimacy and efficiency, in fact, which helps to make it so attractive for both launderers and legitimate capitalists. The shadow economy requires the lit, visible "body" of the legitimate economy for its existence.

The drugs trade provides a good example of how the systems of capital and the military can be regarded as homologous. Singapore comes down very hard on drug traffickers and is particularly sensitive to that fact that, as Wankel puts it, "it is an important financial center for narcotics-related proceeds".[9] Perhaps the most disturbing, yet unmentionable, fact about this is that money laundering – just in terms of the capital it brings into the world financial markets – functions as an undeniably efficient form of capital growth, just as colonial power functioned as an undeniably efficient form of capital growth. Any attempt to maintain a strict distinction between *dirty* and *clean* money is bound to stumble, not only because the majority of laundered currency remains hidden, successfully distributed throughout the world's banking systems, but also, and more crucially, because (if it was only recognised as such) it is the apotheosis of the logic of capital and its insistence on increasing the levels of surplus value. It also brings into relief the double meaning of the phrase *use value* and the insistence a priori of *surplus* as the basic economic condition. There would be no *use* without the surplus that currency always just is and there is no better demonstration of this fundamental economic condition than dirty money.[10]

The (post)colonial military body has always allowed for both the emergence and attraction of capital, both visible and invisible, clean and dirty, lit and shadowed. The use of military bodies in South East Asia to generate wealth within its own ranks, and for those willing to collaborate with them from abroad, has a history as long as the postcolonial/Cold War era, which is a reiteration of colonial arrangements. Marcos in the Philippines, Suharto in Indonesia, and the numerous Thai generals-cum-prime ministers through coups (from Prem to Suchinda) lead a list of "strong man" governments friendly to the flow of global capital. Today the Myanmar military junta provides an egregious example of local military exploitation for global gain, as many human rights and labour organisations have documented. In so doing, it provides an inverted image of Singapore, but one with similar results. The insignia of the military in Myanmar is more visible than it is in many other nation-states, and no more so than in its relation to enforced labour. Prison labour and enforced labour work to build runways, roads and other transportation infrastructure for the military government. Oddly, the practice of enforced labour through the military body includes those in uniform, for the Myanmar military often relies on enforced conscription to fill out its ranks, especially when they have border skirmishes with the Thai military or when they have a particularly large construction project to oversee. The International Labour Organization (ILO) cites over 300 transnational companies working in Burma and argues that it is impossible to do so without indirect or direct support of the military junta, usually through financial means.[11] British Petroleum, through its links with Unocal, has come under recent scrutiny for supposedly profiting directly from conscripted labour and prison labour. Just as Singapore's open and uncorrupt status makes it vulnerable to money laundering schemes, Myanmar's egregious non-participation in neo-liberal global market practices make it an attractive and efficient site for capital growth in the eyes of transnational corporations (as evidenced by the ILO list). That it does so under the camouflage of the insignia of the military provides further attraction, as well as (post)colonial reiteration.

The transformation of colonial Burma into postcolonial Myanmar provides us with several joints, or *taches*, in the re-iteration of the colonial military body in the postcolonial military body, and in many sites. When Burmah Oil left Burma, it operated out of India through joint ventures with Shell and British Petroleum.[12] The same company is currently involved in the Timor Gap through another joint venture, this one with Woodside Petroleum. Along with other oil interests, it lobbied Australian prime minister Gough Whitlam to allow Indonesian annexation (under Suharto) of East Timor, with the civil war, bloodshed and military intervention that has followed ever since.[13] The colonial and postcolonial military bodies of Britain, Australia and Indonesia allowed for the mobile sovereignty of oil companies to attach and detach itself at will, operating from bases not bound by territorial constraints. In the instances just cited, the generation of capital attracted more capital because it was protected and produced by military bodies capable of guaranteeing its flight if things got too rough on the ground.

Just as the power of sovereignty is found in diasporic groups and the abbreviation of the military, so the power of global capital as "a good" is found in the ability to identify and mark some capital as dirty. This power relates explicitly to visibility and invisibility, the *capability* to render the visible *as* visible and the invisible *as* invisible. This power, we would argue, rests in the *tache* that allows for the military body to attach and detach its constituent parts at will, to perform transformation, and to provide capabilities.

We want to conclude with a brief reference to a contemporary novel from South East Asia, Tunku Halim's *Vermillion Eye*, which features the caricature ghost of Malaysia's pre-independence British past, Claymore, possessing the bodies of similarly caricatured present-day Sydney citizens.[14] Reversing the direction of Whalley's uncharted route in Conrad, Halim's colonial ghost has travelled from Kuala Lumpur to Australia and is engaged in a series of cannibalistic murders while in possession of the grotesquely obese Jim Oxley, whose body is "made for limitless consumption" (*Vermillion*, 128). There is none of Conrad's subtle rhetoric here. Halim's chief rhetorical device is the pun, the caricature and the visual culture analogue, for there is a supernatural counterforce at work – the monstrous reincarnation of a Malay murder victim, who has taken the form of a swarm of vengeful eyes. The caricature and popular culture iconicity are strangely appropriate for a culture almost entirely immersed in the iconicity of the forces it cleverly mimics and at one point it accurately identifies those forces. In the body of Jim Oxley, Claymore has just enjoyed a feast of flesh, blood, cartilage and bone: "Feeling the effects of the wine and the mountain of meat in his stomach, he turned on the television and watched a cartoon with robots that could turn into high-speed cars and jet fighters" (*Vermillion*, 128). Hidden here in a representation of the chief source of global representation, we find the siglum of the military body itself – the transformer.

Notes

1. Joseph Conrad, *The End of the Tether*, in *The Eastern Stories*, ed. Ban Kah Choon (New Delhi: Penguin, 2000) p. 163.
2. Michel Foucault, "Body/Power", in *Power/Knowledge: Selected Interviews and Other Writings: 1972–1977*, ed. Colin Gordon (New York: Pantheon Press, 1980) pp. 55–62.
3. THAAD is "an aggressive initiative to field the first endo/exoatmospheric system for defense against Theater Ballistic Missiles" (http://lmms.external.lmco.com/thaad/).
4. For an extended discussion of Tesla's futuristic writings on war, as well as for an excellent discussion of early twentieth-century military imaginaries, see H. Bruce Franklin's cultural history of superweapons, *War Stars* (Oxford: Oxford University Press, 1990).
5. See Wilfred Bion *Transformations* (London: Heinemann, 1965) for the subtleties involved in thinking through the "invariants" of a transformation.
6. Michel Foucault "What is Enlightenment ?" ("Qu'est-ce que les Lumières?"), in Paul Rabinow (ed.), *The Foucault Reader* (New York: Pantheon Books, 1984) pp. 32–50.
7. The CIA identifies Singapore as a transportation and financial services hub and observes that, as such, "Singapore is vulnerable, despite strict laws and enforcement, to use as a transit point for Golden Triangle heroin and as a venue for money laundering" (http://www.cia.gov/cia/publications/factbook/).
8. http://www.dea.gov/pubs/cngrtest/ct960228.htm
9. He goes on to point out that, "Officials in Singapore believe that between 1989 and 1992 a drug trafficking group funneled approximately $100 million in US currency through one underground bank in Singapore to Bahrain and ultimately to the organization's worldwide bank accounts."
10. On the role of surplus and economy a daunting list of essential references is available. We would isolate a few: Aristotle's Fifth Book of the *Nicomachean Ethics* (on justice – and see John Phillips, "Just Sentences" for a reading of it); Shakespeare's *King Lear* and Derrida's *Specters of Marx*, last chapter, which links us back with *The End of the Tether* and the Captain's pathological fixation on the whole £500.
11. www.global-unions.org
12. See Anthony Sampson, *The Seven Sisters: The Great Oil Companies and the World They Made* (New York, Coronet 1975).
13. See George J. Aditjondro, "Sacrificing the Poor People's Fish for the Rich

People's Oil", in Richie Howitt, John Connell and Philip Hirsch, *Resources, Nations and Indigenous Peoples* (New York: Oxford University Press, 1996).

14. Tunku Halim, *Vermillion Eye* (Kuala Lumpur: Pelunduk, 2000).

Chapter 7

Manufacturing Emergencies

And they must have learned how to keep silent in order to remain your friend. (Friedrich Nietzsche)[1]

Not that friends should keep silent, among themselves or on the subject of their friends. Their speech would perhaps have to breathe with an implied silence. This is nothing other than a certain way of speaking: secret, discrete, discontinuous, aphoristic, elliptic, just in disjointed time to avow the truth that must be concealed; hiding it – because it is deadly – to save life. (Jacques Derrida)[2]

If straight thy tack, or if oblique, thou know'st not. (Tennyson, *Two Voices*)

Prior to the war in the 1990s, Bosnia figured in the consciousness of US citizens, if at all, as a site of miracles. In the mountain village of Medugorje, two children (young teenagers, actually) spotted the Gospa, or Virgin Mary, walking by a river. The next day, they brought four friends to the same spot, met the apparition again, and conversed with her. Since 1981, the epiphany has been repeated on a daily basis, even during the Yugoslavian civil war. The Catholic Church has not officially authorised the sightings but, significantly, it has not condemned them either. Once word spread out about this specific Marian apparition, Medugorje – while not Lourdes – got its name on the map of religious hotspots, attracting over a million pilgrims a year. Bus loads of them poured into a village that once had only 400 souls dwelling there, and the economy took off. To reach various sacred spots, the pilgrims had to muscle their way through armies of vendors hawking icons, prayer books and other tokens commemorating their journey. Quite popular in the late 1980s were chains and bracelets of "silver" that later turned to "gold" symbolising in concrete form Our Lady's blessings on the bearer. Planes jammed with pilgrims from North America filled the skies and, on their return, excited devotees raced up and down the aisles showing each other and their priests the miraculous alchemy wrought by divine design. That the chains were brass with a silver coating easily rubbed off through handling, and therefore mimicking transformation, never entered the pilgrims' minds. The individual emergencies that propelled their pilgrimages to the

Balkans overwhelmed any quotidian explanation, allowing only the meta-physical answer, which thus confirmed their own crises and the passing of the same.

The war came to Bosnia and killed off the pilgrimages. The children continued to speak to the Gospa but their conversations faded into the smoke of mortar rounds and the darkness of ethnic cleansing. The village took its share of artillery shells and the opportunistic vendors took their shady operations into even shadier territory: black market cigarettes, passports, electronic goods and weapons. Mafia warlords fought the underground war for economic turf in the guise of, and as a result of, the nationalistic armies waging the visible, "legitimate" war above ground.

What the Gospa shows is that the distinction between the hidden underground war and the visible legitimate one cannot be maintained. Her persistence as an absent or spectral presence both before and during the war exemplifies the structural condition of emergency (and emergence), which operates from peace time to war and back again with increasing intensity and momentum independent of the actual state of affairs. Just as the economy works both above ground and underground whether a nation is at war or not, the Marian apparition makes apparent through her transparency how the visible requires the invisible – either as threat or salvation – to justify the visible's very visibility, as well as the need to have more of it. The Gospa, as exemplification of the state of emergency, shows that the distinction between the visible and the invisible serves as a mystification, perpetuating the state of emergency itself by disguising the intrinsic connection between the two domains. The Marian apparition thus provides us with a way of focusing on the politics that follows from this kind of mystification, in that it allows the illusion of a possible distinction between a state of emergency and its subsidence.

Bosnian director Emir Kusturica's 1995 film *Underground* follows the Rabelasian exploits of Marko and Blacky, two World War II gun runners who arm the partisans fighting against the Nazis, thus merging nationalism and profiteering. After Blacky shoots a Nazi officer in a Belgrade theatre (over the love of an actress), he is forced to go underground and hides in the elaborate cellar beneath Marko's family home. As bombing raids by fascist fighter planes give way to bombing raids by Allied aircraft – that is, as "enemy" bombers yield to "friendly" bombers with similar results – Blacky (along with others hiding in the cellar) begins manufacturing arms for the cause, and for Marko's profit. Eventually, a miniature village emerges underground, complete with a village square and the ubiquitous urchins kicking a football. When the war ends, the life and work underground does not, as Marko converts his wartime venture into a highly profitable peacetime enterprise. The black market weapons business is *always* good.

To keep Blacky and his labourers cranking out the goods, Marko manufactures the emergency of perpetual war, pretending that the fight against "the fucking Fascist motherfuckers" continues for decades. To sustain the illusion, Marko, at random moments, stages mock air raids, complete with taped radio announcements from the war and appropriate sound effects, including an amplified hand-cranked portable air raid siren. (Kusturica here takes a page from Enver Hoxha's book, as the Albanian dictator used to stage similar fake air strikes over Tirana long after World War II had ended.) During Marko's mock air raids, the entire manufacturing village runs for cover and takes refuge in a tank housed in the cellar.

Kusturica's deliciously surreal allegorical images are bitterly apt: a manufactured state of sustained emergency allows for and increases the manufacture of weapons and profits. An underground, shadow economy generates contraband weapons, and the workers labour under their belief in a struggle against a manufactured enemy that perpetuates, and perpetrates, the emergency under which they suffer. Delusion and faith, fear and patriotism, deception and dedication, theatricality and economics cooperate when the underground produces profits and a luxurious life for the illusion-spinners above ground. The hallucination of – or apparition of – nationhood emerges from the two-tone drone of the air raid siren and the emergency it manufactures.

But it is to the air raid siren itself that we turn our attention. The dire whine of the hand-cranked air raid siren, and more so its electrical cousin, can still cause traumatic responses in people over the age of sixty in Coventry, Dresden, Tokyo, and so on. The machine embodies the technicity of the military formalised and applied in World War II that broadened and deepened – became molar – during the Cold War. Its forlorn mechanical cry told citizens that the "death from the sky" imagined by H. G. Wells, Jack London and numerous other popular writers in the 1890s and 1900s – that is, the use of air power against civilians as practised by Europeans against their colonies (including Iraq in the early part of the twentieth century) – had come home to them. The sound of the siren manufactured warning and fear, a psychological terror that gripped the world's citizens once "total war" was taken in hand by Axis and Allied forces alike. The mushroom cloud that ushered in the nuclear dawn meant emergency would always be our state, and the vegetable growth of air raid towers in every village and city bespoke the looming horrors of a nuclear nightmare to come. Civilian defence and preparedness became the state's watchwords to protect citizens' lives. They assured access to and from the sites of production, where workers laboured by day in the factories that manufactured the hardware they prayed would not drop on their heads at night. Over all of this, the air raid siren stood vigil. Many of these sirens in North America were made by Chrysler and, during the Cold War, an increasing number of those who manufactured them could drive to work in their own Chryslers.

But it is the apparatus itself, especially the crank or lever, in the early, manual sirens that enacts issues we find of interest, for the lever that so easily turns (which Marko pushes with barely a finger, allowing the momentum to carry the sound up and forward) provides us with a way to think through the technics of manufactured emergency and terror. The manual air raid siren is small and portable. It contains a single-hand "impeller", which allows a clutch to turn the motor shaft and rotor together. This allows the fan or impeller to spin after power (muscle or electricity) has ceased. It has a momentum all its own. And the two-tone whine it produces results from a centrifugal fan that simultaneously pulls air into the siren on the axis and blows it out on the radial. The rotor chops the air, slicing and dicing the air stream into "impulsive bursts", creating a "perfectly harmonic, or Just, minor triad".[3] Engineering and aesthetics combine to create aural terror. In the air raid siren apparatus resides the state of emergency.

The momentum of emergency, a momentum projected consistently in Kusturica's film – as it starts in high gear and never lets up – can be tracked in the development of air raid sirens. The technology, as with all military technology, propulses in an unswerving trajectory, making the sirens bigger, louder and applicable to an increasingly wide range of situations and conditions. Such sirens now are attached to an array of sites: nuclear power plants, chemical plants, and other hazardous manufacturing locales. The military use has merged fully and completely with civil defence, protecting the populace from disasters such as tornadoes, earthquakes, chemical spills and inadvertent radiation releases. Emergency – being on the alert, preparedness – has been our steady state for some half a century; only now, we have more of it and the stakes get ever higher.

The Song of the Siren

The first siren, invented by the French physician Charles Cagniard de la Tour in 1819, calculates the number of vibrations needed to produce a certain level of sound. Named after the mythological creature because it functions well in water (normally air is passed through it), the siren is set into motion with an increasing velocity, obtaining an increasingly acute sound until the listener hears a sound that has the same level as the external one to be calculated, that is, until the two sounds are unisonous. It is this same instrument, only larger, that finds its way onto steamships, its muffled shriek warning unwary vessels in fog. Steam is the ideal breath for animating the acoustical mechanism. It is this signal, the sound of the siren, which we now associate with alarm in general, its warnings, its calls to arms, to alertness and to response, as if the level of noise were a means of calculating the measure of alarm. By the 1940s sirens like Chrysler's *Big Joe*, designed to stand guard over Pearl Harbor, are so powerful that their vibrations can start fires.

Steven Connor, in an elegant BBC broadcast on "Noise", finds it strange but also appropriate that the word siren, for alarm, derives from Homer's maidens of *The Odyssey*. He notes that, like Ulysses, "we are all tied to the mast of indifference and disregard", surrounded by the modern city's noises of warning and alarm:

Figure 7.1   'Big Joe' Chrysler Siren Advert. Scanned from a military magazine by Bishop and Phillips

> The care taken to make sirens unignorable is matched by the slowly and carefully learned capacity of the city-dweller to filter them out. Alarms strive to nullify this auditory anaesthesia. But there is always a cost. Perhaps what is most stressful about a world full of alarms is the generalisation of a readiness to act which does not find adequate discharge in action.[4]

It is hard to imagine a talk on sirens less strident, less urgent or more languorously reflective than Connor's but concealed in his increasingly lyrical presentation lurks a nagging question about the relationship between the event and the decision. If the alarm speaks in a voice at once like the cry of the infant and an automated shriek, where, as he says, "the body speaks from a place beyond or before culture, before or behind the human", then the response – the potential at least for an adequate discharge in action – must respond to something otherworldly, unearthly. The decision itself would thus be made from a place beyond or before culture. So while we would not want to be too quick to respond to the call of the siren – measuring instead the extent to which the call demands our passive response and refusing the grand seductions of alarm – we also wish to dwell for a while, oscillating with the vibrations, between refusal and acquiescence. The agitated yet still passive response would have had us running underground in the way described by a famous line from George MacBeth's war elegy, "Then the sirens went, Sucking life underground".[5] Or, as in the case of Kusturica's allegory, *keeping* us sucked underground. The incessant repetition of our states of alarm would itself be alarming if it was not for this proviso, that is, there would be a real feeling of urgency about this if it was not urgency itself that we felt impelled to resist. The lever of the hand-cranked siren moving with ghostly momentum impels this urge.

Geoff Bennington, in his article "Emergencies", provides an exemplary account of what we might call the aporia of urgency (though a very similar aporia applies to justice and to philosophy generally). He draws attention to the strident clamour of the alarm(ist)s and identifies "a concomitant hectoring tone [generating] a sense that someone has to give orders if all is not to be lost".[6] And he focuses on the paradox that afflicts those who attempt to confront what is urgent, according to which, "what is urgent is to hold up against urgency so as to think it, to be patient enough with the emergency to do its urgency justice by not just running with it: the thinking of urgency will, then, also be a thinking of the resistance to urgency" (Bennington, "Emergencies", 165). What is urgent is to think urgency and to think the resistance to urgency without succumbing to either. The notion that emerges out of Bennington's syntax and that fails to succumb to the terminal dialectical cancellation of urgency and its resistances is *thinking*. A thinking of urgency that is simultaneously a thinking of the resistance to urgency would be reducible neither to urgency (the moment) nor to its resistance (and the continuation of the interminable journey). Perhaps what is most alarming about this thinking is that it would no longer be the thought of a conscious subject. The paradox is not unfamiliar because it concerns the problem of the relation of the event to its eventness, or as we shall say, to decision.

The Greeks remind us that sirens have many voices. Their names are often words distinguishing qualities of noise: Ligeia is shrill, Aglaophonos is beautiful voice, Molpe is music. Others, like Peisinol (persuading mind), Raidne (improvement), Thelxepeia (soothing words) and Thelxiope (persuasive face) help to give an indication of the mythopoetic significance of these figures. They are figures of influence, representing the artful seductions of persuasive argument or entertainment designed to draw attention away from life and so they belong squarely within the demonised figures of a long tradition that includes the latecomer Plato: these alarming distractions that lure the wayfarer to his death stand for the threatening influences – sophism, poetry, theatre – that must remain outside the walls of the Republic. When Odysseus listens but fails to be lured, the sirens cease to exist. Apollodorus notes that, "it was predicted of the Sirens that they should themselves die when a ship should pass them; so die they did".[7] The mythic wish fulfillment – ignore them, resist them, then they will disappear – supports Aristotle's harsh judgement about Greek audiences and their need for catharsis: the uplifting disavowal of the truth of death (in contrast the Homeric version filters out the moralising allegorical aspects, playing up instead an anthro-pomorphic suicidal rage on the part of the frustrated sirens). *Underground*'s siren plays a similar role; in this satire on false alarm, the siren plays the role of the Greek siren robbing the underground population of its above-ground life. But if their catastrophic re-emergence signals the end of the siren, then emergence is not the end of emergency but the start of a new confusion.

What the mythopoesis of the sirens does not quite capture – which is what the modern powerful instrument more than ever emphasises – is that the most forceful of the siren's voices would be heard in the mode of its keeping silent. Veterans of the Cold War (if there were any) would remember only this about the powerful sirens: their ominous silence. This silence is infinitely more powerful than any of the extra-worldly noises identified by Connor and others because its source is the spring of both life and death, before and after, prefacing and articulating in a dire prolepsis the post-apocalyptic event before the event. Tempted with Connor to develop the tendentious his-torical connection between the Greek siren and the modern device, wouldn't one be led into error? The story of the sirens, as an allegory for the danger they represent, becomes the danger itself. The myth of the siren simply *is* the siren, manufacturing alarm, contaminated by the danger it warns against. But if we cannot always rigorously distinguish between the alarm and the cause for alarm, then that does not mean we can choose to ignore the siren. Perhaps there would be a way of listening for its implied silence. It would be a matter of listening out for what the decision, made in a state of emergency, has failed to keep in living memory, a way of re-membering or dis-closing the conditions of possibility for ethical and political decision – its own uncer-tainty in the face of perceived danger.

The Aporia of the Perhaps

> The aporia of the *event* intersects with, but also capitalizes or overdetermines, the aporia of *decision* with regard to the *perhaps*. There is no event, to be sure, that is not preceded and followed by its own *perhaps*, and that is not as unique, singular and irreplaceable as the decision with which it is frequently associated, notably in politics. But can one not suggest without a facile paradox, that the eventness of an event remains minimal, if not excluded by a decision? (Jacques Derrida, *Politics*, 68)

The decision would relegate the siren's voice – its articulation, no matter how cynical, beneficent or ambivalent – to a mode (or modes) of silence, if it was not for the fact that an inescapable mutual interference of decision and event implies that the responsible decision could not have been the work of a con-scious subject, though such a subject (if there was any) can always set things in motion, like Marko at the lever. What is *normally* understood by responsi-ble decision can easily be revealed as incessant unconscious repetition. That is, one's decision might always have been determined, or overdetermined, by some institution or structure according to which what comes to us as possibility is already predetermined, on the model of the consumer's choice in the logic of the commodity, so that what one decides makes no difference to the structure of choice itself. And according to the same logic we'd find that a conscious repetition might always turn out to have been an *unconscious* decision, which would leave most of our thoughts about democracy, subjectivity, agency and consciousness at a loss. That is, some form of moving forward on the basis of repetition, following the path of a precursor, operating on a historicity of possibilities, might turn out to condition the most powerful decisions – those which move beyond the realm of the possible. By this we mean the kind of decision that would auger something that would count as an event – something unpredictable, something new. As this notion of decision is one that can affect how we respond to the call, we acknowledge that its condition – far from certain and anything but authoritative – can be found in the logic of the perhaps, which always implies, as its strongest indicator, perhaps *not*.

Perhaps: a word qualifying a statement so as to express possibility with uncertainty: it may be, possibly. Even the etymology of per-haps must be qualified with a "perhaps": as happens (*per-happens*) or "perhaps" by chance (*per-happas*). A statement qualified by *perhaps* expresses possibility combined with suspicion or doubt and tends to result in avowedly doubtful propositions. At best, the perhaps indicates something that may happen (or exist), or may not. It indicates at best a mere possibility. So what must be affirmed in the *perhaps* is the uncertainty. Because in the uncertainty – and only there – lies the possibility.

More to the point, the *perhaps* allows us to consider – in what is possibly a new way – the *strange* figure that throughout the twentieth century takes shape as the condition of politics per se, that is, the figure of the enemy: the figure of the enemy as necessarily a stranger, alien or other, even when it is the enemy-within. In this respect *Underground*, already a political film in obvious (and thus not necessarily the most interesting) ways, opens onto less apparently urgent but nonetheless decisive political questions. As we have indicated, the lever for this movement, like the lever for the siren, is the siren itself, the mechanical iteration of its alarm, whether its supposed referent – an attacking enemy – is present or not. Marko's use of the siren presents through the film's narrative irony a figure whose friendship is a mask. Masking not only the absence of a friend's true character but also the absence of an identifiable enemy, the siren helps to manufacture the figure of enemy through its mechanical iteration – a kind of historical repetition.

Here we witness the spectacle of two apparently irreconcilable political attitudes. The first belongs to the underground itself, to Blacky, his son and comrades sheltering from the bombs of imaginary enemies. Blacky is never reconciled to a world without enemies and his emergence in the midst of a film-shoot celebrating his own mythologised exploits only reinforces his unshakeable sense of the perpetual war. The second political attitude is more difficult to pin down but belongs with the deceptively complex figure of Marko, for whom (and retrospectively this will have been the case from the beginning) there *just is no enemy*. Marko does not operate according to a theory of the enemy. Rather he operates according to a mythology of the enemy, an understanding of what we might call the psychological dimension of the theory and another form of a phenomenon that we have referred to in a later chapter as the hallucination of alterity.[8] The manufacture of emergency is a repetition of the form of emergency that folds into the hallucination of a radical and threatening outside: the enemy. Thus we see that the event – its emergence and its continuation or prolongation – is both preceded and followed by its own perhaps, with or without an air raid. So Marko represents a figure of the political, according to which, while there is no need to believe in an enemy yourself, you need people to believe in one and, thus, in the absolute distinction between friend and enemy.

Marko's dissimulation thus represents an alarming ambiguity in the politics of enmity, whose most effective and increasingly influential proponent is the controversial Carl Schmitt. His attempt to ground politics in the quasi-metaphysical dimension, *the political*, follows from this absolute distinction and results in his celebrated *decisionism*. It is worth quoting a key statement:

> The distinction of friend and enemy denotes the utmost degree of intensity of a union or separation, of an association or dissociation. It can exist, theoretically and practically, without having simultaneously to draw upon all those moral, aesthetic, economic, or other distinctions. The political enemy need not be morally evil or aesthetically ugly; he need not appear as an economic competitor, and it may even be advantageous to engage with him in business transaction. But he is, nevertheless, the other, the stranger; and it is sufficient for his nature that he is, in a specially intense way, existentially something different and alien, so that in the extreme case conflicts with him are always possible. These can neither be decided by a previously determined norm nor by the judgment of a disinterested and therefore neutral third party.[9]

The quotation here provides an idea of how Schmitt's thought remains firmly bound within the most traditional political thinking. His supposedly radical redefinition of the political decision as the act of a sovereign subject free from all empirical or historical constraints, norms or forms, nonetheless remains bound to the thought of the decidable decision. The absolute distinction of friend and enemy – despite its address to the thought of an absolute alterity – can only really be read as a further attempt to calculate alterity, to calculate the incalculable, and thus to decide on the basis of what a priori was anyway already a decision, so, absurdly, to decide on a decision.

For this reason, we would acknowledge Derrida's *Politics of Friendship* as an effective response to this thought.[10] He formulates the aporia of the perhaps by deriving, from a passage in Nietzsche's *Human All Too Human*, an aporia that irrecoverably disturbs any chance of maintaining a clear distinction between friend and enemy. Nietzsche had opposed the classical address of the "dying sage", "Friends, there is no Friend", to the voice of the "living fool", "Enemies, there is no enemy." While maintaining the strict distinction between the meanings of the terms *friend* and *enemy*, the opposition is not decidable in the mode of address. The address is each time substitutable, no matter whether friend or enemy speaks. The sage is as capable of playing fool as the fool is capable of playing sage. Derrida radicalises the logic further: "Fundamentally, from one address to the other, the same person is speaking – him, me; and language liberates the substitution: 'I' is 'me,' but an 'I' is a 'him.' One is the other" (*Friendship*, 59). This aporia – the friend and the enemy, substitutable, undecidable – operates like an infinite *surenchère* (a build-up, as in the phrase *une surenchère de violence*, or a raising of the stakes, a higher bid): "A *surenchère* that does not even need an author's intention, or a deliberate decision: it is carried away, it carries itself away, it throws itself into turmoil with the disidentification of concepts and terms we are analyzing right now" (Derrida, *Friendship*, 59). This does not, of course, mean that there are no friends or enemies. Rather what it means is that the possibility of the friend or the enemy lies in this undecidability, thought of as *possibility*. One experiences the perhaps when one addresses oneself to the possible. This formulation of the aporia of the *perhaps* indicates the extent to which the decision – in terms of its relation to the undecidable – departs from the traditional notions, not least Schmitt's:

> Without the opening of an absolutely undetermined possible, without the radical abeyance and suspense marking a *perhaps*, there would never be either event or decision. Certainly. But nothing takes place and nothing is ever decided without suspending the perhaps while keeping its possibility in living memory. If no decision (ethical, juridical, political) is possible without interrupting determination by engaging oneself in the *perhaps*, on the one hand, the same decision must interrupt the very thing that is its condition of possibility: the *perhaps* itself. (Derrida, *Friendship*, 67)

The violence of a decision towards its own possibility is an absolutely unavoidable result of the aporia. A decision would thus be, in a way that is traditionally unthinkable, something like an unconscious interruption of the historicity that makes it possible. An unconscious decision, rather than the act or intention of the conscious subject, operates on the build-up – the between friend and enemy of the *surenchère* – which like the siren can be interrupted while keeping its possibility in living memory.

Marko understands this scenario all too well. He indulges in what Peter Sloterdijk calls "enlightened false consciousness", and therefore stands solidly in the line of famous enlightened cynics from Machiavelli's Prince to Stendhal's Julien Sorel, as well as the numerous anti-heroes that populate modern and contemporary literature who reap personal gain by manipulating the belief systems held by others. And his relation to Blacky within *that* politics of friendship is one of sovereign to subject, complete with the paradoxes of sovereignty. As Agamben as well as Deleuze and Guattari, among many others, have noted, the sovereign is both inside and outside the judicial order, or the law. Marko has unilaterally and sovereignly cast Blacky into a group who can be sacrificed for Marko's own good and gain, which is the mark of the sovereign. But he is only able to do so because he knows Blacky believes in the enemy, which necessitates a belief in friends as well. Marko suffers no such beliefs, and his politics, therefore, represents an estranged politics, for politics is traditionally the politics of enmity – the capacity to create the inside of the state and its outside. He consigns Blacky and numerous others to perpetual martial law and a state of siege.

Marko slides easily between true friend and exploiter of a belief in the friend and the enemy. His oscillation between these domains creates (for Blacky, anyway) the illusion – or the hallucination – of friendship, complete with all of its technicity and momentum. The apparent uniformity of Marko's politics of friendship is echoed in and through the air raid siren's capability to seamlessly blend two distinct tones into the apparition of a single sound. Marko's place of enunciation is exactly that of the state's through the mouthpiece of the air raid siren. By apparently demarcating the division between peacetime and wartime, the air raid siren actually forms and articulates a single state: that of emergency. Whether silent or blasting away, the air raid siren bespeaks the emergency that is ever-present, ever-dormant, ever-past, ever-futural. Only apparently dividing the state of the state into peacetime and wartime, the oscillation of the air raid siren between the two reveals them to be the same. The technicity of the siren as metonym for the militarised state allows for enlightened false consciousness to abuse and exploit those it condemns to perpetual emergency. This technicity need not be enacted or spoken for it operates with the momentum of historical repetition that seeks to obliterate *perhaps*. Despite these efforts, however, the Gospa still makes regular appearances, and the uncertainty of *perhaps* haunts the apparition of friendship, the state, war, the event and emergency. The uncertainty that will not be contained, kept outside or underground, hovers near the silent and the wailing siren – a figure of possibility, perhaps.

The siren, then, is more than a mere emblem for the state of emergency, for it manifests the function of state of emergency itself. Emergency can be manufactured through an economics that capitalises on uncertainty by concealing it beneath the polarities of underground and above-ground, friend and foe, figuring an enemy whether there is one or not. The arrival of the event in a state of emergency would thus never have been a surprise (and thus not an event). It would, rather, have been the repetition of the violence of a decision against its own possibility – the *perhaps*, uncertainty itself, which must be both betrayed and kept within living memory if the decision is to retain its ethical and political basis. The Gospa, the siren, its silence and the *surenchère* of the perhaps, each mark and are marked by the process of raising the stakes, within which the build-up and subsidence of the siren serves to reinforce a perpetual build up disguised as benevolent control.

Notes

1. Friedrich Nietzsche, *Human All Too Human*, trans. R. J. Hollingdale (Cambridge: CUP, 1986) p. 148.
2. Jacques Derrida, *The Politics of Friendship*, trans. George Collins (London: Routledge, 1996) p. 54.
3. www.airraidsirens.com
4. Transcripts as well as soundfiles of the talk can be found at the following website: http://www.bbk.ac.uk/eh/eng/staff/noise3.htm
5. George MacBeth, *A War Quartet* (London: Faber 1969) p. 43.
6. Geoff Bennington, *Interrupting Derrida* (London: Routledge, 2000) p. 164. A slightly longer version of the article was originally published in the *Oxford Literary Review* as a review of Bernard Stiegler's *La technique et le temps* and Richard Beardsworth's *Derrida and the Political*.
7. Apollodorus, *The Literary*, trans. J. G. Frazer (Cambridge, MA: Harvard University Press, 1960) E7.19.
8. See Chapter 9 and the discussion of hybridity.
9. Carl Schmitt, *The Concept of the Political*, trans. by George Schwab (New Brunswick, NJ: Rutger University Press, 1976) pp. 26–7.
10. Much of *The Politics of Friendship* engages specifically with Schmitt, and in this respect it offers an important counter-argument against the hasty identification of Schmitt's thought with an emerging "postmodernist" politics. See especially the section "Oath, Conjuration, Fraternization or the 'Armed Question'", pp. 138–70.

Chapter 8

Among the Blind and the Delay

Vicariousness of the senses. – "Our eyes are also intended for hearing," said the old father confessor who had gone deaf, "and among the blind he is king who has the longest ears." (Friedrich Nietzsche)[1]

The Technics of Sensate Transformations

A dominant medical orthodoxy teaches that the organs of perception fall into two distinct types. The first, in the order both of development and in value, receive sensations from light waves, sound vibrations and aromas. E. D. Adrian's influential *The Physical Background of Perception* from 1947 links these perceptions from a distance, the "distance receptors", to the development of intelligence.[2] Second, and lower in order, are touch and other corporeal sensations, the bowel and bladder movements, sexuality and taste. These characterise the middle or close range sensations. The distinction between the receptors of sensation from a distance and those of sensation up close corresponds to a further distinction between thought and action, which in both covert and explicit ways has helped to organise a remarkably wide field of scientific, quasi-scientific and philosophical activity since the nineteenth century. The distinction between thought and action divides up the ways in which an organism reaches consciousness of its external reality.

In 1911, Sigmund Freud designed his perennially controversial hypothetical fiction, "Formulations on the Two Principles of Mental Functioning", to account for human experience and behaviour in a provisionally satisfying way, where actually no sound theoretical grounds are possible. The distinction between the pleasure principle and the reality principle corresponds to that between action and thought. In Freud's ontogenetic narrative the pleasure principle looks for ways of unburdening the mental apparatus of accretions of unpleasant stimuli. A crucial stage is reached when the function of "motor discharge", which sends thrills into the body's interior, thus leading to "manifestations of affect", is "converted into *action*".[3] It is now "employed in the appropriate alteration of reality". However, in the tension, action calls upon a measure of restraint and this is provided by what Freud calls "the process of *thinking*" ("Formulations", 221). Thinking, which develops out of a presentation of ideas, allows the mental apparatus to tolerate increased stimuli, thus postponing the discharge. Thinking, in Freud's narrative, thus replaces direct action with a form of experimentation.

The relation between distance-sensation and thought would thus stack up against a contrary relation, between proximity-sensation and action. The former represents an external relation to the other; the latter an internalised relation to the body. Wilfred Bion's peculiar brand of psychoanalysis (based on his clinical experience as a group counsellor for victims of combat trauma during and after World War I) follows Freud quite freely but with a vocabulary derived from a wide range of philosophical and scientific references including Kant's metaphysics and neurology. He offers a fecund perspective that accommodates both Freud's grumpily acknowledged debts to Schopenhauer and Nietzsche as well as Bion's own debt to Kant (Nietzsche's philosophical adversary). In revising Freud's distinction between action and thought, Bion proposes a hinge that both reduces and maintains the distance between the two:

> Freud distinguishes a stage where muscular action is taken to alter the environment and a stage where a capacity for thought exists. I propose to include in the category presented by the term "action" phantasies in the mind, acting as if it were a muscle and a muscle acting as a muscle, can disburden the psyche of accretions of stimuli. I include the Kleinian concept of the phantasy known as projective identification in the category of "action".[4]

What neither Freud nor Bion explore in these formulations, designed as they are for therapeutic purposes, concerns an implicit and original *technics* of sensation that the *techniques* of psychology would both appropriate and operate on. That is, sensate life operates already as a technics of proximity and distance, attraction and repulsion; and it operates by opening, closing, lengthening or shortening gaps. The gaps it opens can then be operated on. The experimentation that thinking uses to restrain the demands of action serves, in the end, the same function as action (always motor discharge). The watchfulness of the distance-senses can thus undergo what Bion calls transformations into action associated with the proximal-senses and vice versa.

The perhaps most obviously fictional characteristic of Freud's exploratory essay (which he acknowledges as itself a manifestation of the tensions it schematises) would be its linear narrative progression. The mental entity develops, according to this narrative, from murky origins to ambivalently conscious (and mostly screwed-up) ends. Bion, who follows Klein in this respect, reveals instead a situation characterised by both reversible and non-reversible transformations and repetitions of transformations, not so much a linear progression but rather a build-up of tensions and transactions. Klein's concept of projective identification, according to which the mental apparatus identifies itself as sharing physical existence with, and thus able to have a physical effect on, an external object, operates for Bion as a hinge between internal sensation and action on the external world.

These psychoanalytic explorations in what we might call *the technics of sensate transformation* recall Nietzsche's writings, especially those from the 1880s, in which he explores the possibilities of affirming Schopenhauer's dark vision of Kant's *noumenon*, or thing in itself, reconceived as the insatiable will. "Thoughts," Nietzsche writes in *The Gay Science*, "are the shadows of our sensations, always darker, emptier, simpler" (137 (paragraph 179)). In the preface to the second edition, from 1887, he recalls these thoughts: "The unconscious disguise of physiological needs under the cloaks of the objective, ideal, purely spiritual goes frighteningly far – and I have asked myself often enough whether, on a grand scale, philosophy has been no more than an interpretation of the body and a *misunderstanding of the body*." The notebooks from 1885 reveal further the thinking behind this effective transformation of philosophy itself:

> The triumphant concept of "force," with which our physicists have created God and the world, needs supplementing: it must be ascribed an inner world, which I will call "will to power," i.e., an insatiable craving to manifest power; or to employ, exercise power as a creative drive, etc. The physicists cannot eliminate "action at a distance" from their principles, nor a force of repulsion (or attraction).[5]

If these notes serve, explicitly here, to topple the metaphysical category of the transcendental, then, they also refuse to give material science the last word. The emerging doctrine of the will to power, as the internal space of forces in contest, not only displaces but also replaces the "old soul" of philosophy. In a significant note (number 36 from the June-July 1885 notebook) Nietzsche echoes concerns that were emerging contemporaneously, particularly in Paris, as part of a nascent modern aesthetics: "Even today, particularly among artists," he writes, "one often enough finds a kind of wonder and deferential unhooking of judgement when the question arises of how they succeeded in making the best throw and from what world the creative thought came to them" (*Notebooks*, 27). This "unhooking of judgement" would in its own way have been quite a complex unconscious procedure that – in Nietzsche's own terms (had he expanded them) – followed those laws that escape judgement once it had been unhooked: the will to power disguising itself, or withdrawing itself from the observation it has made possible. Nietzsche's unpublished drafts resonate with a contemporary aesthetics, which explicitly contests the dominant aesthetic ideology of the nineteenth century. The aesthetics that Nietzsche mocks here defers, against all evidence, to a transcendental source and aliment for art. Against this, and following Schopenhauer, Nietzsche regarded the work of aesthetic production in terms of its capacity for elevating itself beyond the will from which it must always have emerged. But the doctrine of the will to power needs supplementing further if we regard it, as he did, as already a supplement to the concept of force.[6] The nascent aesthetics of the period, which as we have shown explicitly engages and mobilises an upsurge in technological activity, does so in such a way as to establish a common basis both for what Nietzsche affirms in the "astonishing idea" of the body and for the astonishing progress of science and technology.

Neurology and psychoanalysis throughout the first half of the twentieth century repeat the story Nietzsche tells regarding the toppling of the transcendental in philosophy and the emergence of an empirical basis to replace it. This empirical basis would never have been simply evident. Its absence, a withdrawal, complicates things and calls for supplements. The basis must instead be inferred, induced or hypothesised on the basis of partial or oblique evidence. However formally it is dressed (in the several registers of scientific discourse), a narrative always needs to have been invented, and, as we have shown, a technology exists for the construction of narratives too, unhooking judgement from its domination by one narrative but available perhaps to be hooked back up to an alternative one. The supplements of aesthetics and military technology, against the stories that divide them and reconnect them in particular ways, can be instructive here. The idea of projective identification (an extension of Nietzsche's idea of action at a distance) is extended further by military technology in what we might call *projectile identification*, which invests the object relation with a ballistics that increasingly quickly closes the gap between distance and proximity.

We must therefore be careful to read these diverse discourses in a certain way. It would not be a matter of constructing a theory, as if from, say, the philosophy of Nietzsche, as Bion does from his several sources (for example, Kant, Nietzsche, Freud, Klein). Nothing here would resemble a psychoanalysis of culture or history, let alone of aesthetics or military technology. Nor would it resemble the authority of a science. But if our reading remains attentive to the build up, the *surenchère*, manifested in all the discourses under study (military technology, aesthetics, philosophy, science and quasi-scientific psychologies), we might proceed according to the following observation: all tell the same story from different angles, different perspectives: the horizon has either already disappeared into the absolute distance or a spectral remnant of it remains in sight, the target for an action that would reduce it and bring it back entirely into its range.

As is well known, the explicit goal of C³I (containment, control, communications and intelligence) in US and allied geo-political policy is perfect, real-time visual control of the entire planet to contain Communism. The substantial intensification of opto-electronic technologies for military targeting and surveillance manifests an intensification of the desire to render the horizon obsolete, to make the unwieldy three-dimensional orb of the earth a two-dimensional map easily en-framed and controlled. This desire so obviously repeats the circular mode of life in Heidegger's "bad present" that its inevitable failures should follow as a matter of course. The equation, for instance, of visual technological domination with geo-political military domination ignores the momentum of a technology that generates illimitable unintended consequences, each requiring another set of technological fixes that will result in further unintended consequences, each requiring . . . and so on.

Gaining Momentum

H. G. Wells again addresses several of the issues that concern us here, bundling them into the popular form of the short story, compact narrative fictions published in popular magazines. The idiom allows a considerable relaxation of the tension building up in the grand narratives of western science, technology and aesthetics while at the same time acknowledging the stakes of this build-up with facility and wit. Attentive to the possibilities of the idiom, these tales offer gently allegorical twists, spicing up their concerns with scientific speculation and technological possibility. Certain kinds of motif turn up repeatedly in the stories, especially those written between 1894 and 1905. The setting often evokes those emergent spaces of research and development that mark the twentieth century: laboratories and workshops, industrial parks and technical facilities. If not, the narrative is often anyway driven by the paraphernalia of experimentation and the sometimes accidental circumstances that turn the spaces of everyday urban life – schools, parks, roadways and private rooms, the crowded city late at night or through the day – into dangerously uncontrolled experimental fields. The uncontainable elements of scientific experimentation often convert the city into an unwitting and accidental laboratory in many of Wells's short and longer fictions and do so in ways that underline the vulnerability of the urban to increased technicity because the city, from the outset, would have always been such a site for scientific and technological experimentation, implementation and accident.

Wells sometimes attacks the nineteenth-century fascination with the occult in these humorous tales, often evoking the accidental discovery of gateways into invisible worlds of disembodied spirit peoples, ghosts, invisible observers, ravenous revenants and imaginary friends. In "The Crystal Egg", such a gateway operates like a remote two-way video monitor (the egg) giving viewers access to aliens viewing them back from, perhaps, Mars. In "The Plattner Story", the bewildered protagonist, a village schoolteacher, accidentally sets fire to a green powder during a chemistry class and disappears from this world for nine days, only to return with his internal organs reversed and outwardly a mirror image of his previous self. In these and in similar stories the real protagonist is not any of the named characters but an anonymous narrator, whose satirically scientific discourse keeps its judgement firmly "hooked" to its evidence and proofs. The motif of the disembodied spirit (and the liminal, invisible space it inhabits) features prominently in several tales about mutually separable minds and bodies. "The Stolen Body" concerns an experiment with corporeal projection that goes terribly wrong. A Mr Bessel of Piccadilly, interested in "the questions of thought transference and of apparitions of the living", commences a series of experiments "in order to test the alleged possibility of projecting an apparition of oneself by force of will through space". Bessel manages this only to leave his body free for one of the ravenous disembodied and demonic spirits that invisibly people the occult world to colonise this conveniently empty living corpse for the purposes of running amok through Covent Garden, causing damage and mayhem all the way. "The Story of the Late Mr Elvesham" involves a prize-winning scientist (Elvesham) perfecting a procedure that allows him to exchange his dying body with the healthy one of a younger man (the narrator), whom he tricks into the exchange by promising all his wealth (which he has thus simply made over to himself in his outwardly new identity).

The fantasy of unhooking mind from body takes the more specific form, in several interesting variants, of the unhooking and re-hooking of the senses from the body. "The Remarkable Case of Davidson's Eyes", for instance, involves a research experiment that goes interestingly wrong. Davidson finds that his visible field has suddenly been transported from his workshop in King's Cross to an island apparently off the coast of Malaysia, while his body remains in London. Wells explores in the fiction of televisual transport what it might be like "to live visually in one part of the world, while one lives bodily in another", His sceptical though persuaded narrator suggests that "it's perhaps the best authenticated case in existence of real vision at a distance",[7] as opposed presumably to the no doubt disappointing forms of stereoscopic illusion that saturated the gimmicky market of the time, like the Keystone stereoscope we discussed in Chapter 1.

These various kinds of fictional projection, the narrative equivalent, perhaps, of thought flexing its muscles, take a slightly more technologically and historically literal turn in the story "Argonauts of the Air", from 1895 (a momentous year for the idea of the flying machine, which nevertheless may have seemed almost as preposterous as disembodied demons or disembodied perceptions to those outside the world of the adventurous technician). There are many suggestive dimensions to this affectionately mocking parable of private hubris in an industrial milieu. Monson, the inventor and builder of the flying machine, and his engineer, Woodhouse, are not the only ones affected by the five years of building, development, testing and adjustment – with no sign of a launch date – that the experiment has cost: "When a millionaire who has been spending thousands on experiments that employ a little army of people suddenly indicates that he is sick of the undertaking, there is almost invariably a certain amount of mental friction in the ranks of the little army he employs" (Wells, *Complete Stories*, 119). The industrial magnate as benefactor of a little army and the community that inevitably evolves around this industry forms the microcosmic social setting for the project – part of a growing urban sprawl. To describe the flying machine, Wells draws on existing experiments in flight, like Otto Lilienthal's gliders, which allowed a kind of sport in human flight, and Hiram Maxim's experiments in the technics of bird flight.

Lilienthal's talks on the difficulties of experimental flying projects are perhaps echoed by the hubristic tone of Wells's tale. In 1891 Lilienthal had built and flown the first successful glider. Gradually modifying his design, he made over 2,000 flights over the next five years and in 1895 he flew a biplane glider that lifted with hardly any running start from the 50-foot hill he had constructed, and carried him distances of a quarter of a mile at heights of 75 feet. He also gave notice of his plan to attach a motor that would drive a mechanism to flap the wing tips and, he hoped, extend the duration of his flights. But Lilienthal had warned:

> We are not yet capable of constructing and using complete flying machines which answer all requirements. Being desirous of furthering with all speed the solution of the problem of flight, men have repeatedly formed projects in these last few years which represent complete air-ships moved by dynamos; but the constructors are not aware of the difficulties which await us as soon as we approach the realizing of any ideas in flying.
>
> All those, who have occupied themselves to any extent with actual flying experiments, have found that, even if they mastered theoretically the problem of flying, the practical solving of the same can only be brought about by a gradual and wearisome series of experiments based one upon the other.
>
> Also the practical tasks of the technics of flying should be simplified and divided as much as possible instead of steering straight to the final goal.
>
> As these principles have been seldom carried out, the practical results in human flight have remained very scanty up to the present day.
>
> One can get a proper insight into the practice of flying only by actual flying experiments. [. . .] It is in the air itself that we have to develop our knowledge of the stability of flight so that a safe and sure passage through the air may be obtained, and that one can finally land without destroying the apparatus. One must gain the knowledge and the capacity needed for these things before he can occupy himself successfully with practical flying experiments.
>
> As a rule the projectors and constructors of flying machines have not gathered this absolutely necessary practical experience, and have therefore wasted their efforts upon complicated and costly projects.[8]

In efforts of his own to carry out these necessary flying experiments, Lilienthal devised a movable elevator that was attached to his head in order to free his legs. While Lilienthal was testing this device, something failed; he fell 50 feet and died the following day. Maxim was no less prodigal, for after making his fortune inventing the machine gun (which would a few years later routinely be attached to flying machines) he built a large testing facility in England and established some influential principles of aerodynamics: "There is no magic in a bird soaring," he wrote,

> constant interchange of air is taking place, the cold air descending, spreading itself out over the Earth, becoming warm and ascending in other places. Soaring may be accounted for on the hypothesis that the bird seeks out an ascending column of

air, and while sustaining itself at the same height as the air, without any muscular exertion, it is in reality falling at considerable velocity through the air that surrounds it.

With his considerable wealth Maxim built large elaborate aircraft, like the steam-driven Goliath, to match his aspirations. Monson and Woodhouse are no doubt partly Wells's ambivalent tribute to these actual "Argonauts" of the air. His description of Monson's apparatus calls on both these men yet he adds a fictional element of his own, based on the principle of mechanical *propulsion*, which allows him fictionally to jump the gun:

> Monson, guided perhaps by a photographic study of the flight of birds, and by Lilienthal's methods, had gradually drifted from Maxim's shapes towards the bird form again. The thing, however, was driven by a huge screw behind in the place of the tail; and so hovering, which needs an almost vertical adjustment of the flat tail, was rendered impossible. The body of the machine was small, almost cylindrical, and pointed. Forward and aft on the pointed ends were two small petroleum engines for the screw, and the navigators sat deep in a canoe like recess [. . .] The machine was not only not designed to hover, but it was also incapable of fluttering. Monson's idea was to get into the air with the original rush of the apparatus, and then to skim, much as a playing card may be skimmed, keeping up the rush by means of the screw at the stern. Rooks and gulls fly enormous distances in that way with scarcely a perceptible movement of the wings. The bird really drives along on an aerial switchback. It glides slanting downwards for a space, until it has gained considerable momentum, and then altering the inclination of its wings, glides up again almost to its original altitude. (Wells, *Complete Stories*, 121–2)

The description utilises the principles established by Lilienthal and, more particularly, Maxim, yet the machine is nothing but a rocket with seating for navigators and is to be driven by the fictional conceit of a powerful screw. Wells seems to have taken the case of Lilienthal's tragic misadventure and re-imagined it in the case of a fuelled and powerfully driven machine. He gives two accounts of the calamity, the first from the navigator's point of view:

> Woodhouse, sitting crouched together, gave a hoarse cry, and sprang up towards Monson. "Too far!" he cried, and then he was clinging to the gunwale for dear life, and Monson had been jerked clean overhead, and was falling backwards upon him.

The second account is written from the point of view of spectators on the ground:

> A distant winged shape had appeared above the clustering houses to the south, had fallen and risen, growing lager as it did so; had swooped swiftly down towards the Imperial Institute, a broad spread of flying wings, had swept round in a quarter circle, dashed eastward, and then suddenly sprung vertically into the air. A black object shot out of it, and came spinning downward. A man! Two men clutching

each other! They came whirling down, separated as they struck the roof of the Students' Club, and bounded off into the green bushes on its southward side. (Wells, *Complete Stories*, 124)

The machine ultimately smashes down into the Royal College of Science, splintering, catching fire and taking much of the building with it. Wells's story was published in December 1895. The narrator's eulogy for Monson's disastrous failure foreshadows similar ones that pervaded the international press in words and pictures after Lilienthal's own fatal failure in August of the following year: "Though he failed, and failed disastrously, the record of Monson's work remains – a sufficient monument – to guide the next of that band of gallant experimentalists who will sooner or later master this great problem of flying" (Wells, *Complete Stories*, 125).[9] In Wells, though, the hint of hysterical irony is unmistakable. The stakes are raised: the city itself and, emblematically, its scientific institutes have now become the targets of their own accidental follies; the dream of flight, which Wells connects here to the fantasy of rapid action at a distance (projective identification in the projectile), has passed from the action of the lone experimenter to the community itself, and from the glider to the rocket. What stands out (recalling Lilienthal's prophetic words, "Sacrifices must be made") is the rapid raising of stakes when the industrial, technological and military machines take over.

The kind of science fiction premise mobilised by Wells would seem to exploit a logical condition which cannot be reduced to the normal notion of hypothesis. A writer does not simply answer the question "What if . . .?" with a fictional reconstruction. Rather, science fiction seems to follow a more powerful logic of "as if". The first serious formulation of the philosophy of as-if is probably to be found in Immanuel Kant's *Critiques*, where it functions as the crucial hinge between pure and practical reason and thus, no doubt at first obscurely, as the ground of the power of judgement itself (which by its own logic remains inexistent). Kant would thus confirm before the act that Nietzsche's "unhooking of the power of judgement" is only possible on the basis of that power itself: only judgement has the power to unhook the power of judgement. Or, in a more powerful formulation, the power of judgement is grounded only on the necessity of its own invention: no such power exists so one must operate as if it did; the power of judgement is nothing other than the power of its own invention. By the time Hans Vaihinger's mobilisation of the as-if function (culminating in his *The Philosophy of As If* from 1911) had become one of the more popular of the early twentieth-century works in that idiom, both science and fiction had developed considerable resources that, it would seem, were designed to exploit the groundless function of *as if*.

It is possible to trace an increasing division between two dimensions of this groundless logic across several often seemingly incompatible and anyway obliquely connected idioms and institutions of the twentieth century. The division is one of the key driving forces of the intensification of industrial, technological and military technology. The first, theoretical, dimension gives its law to the technical sciences whose operations proceed as if its final aims were possible, as if the final scenario was already an actuality. The second, fictional, dimension develops in the mobilisation of the *impossibility* of this final aim, as the *possibility* of its perpetual invention.

In the Country of the Blind

A strange and poignant link between the emergent sciences of aerodynamics and neurology becomes apparent in Ernest Starling's "Editor's Preface" to an edition prepared by E. D. Adrian in 1917 of *The Conduction of the Nervous Impulse*, based on the work of his friend and colleague Keith Lucas. Lucas had died before having time to write up his research. Starling offers the following brief eulogy:

> The qualities, which had rendered Lucas eminent as a physiologist, are just those required in the new science which set out on the conquest of the air; and from the beginning of the war he applied all his inventive faculties to solving the practical problems which confront our aviators. His loss to the flying service is as great as his loss to physiology. But his work is for all time, and will serve as a sure vantage ground from which other men will carry on the quest so ably initiated by Lucas.[10]

The vantage ground that Starling evokes concerns the question of how the mind is controlled by what is "sent to the brain from the sense organs". And human awareness is dependent mainly "on what is coming into the brain from our eyes and ears"(Adrian, *Conduction*, 18). This sensate determinism and the hierarchy that privileges the seeable and hearable (with vision first) characterise a corresponding blindness to the conditions of possibility for the technics of scientific observation and, by association here, the active technologisation that is its inseparable counterpart.

Wells also addresses the quandaries posed by problems of vision and its attendant desires in his 1904 story "The Country of the Blind". The general milieu of the early part of the twentieth century is represented here by a text that engages with vision, technicity, science, and what we are describing as the ineluctable undecidability of the conditions that give rise not only to modernist aesthetics but also to the optoelectronic technologies that allow for prosthetic extension of the capacity to see.

In Wells's parable, a mountaineer ventures into a fabled valley populated by a physically isolated race of blind people. Believing that his sight will make him their immediate superior, he attempts to enact the mantra that drives his desires and which he repeats incessantly: "In the country of the blind the one-eyed man is king". Wells, in a sense, updates Plato's myth of the cave by having the blind utterly unpersuaded by the explanations of the world that sight provides, as offered by the mountaineer. After all of his efforts to control these blind people fail and as he is increasingly forced to live within their conceptions of how reality is constituted, the mountaineer attempts to run away, only to return cowed and subdued. He acquiesces to his fate amongst the blind on their terms and falls in love with a blind woman whom he wishes to marry. Opposition to the marriage is strong since relatives and others believe that he will weaken their race (especially as he has earlier spoken of such gibberish as "sight" and "vision") – a sly stab at eugenics and its techno-socio application. A doctor is called to examine him and decides his weakness of mind results from the "irritant bodies" that the mountaineer believes provide him sight, and an operation to remove them is suggested. (The woman's uncle cries, "Thank heaven for science!" at this solution to their familial problem.) Wells's text explains the position the sighted mountaineer finds himself in: "For a week before the operation to raise him from his servitude and inferiority to the level of a blind citizen . . . he sat brooding . . . trying to bring his mind to bear on his dilemma."[11]

Wells might have been influenced by various modernist experiments, as his tale opens with a series of embeddings, indirections and false starts that make it difficult for readers to get a clear sense or picture of what is going on – making the piece an ill fit for realist fiction. An opacity of sorts occludes the opening sections (a kind of Joycean darkling), and a lack of focus unusual in popular magazine fiction holds for several paragraphs until the tale settles on its protagonist and his travails, as recounted in traditional realist mode, but one laced with heavy irony. In these ways, Wells's work also echoes Conrad's nearly contemporaneous writings, especially his *The End of the Tether*. This Conrad story with its thematisation of blindness, discussed earlier, also relies on ocular obscurity in its opening paragraphs before it, too, settles into the more linear but deeply ironic account of the visually impaired Whalley's last trip as ship captain. While operating within a more popular idiom than Conrad, Wells nevertheless addresses the intimate and fundamental connections between the blindness wrought by vision, the forms of vision that sightlessness enables, and the role of science in at least its promise to "remedy" both situations – itself another type of blindness about technicity and its operations. Wells in these ways returns to dilemmas posed in the perennial conflict between empiricism and rationalism. In this way he belongs, perhaps, to that populist tradition marked by the critical challenge to all dogma in knowledge, and characteristic of a long line of writers from the seventeenth to the nineteenth centuries, including Locke, Swift, Pope, Berkeley, Diderot, Rousseau, Voltaire and Goethe, among others. But as a writer of science-based fiction and largely in support of technology's con-tribution to questioning the grip of religion and other belief systems on the imagination, Wells invokes the uncertain and ultimately undecidable nature of empirical evidence, technology and nature itself. The paradox of the sighted man actually knowing more about the material and empirical world inhabited by the race of the blind but being incapable of expressing himself in a meaningful way and so, eventually, acquiescing to their world-view, suggests a lack of solid grounds for even scientific/empirical knowledge. This kind of proposal is not often found in the type of popular fiction for which Wells made his name. The ironic turns of the protagonist's fate show that Wells obviously enjoys having a sighted egoist brought low by the very sense which he believes will allow his individual colonial ambitions to be realised, and he tweaks staid beliefs of superiority by making the mountaineer an idiot, not a king, in the country of the blind.

A key to Wells's questioning of visual superiority might reside in the proverb the mountaineer repeats – "In the country of the blind the one-eyed man is king" – because the mountaineer is endowed with both eyes. The point of scientific inquiry into biocular vision is, after all, the vanishing point: the insight of perspectival painting and geometry. That is, the placement of two eyes in the face can allow for "perspective" as we have come to literally understand it, and the mountaineer lacks figurative perspective because of the omnipotence of visual space accorded to and by literal perspective. And it was the stereoscopic nature of vision itself that received an inordinate amount of manipulation in nineteenth-century experimentation on perspective, depth-of-field and movement. Marey's photo-gun that "shot" the phases of a bird's flight preceded Wells's story by about two decades and pushed scientific inquiry into vision into areas other than the entertaining effects of stereoscopes that dominated the middle and late parts of the nineteenth century.

The links between Marey's visual investigations and Marcel Duchamp's avant-garde works are well known and have been explored.[12] As we have shown, Duchamp's 1913 *Nude Descending a Staircase* clearly incorporates the statement of Marey's and Muybridge's studies of movement if not their performance, for Duchamp's interest resides not in the technology of documentation nor in the mechanics or automation of vision, but in the aesthetics of blindness that opens rather than closes the gap of apprehension and that slows down the technology of increased speed. "Duchamp set up a vertigo of delay," as Octavio Paz perceptively argues, "in opposition to the vertigo of acceleration".[13] Duchamp's nude perpetually flows in a frozen stream of points of movement, invoking what Duchamp considered to be the Zeno's paradox-like nature of such technological explorations of movement and vision. The nude's movement is not caught in technovisual or optoelectronic mimesis, but delayed in the slowness of paint. "I wanted to create a static image of movement," Duchamp said of the piece; "movement is an abstraction, a deduction articulated within the painting".[14] Duchamp wields the power integral to modernity, which we have been arguing throughout the book, by demarcating the capacity to divide the fast from the slow, the kinetic from the inert, and the invisible from the visible.

The avant-garde magazine Duchamp, Loy and others produced in New York during the 1910s was called *The Blind Man*. Devoted to jury-less exhibitions, the new magazine editors continued the same democratic spirit with the magazine itself, offering a venue willing to publish anything submitted to it by writers and artists. In a telling repetition of blindness, though, the first issue neglected to include the address to which potential contributors could send their work.[15] The second issue took up the controversy surrounding Duchamp's *Fountain*, a work that in itself reveals the hinge at work.

Duchamp's "ready-mades" explicitly evoke the strange power of division, the ability to divide, that underlies techno-scientific development, especially as it is manifested in military technology of the visible. The ready-made imposes itself between object and art-object, between technological production and aesthetic object, the latter being what the museum-goer expects to see and what the artistic/institutional logic-of-art renders visible. The power of the ready-made is not just the Adamic power to name, but that of divisibility itself. "As a hinge," Dalia Juodovitz asserts, "the ready-made is the doorway between art and non-art, whose 'objective' character is merely the construct of this interplay as a 'delay' effect".[16] And, yes, the ready-made operates the delay and instantiates what we have called the curious logic of the hinge. Duchamp explicitly evokes the delay in his most celebrated piece (executed between *Nude* and the ready-mades), *The Bride Stripped Bare by Her Bachelors, Even (The Large Glass)* – designating it a "delay in glass." The aesthetics of the "delay effect" reinserts the gap of perception and decidability that military and other technologies (usually) seek to reduce. However, at the same time, the ready-made deploys the logic of the hinge, which provides the capacity to transform and appropriate into the corpus (military or otherwise) that which lies outside it and which cannot ever be fully contained. According to this same logic, the organisational and strategic dream of the Cold War's full implementation of the military's entire technological prowess, articulated as C^3I, could not ever be realised under the terms of its own constitution. The aesthetics of the ready-made, then, allows us to access the logic of military technology while also pointing toward those aspects of the logic that simultaneously make it possible but unrealisable.

A related kind of distancing, imposing delays and detours in the route that perception must take in its passage through these works, occurs in Duchamp's final work, the posthumous installation *Etant donnés*, on which he laboured for about twenty years. By 1947 he had established the full title: *Etant donnés: la chute d'eau et le gaz déclairage* [Given: The Waterfall and the Illuminating Gas], repeating a note from *The Green Box* (1916) and thus linking this final contrivance to *The Large Glass*. Duchamp, who died in 1968 before this final work was revealed, had worked on it with two accomplices in absolute secrecy and had subtitled it "Collapsible mock-up made between 1946 and 1966 in New York with scope for ad-libbing during assembly and disassembly". In 1969 *Etant donnés* was installed using his instruction manual (an integral part of the work) in The Philadelphia Museum of Art, which was then (and remains) home also to *Large Glass* and other works.

Etant donnés stands in a bare room, in an unpromising, dark space that resembles an emergency exit. Starkly visible is a large solid wooden door (from an old garage) set in an arch of brick. The door cannot be opened but two small holes at eye level invite closer inspection, placing the viewer in a spot of immobility and enforced visual circumscription rather like the pilot in the Apache. A dark space opens through a ragged hole in a brick wall onto a brilliantly lit landscape with a figure of a woman in the foreground, prone, naked and with legs splayed towards the viewer. The figure is a palpable thing in real space – a three-dimensional sculpture, like many of Duchamp's works – but this sculpture is for the eyes only and only from this viewpoint. The work cannot be accessed in any other manner. Dawn Ades offers the following description:

> The two small holes, allowing natural bifocal looking rather than the single view-point that would be allowed by a keyhole, gives visual access onto further open-ings. The rough hole in the brick wall is separated from the door by a short dark passage (lined in black velvet), through which the nude is seen, lying on a bed of twigs. Her head is hidden by the edge of the brick wall, and the spectator's first instinct is to shift position to try, in vain, to see the whole figure.[17]

The invention clearly displays the limits of vision and the seductive promise of what lies beyond these limits. Working as it does on the implicit promise of seeing more while actually delivering less, Duchamp's last work provides commentary on all of the optotechnical enhancements of the first half of the twentieth century (including the museum as institution). For the first time since the early days, the figure itself, unlike the bride of *Bride* and *The Large Glass*, gestures to some kind of realist principle (however lifeless and pale). This truncated figure, missing a head and most of the legs, at least from the viewer's perspective, is the prone victim of visual focus and targeting. The promise of the voyeuristic gaze is delivered but only in the most limited and crudely salacious ways. As with the whole run of visual tele-technologies, the punchline of *Etant donnés* is, "the more you see, the less you see". One's sight is hijacked by the very means by which one is allowed, in an infinitely curtailed manner, to see more.

This work also suggests a commentary on the limits of reproducibility of art in the twentieth century. One of the features of this work is that it sub-verts the conditions described by Benjamin in "The Work of Art in the Age of Mechanical Reproduction". Here is a work that simply cannot be repro-duced technically. If you want to view it, you must go to Philadelphia. The artwork, taken as a whole, is an experience that cannot be achieved without a single and present observer – viewing it is part of the action comprising the work – one looks through two holes and then on through another, sug-gesting a series of embedded visual horizons and foregrounds. The "given" of the piece might among other things evoke the horizon, the irreducible distance between the viewer and the object of perception, for having stepped onto the mat the viewer is there confronted with a scene of shocking banal-ity and seemingly frivolous titillation that has captured the attention and debates of many critics. However, the figure holds aloft an oil lamp, gestur-ing in an offhand manner toward further sights of potential illumination if

Figure 8.1   Marcel Duchamp, *Etant Donnés: 2. The Illuminating Gas* (1946–66). Permission by Adagp, © Succession Marcel Duchamp/ADAGP, Paris 2010; image provided by the Philadelphia Museum of Art

only the viewer could see, if only the viewer could move, if only the viewer were allowed. Both the lamp and the body are decoys, the false delivery of a promise.

The tableau Duchamp reveals at the moment of viewing contains both static and dynamic elements. A flickering light makes the waterfall shimmer, though the nude beside remains frozen. Duchamp's piece reinforces the deadening effects of mechanisation and blind repeatability we observed in Barnes's automata (personified malfunctioning talking machines) while reminding us that he, too, has harnessed the same power of repeatability manifested by mechanisation and technology in these *delays*, each of which serves as a commentary on or an addition to his own earlier productions and an adumbration of what will come.

The effect of movement made by the waterfall hearkens back to the earliest projected images, such as those found in magic lanterns and on painted glass, reminding us that the effect of visual realism – no matter how effective or eerily real – is no more than an effect. "This door thus emerges as a pun on the immediacy of the visible," Judovitz argues, "since it also acts as an obstacle" (*Unpacking*, 202). Judovitz links the obstacle to the structures of spectatorship, so that what one sees would be the otherwise invisible structure of seeing rendered visible. The obstacle renders concrete the inexistent gap of perception, and it is this that technologies of vision would erase in the prompt union of a moment with itself. "The illuminating gas" of the installation's subtitle, then, indicates that Duchamp has taken visibility itself, and the technicity of the visible that has increasingly dominated for almost three centuries, as the subject of his final piece. "The illuminating gas" that turned Paris into the City of Lights – a city without clear divisions between night and day yet depending on them, as the doctor from Barnes's *Nightwood* evocatively notes – continues to flicker in the various technicities of sight that manifest modernity's power to divide the visible from the invisible. "The illuminating gas" gives the AH-1Z's pilot the power to see the enemy over the horizon and reveal the helicopter's invisibility as visible.

What The Decoy Reveals, or The Blind Man Becomes the Blind Missile

> But the world, mind, is, was and will be writing its own wrunes for ever, man, on all matters that fall under the ban of our infrarational senses fore the last milch-comel, the heartvein throbbing between his eyebrowns (James Joyce, *Finnegans Wake*, 19.35-20.2)

> The decoy can be used in the seduction, distraction, confusion and signature management roles. (Marketing information for naval decoys)

The advances made by over-the-horizon and sighted or intelligent weaponry have resulted in a supplemented field of vision for combat, almost a complete transformation of the earth's three-dimensional globe into a two-dimensional map. But the increased field of vision also means, of course, an increased field of blindness. Similarly, the power to divide the visible from the invisible is not solely the purview of the attacker, but also that of the target – *if* the target desires to engage and deploy the power to so divide. The challenge posed by advanced targeting systems becomes an opportunity for the targeted to turn the enemy's reliance on this weaponry to its advantage, that is, by distracting the guided weapon and making the enemy waste sophisticated and expensive weaponry on targets that are not real – or the intended – targets. The entire range of stealth-, decoy- or deception-based military systems and counter-measures seeks this turning of the technological tables, and therefore manifests "an aesthetics of disappearance," to borrow Virilio's terminology.[18] The decoy differs from its related counter-measure of "camouflage" in some important ways. The decoy assumes that the enemy knows of one's presence, or that this knowledge is not to be hidden, while camouflage presumes the enemy does not know one is present. Additionally the decoy seeks to turn visibility into a defensive advantage while camouflage deploys invisibility.

The infrared or radar decoy is one of several measures that military vehicles can take in throwing off guided missiles. It is currently fitted routinely into most mobilised military craft and acts as an additional layer of armour. The operation is relatively simple. A heat-seeking missile either locks onto the bright heat sources on a craft (nose, engines, exhaust) by infrared tracking or it uses radar emissions that are reflected back from its target. The three images below show the difference between what the eye sees, what an infrared guided missile tracks (heat sources) and what a radar guided missile tracks (reflected signals). The decoy involves flares fired from the targeted vessel that approximate the signals that the missile has been programmed to

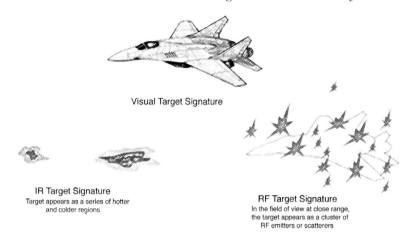

Visual Target Signature

IR Target Signature
Target appears as a series of hotter
and colder regions

RF Target Signature
In the field of view at close range,
the target appears as a cluster of
RF emitters or scatterers

Figure 8.2   Decoy, permission and image provided by Jordan Crandall

locate. Strong reflective material called chaff (composed of millions of pieces of aluminum-coated glass fibres) can be expelled to either lead a missile away from its target or cloud the target area, thus obscuring the target. The length of the chaff is dependent upon the radar frequency one wishes to counter.

The connection between radar or infrared detection systems and animal eyesight remains obscure, yet the language and imagery employed in the marketing and application of decoy systems suggests a curious analogy. The missile supposedly in some sense "sees" a ghostly doppelganger of its target and is fooled into missing it (like Duchamp's Bachelors in *The Large Glass*). The Lockheed Martin marketing material actually uses artistic renderings of ghostly ships, which have apparently led buyers into believing that the technology is capable of this kind of doubling trickery. In fact, eyesight is bypassed completely in a process that is entirely technical. It therefore looks as if the eye can see the difference between the real target and its doppelgänger, while the missile sees only the decoy, which thus turns the missile's artificial prosthetic sight advantage against itself. Believing it sees the ship, the guided-missile mistakes the infrared simulacrum for the vessel and strikes elsewhere than its designated target.

The image of the missile mistakenly striking the doppelgänger ship created by infrared projection is reminiscent of such ghostly apparitions as those projected by late nineteenth-century optical devices (such as Pepper's ghost, the glass image slide shows invoked by Duchamp's *Etant donnés*). But this is not an expansion of the visible spectrum; it is, rather, the infrared and radar supplement of sight. The marketing material evokes backgrounds reminiscent of Turner and his experiments with twilight diffusion. Yet the technology has nothing to do with what is seen or unseen and remains crudely mechanical despite the sophistication of its various sensing systems.[19]

Notes

1. Friedrich Nietzsche, *The Gay Science*, ed. Bernard William, trans. Josephine Nauckhoff (Cambridge: Cambridge University Press, 2001) p. 223.
2. E. D. Adrian, *The Physical Background of Perception* (Oxford: Clarendon Press, 1947) pp. 48–62.
3. Freud, Sigmund, "Formulierungen über zwei Prinzipien des psychischen Geschehens", *Gesammelte Werke* VIII (Frankfurt: Fischer, 1999) pp. 229–38. Translated as "Formulations on the Two Principles of Mental Functioning", *Standard Edition* (London: Hogarth, 1958) pp. 213–26.
4. Wilfred Bion, *Transformations* (London: Heinemann, 1965) p. 36.
5. Friedrich Nietzsche, *Writings from the Late Notebooks*, ed. Rüdiger Bittner, trans. Kate Sturge (Cambridge: Cambridge University Press, 2003) p. 26.
6. See Martin Heidegger, *Nietzsche*, vol. 4, ed. David Farrell Krell, trans. Frank A. Capuzzi, Davis Farrell Krell (New York: Harper and Row, 1982) for Heidegger's reading of nihilism in Nietzsche but see also Jacques Derrida, *Of Grammatology* (Baltimore: Johns Hopkins University Press, 1978) p. 36, for how Nietzsche's text escapes Heidegger's otherwise compelling criticisms.
7. H. G. Wells, *The Complete Short Stories* (London: Phoenix, 1998) p. 70.
8. Otto Lilienthal, "Practical Experiments for the Development of Human Flight", in James Means (ed.), *The Aeronautical Annual*, ed. James Means (Boston, MA: W. B. Clarke & Co., 1896) pp. 7–20 (a year after Wells's "Argonauts").
9. The eulogy echoes the tone and style of Lilienthal's own quietly inspirational writings. In an article written before, but published after, his fatal accident, he had written: "Can any sport be more exciting than flying? Strength and adroitness, courage and decision, can nowhere gain such triumphs as in these gigantic bounds into the air, when the gymnast safely steers his soaring machine house-high over the heads of the spectators. That the danger here is easily avoided when one practises in a reasonable way, I have sufficiently proved, as I myself have made thousands of experiments within the last five years, and have had no accidents whatever, a few scratches excepted. But all this is only a means to the end; our aim remains – the developing of human flight to as high a standard as possible. If we can succeed in enticing to the hill the young men who to-day make use of the bicycle and the boat to strengthen their nerves and muscle, so that, borne by their wings, they may glide through the air, we shall then have directed the development of human flight into a course which leads towards perfection" (Otto Lilienthal, "Fliegesport und Fliegepraxis: Prometheus, Illustrirte Wochenschrift über die Fortschritte in Gewerbe", *Industrie und Wissenschaft*, no. 322, vol. VII, 4. XII. 1895.
10. Keith Lucas, *The Conduction of the Nervous Impulse*, revised by E. D. Adrian (London: Longman, 1917) vi–vii.
11. H. G. Wells, *Collected Stories*, (Harmondsworth: Penguin, 1958) p. 144.
12. For more than half a century, since Sigfried Giedion at least. See Giedion, *Mechanization Takes Command: A Contribution to Anonymous History* (Oxford: Oxford UP, 1948).

13. Octavio Paz, *Marcel Duchamp: Appearance Stripped Bare*, trans. R. Phillips and D. Gardner (New York: Grove Press, 1978) p. 2.
14. Pierre Cabanne, *Dialogues with Marcel Duchamp*, trans. Ron Padgett (New York: Da Capo Press, 1987) p. 3.
15. Irene T. Hoffman, "Documents of Dada and Surrealism: Dada and Surrealist Journals in the Mary Reynolds Collection", http://www.artic.edu/reynolds/essays/hofmann.php
16. Dalia Judovitz, *Unpacking Duchamp: Art in Transit.* (Berkeley: University of California Press, 1995) p. 201.
17. Dawn Ades, *Marcel Duchamp* (London: Thames and Hudson, 1999) p. 190.
18. Paul Virilio, *The Aesthetics of Disappearance*, trans. P. Beichtman (New York: Semiotext(e), 1991).
19. The decoy need not be of this high-tech nature, as the various tactics deployed by the allies in Britain during World War II to fool the *Luftwaffe*, by the North Vietnamese on the Ho Chi Minh trail to defeat Operation Igloo White, and by the Serbians against the more sophisticated NATO weapons systems attest. See Virilio's *War and Cinema: The Logistics of Perception*, trans. Patrick Camiller (London: Verso, 1989) for a discussion of British tactics, and Paul Edwards's *The Closed World* (Cambridge, MA: MIT Press, 1997) for an insightful reading of Operation Igloo White.

PART III

Surveillance, Targeting, Containment

Chapter 9

Strategies and Technologies of Containment: Containing the Political

The "deportees" in the "camps" of our urban wastelands are . . . merely indicating the irresistible emergence of a previously almost unknown level of deprivation and human misery. They are waste-products of a military-industrial, scientific civilization which has applied itself for almost two centuries to depriving individuals of the knowledge and skill accumulated over generations and millennia, before a post-industrial upsurge occurred which now seeks to reject them on the ground of definitive uselessness. (Paul Virilio, *Strategy of Deception*)[1]

> Ostracized as we are with God
> The watchers of the civilized wastes
> reverse their signals on our track (Mina Loy, "The Apology of Genius", *The Lost Lunar Baedeker*)[2]

Narratives of diasporic movements often structure them as exemplifying what we identified in Chapter 5 as a kind of excess (Excess 1), according to which they would represent a superfluous and unnecessary fallout from ideal social conditions. The epigraph from Virilio suggests that the increasing instrumentality of the past two centuries, revealed in specific geo-political economies of production and consumption, has rendered a segment of the population once deemed necessary for production as now worthless, because production occurs elsewhere and consumption is beyond this segment's means. Because they neither produce nor consume, they are the useless excess of the social order and its inexorable logic that then spews them out for the greater good of the state.

Later in this chapter we focus on ways of thinking that valorise this excess, as if to confer strength and solidarity on a diverse multitude's powers of resistance to its state persecutors. The alternative perspective on this excess (Excess 2) identifies a kind of internal criticism of these processes, and affirms instead the ideal's dependency on its fallout, a parasitism that reverses the dominant idea (the migrant poor as parasitic on established states), to reveal, at the shifting boundaries crossed by peoples on the move, a prior condition that divides the stranger from the settled and law-abiding global citizen and yet grounds them in their difference. A theoretical jumble sweeps up into its polemic the themes of diaspora, migration, exile and refuge, all regarded as spatio-historical marks of a wandering in general. This assemblage of divergences from continuity includes the celebrated "drift" of postmodernist thought, the identity politics of cultural studies, and a beleaguered postcolonial criticism that continues to valorise the displaced yet resistant subjects of colonial, neocolonial or postcolonial powers.

Excess, though, occupies, or at least emerges from, a sphere that eludes and subverts any passionate claim for recognition and thus any principle on which the active struggle of the postcolonial subject (as either colonial victim or postcolonial agent provocateur) can be grounded. This elusive sphere (which is not an actual sphere for this reason) emerges only negatively in reference to geography and identity, but it can be pursued, nevertheless, because without it there would be no excess whatsoever. As we have consistently shown, two kinds of procedure aiming either to expose or to destroy it demonstrate the elusive insistence of this sphere, as a condition of life or field of potential activity: the aesthetic procedures of certain modernist artworks and writings in their struggle to represent it; and the increasingly intense operations of military technologies in the struggle to eradicate it. This excess of a third kind operates as if from a non-dimension, as a function, without which neither the marked nor the unmarked occupants of a nation would ever have had a place. The nation-state with its several apparatuses of division and inclusion, at once manning and unmanning the homeland, cannot operate without some engagement with this function, which we have designated with the nomination *Excess 3*, thus avoiding either negative or positive determinations (Excess 1 and Excess 2).

The attempt to eradicate excess in general can give rise to the illusion that this attempt is mobilised primarily against the actual victims of the operation, which inevitably bears the insignia of military technicity, with its assemblage of techniques and technologies. The primary target of the military is better understood as the sphere of possibility itself. The necessarily potential relationship between the state and its citizens operates as a paradoxical distribution of forces, which must be somehow contained but which always leave a remainder. To recognise in this remainder the power of the state is to see that a state need not have any concrete political relationship with the multitude that includes both its citizens and its excluded remains. The eradication (exclusion or control) of this remainder would thus function as a contingent effect of the attempt to eradicate the difference between a constitution itself (a powerful abstraction) and the individuals that supposedly constitute it. It thus operates in the difference of the constitution from itself.

The reserve, symbolically expressed in capital (as Virilio suggests), provides the state with its most powerful narrative of diaspora, regarding it as a kind of waste. But it also can function to reveal the elusive conditions of its constitution. At the level of the statement, the narratives of diaspora seldom diverge from the sense of Excess 1 – the uselessness of or the danger posed by those marked as diasporic. But the performative dimension of the narrative reveals that the demarcation of the populace operates as capacity or state power per se (Excess 2). Between the statement and the performance of it one can try to dwell in the discomfiting space of the population's vulnerability. The waste, in this sense, allows not only the sphere of economic gains and losses in the incalculable elasticity between, for instance, purchase and sale (an elasticity that every economic system must negotiate as its reserve, or *achresis*, in Aristotle's term), but it also generates the sphere in which populations are organised or mobilised. In the formation of diasporic communities the military, with its ensemble of technologies and technicities, operates again as an attaching/detaching hinge, allowing groups to be unhinged from the state and abandoned to their various diasporas. The non-sense of Excess 3 (*achresis*) emerges only when we follow the simultaneously economic, existential and aesthetic operations that negotiate between usefulness (necessity and demand, or Aristotle's *chreia*) and wastefulness (abusage, *catachresis*) in the divisions of populations.

This chapter proceeds in three stages. Looking first at the destructive properties underlying the evident effects of diaspora on the politics of global populations, we examine powerful instances of the valorisation of the excluded multitude and dwell on the enduring difficulties that challenge anyone wanting to avoid repeating the conditions that they object to. Homi Bhabha's identification of wandering people, "colonials, postcolonials, migrants, minorities", as the marks of the so-called "shifting boundary" represents a powerful, perhaps the most radical, insistence of this political imperative and for this reason demands serious consideration.

Secondly, we return to the field of modernist aesthetics as a way of outlining yet more clearly how an operation can be produced that affirms a condition irreducible to any identity grounded whether positively or negatively on existing institutional marks of community. Mina Loy's "Apology of Genius" might appear at first to be merely a rude satire evoking the avant-garde's response to a mystified public. But after careful reading we will see that by hinging two incommensurable (but confusable) literary traditions – the *apologia* and the *apology* – the poem creates a single fascinating and paradoxical statement about the difference between art and life, grounding life itself on this difference. This paradoxical hinge turns out to be at once the very source of what today we recognise as the power behind the military, and yet this is precisely what the military is mobilised primarily to eradicate.

Finally we examine the seemingly utopian projection, related to contemporary technological developments in unmanned vehicles, of a militarised sphere that has eradicated the human requirement altogether.

Diasporic Communities and the Insignia of the Military

What, then, marks the diasporic narrative? What shapes diasporic communities in ways unique to them? Perhaps the answer can be found in the violence of its peculiar community formation, the traumas that led to migration and the terrors of carving out a space in a new country and culture, the inevitable rending wrought by forced evacuations from and insertions into the complex webbing of geo-political sites, the tearing of roots from the earth's surface coupled with the tenuous act of transplanting. The patterns evoked here contain synchronic similarities worth noting, but the diachronic differences – that is, the elusive specificities of founding events – assemble to help produce the kind of collective memory that marks diasporic experience.

The violence inscribed on Asian diasporic communities, for instance, reads, appropriately enough, like a list of trials and punishments in the Torah. Floods, droughts, civil war and rebellions in mid-nineteenth-century China poured forth massive numbers of émigrés to a range of locations. Some of these ended up on the West Coast of the US, and anti-Chinese violence perpetrated by white workers in the 1870s helped form Chinatown in San Francisco from an inchoate clustering of shops and residences into a segregated ethnic enclave that provided protection from a hostile social environment. This violence, too, spurred Chinese migration in the US toward the East Coast, eventually making New York's Chinatown the largest such community in the world. The end of the nineteenth century saw the US military brutally and bloodily taking hold of the Philippines from first the Spanish and then Filipino nationalists, causing flight from the archipelago that was to be sustained for almost 100 years.

Japan's self-imposed isolation ended, of course, at the hands of Perry's gunboat actions, starting a period of interaction with the external globe that exacerbated political crises within the country. Meiji modernisation policies created agricultural pressures and landlessness among farmers, leading to nefarious dealings of conscripted labour to work in Hawaii, Guam and California, where labourers were treated brutally by bosses and co-workers alike. Korea suffered invasions from without as well as religious rebellions from within, especially in the late nineteenth century, not to mention the Sino-Japanese war being fought on its soil in the first decade of the twentieth century. Again, the export of labourers played a pivotal role in the formation of Korean diasporic communities during these periods and, again, violence marks the experience. When the Cold War became a hot war for the first time, in the Korean Peninsula, new diasporic groups came from there as well. A second major hot war of the Cold War was also fought on Asian soil, leading to massive diasporic movements from Laos, Cambodia and Vietnam – once more, with violence being the bookends of the diasporic experience. This is but a brief, grossly truncated list of atrocities that led to the formation of Asian diasporic communities and that marked their reception. European, African, Middle Eastern and South American geographies yield different but similar lists of horrific tales of wanderer creation.

We would draw attention in this list to the complex interaction of economic, technological, state and martial forces at play in the constitution of all of these Asian diasporic communities. This is what we call *the insignia of the military*, which inscribes diasporas past and present. The term "insignia" probably comes from two Latin roots: *signum*, which is "a distinguishing mark" and *sec-*, "to cut". The distinguishing mark, then, is a cut, forming an integral connection to the severing operative in diasporic experience. The "military" involved in our analysis is both military-as-entity, and military-as-*technē* (or organising, operating and executing principle). Regardless of whether we are discussing actual military operations or events that have militaristic logic, violence is the tool of implementation, and severing results. Thus, even when diasporic communities result from civic conflict, for example religious or ethnic violence resultant from political decisions, such as the partition that created Pakistan, we would argue the insignia of the military marked the event of diasporic sufferings. The "spontaneous" outbreak of violence and the dislocation of millions of people during the 1947 event had both militaristic origins and implementations. And the distinguishing marks of this event that severed peoples from lands long held as familial property were sustained physical and symbolic violence.

The marks inscribed as insignia of the military cannot always be easily distinguished from those of civil or ecclesiastical insignia – either as manifestations or as significations (senses which anyway overlap and recall each other). While the dominant insignia – the uniforms, arms, units, divisions, armies – help to play this distinguishing role by marking out an armed and mobile force in the service of some sovereign state, the insignia of the military in fact disperse in fragments into all aspects of experience, emerging for instance both in the form of monuments (memorial structures, museums, coats of arms, titles, tombs and public marches) and in the form of ruins and remains (bunkers, rubble, cripples, killing fields and dispersion). The overlaps between monument and ruin, one standing for the other falling, help to mark out the sense of *abbreviation* that the insignia of the military imposes, cutting short or cutting out. In some very important ways, the power of the state is borne by and through the *abbreviation* of the insignia of the military. The *abbreviation* reveals the state's sovereignty to cut out, to mark citizens, territory and language; that is, to cut short lives, borders and words.

Diasporic communities result from the power of sovereignty to expunge those who oppose it, and are, indeed, the manifestation of this power. Because the military provides the most crucial and visible means of implementing state sovereignty, the very existence of diasporas reveals the insignia of the military through the state sovereignty manifest in and apparent through its creation of wandering peoples. The insignia of the military, then, is part of the invisible trace diasporic communities bear *in* and *for* their "home" sites, as well as in the sites of exile. In this fashion, Ambrose Bierce's definition of an exile as "one who serves his country by residing abroad, yet is not an ambassador" is as accurate as it is satiric. In its scopic role for the state, functioning in its episcopal role, the military marks and targets a segment of the population for excision.

The singular unit of the military, the *milēs* (or soldier) must be employed to bear arms potentially against other soldiers but not necessarily. Thus it is that civilians also can bear the marks of the military. Everyone is potentially a soldier, especially with the advent of "total war" and its intensification during the Cold War. From this fact derives the *power of sovereignty*, which thus shapes political communities according to the relative capabilities that individuals can learn, a point that manifests itself in a range of institutions. It is no accident that the word *discipline* (from *discere*, – to learn) finds its most appropriate usage today with reference to the modern military whose armies command great skill and great force and so must be managed through the exercise of great discipline. In this way the insignia of the military inscribes itself on the academic disciplines too, and it is this aspect that tends to get lost in the identity politics of contemporary intellectuals. In the university-qua-institution, a cool debate about who and what we are serves the military function of drill, and a delimited debate about "the political" effectively serves as an abbreviation of *thinking* about "the political".

The insignia of the military in diasporic community formation operates in many ways, from the visible to the invisible, from the explicit to the implicit. Direct military conflict – such as the Taiping Rebellion, or Perry's arrival in Japan, or China and Japan at war on Korean soil, or the Vietnam war – is only the most blatant, or visible, means through which the insignia of the military results in diasporic movements. But when the insignia of the military manifests itself in other systemic forms, for example technology, economics, political apparatuses or global linkages, then the full complexity of the phenomenon and its capacity to shape human organisation can be glimpsed.

The bombing of Kosovo in the 1990s, for example, by an international force deploying the most advanced high-tech weaponry resulted in large-scale movements of people who were not welcome at any nation's borders, except in the most minimal numbers. This war that was not a war resulted, therefore, in refugees who were not refugees. That is, other, systemic dimensions of the insignia of the military prevented the conflict from being defined as a war and its wandering victims as refugees worthy of designation as diaspora. Or, the fact that their evacuations were externally imposed, and thereby superseding the power of the state, might explain why they were denied diasporic status. Not allowing the state the power to demarcate its own populace as no longer members of its state cancelled their claims to be counted as a diasporic community. Alternatively, the transfer of Hong Kong to the People Republic of China (PRC) led to thousands of wealthy Hong Kong Chinese fleeing to North America and Australia. In this case, the peaceful transfer of power intended to facilitate both state sovereignty and market access resulted in a new diasporic community significantly different from most Chinese immigrants past and from those huddling along Macedonia's borders: one that was well heeled and therefore capable of attaining (or purchasing) diasporic status. The relatively comfortable status of immigrants during and after flight does not ameliorate the genuinely traumatic effects of political and economic violence wrought by the transfer of Hong Kong to the PRC. The Hong Kong and Kosovo examples reveal the difficulty of containing excess (as Excess 1) in the confusion of diasporic narrative techniques. They also show the difficulties in manifesting state sovereignty in and through the capacity to mark diasporic communities, because the diaspora must, by definition, function in the international sphere that provides the state with its capacity to achieve statehood.

Another densely complex example of how the insignia of the military creates diasporic communities can be found in the 1997 South East Asian Economic crash. The globalisation thrust that allows for "real-time" military surveillance of the earth necessary for waging the Cold War also provides the means for uniting the earth in interrelated markets. Technologies designed to take snap-second decisions out of human hands in military situations function in a similar fashion for currency exchange markets and other global investment strategies. Maximum control by these technologies led to maximum economic meltdown in 1997, resulting in capital taking the mantle of the diaspora. Capital fled the region, and, as it always can and does, found harbour elsewhere. People who suffered the adverse effects of this flight, on the other hand, did not always have the advantage of flight themselves – capital having the inherent attribute of mobility that people do not, unless it is forced upon them. The insignia of the military, then, provides a means for reading a myriad of diasporic phenomena in subtly but profoundly interconnected ways, thus keeping a range of causes and effects, forces and resistances, and modes of violence simultaneously under consideration. In other words, the insignia of the military does not isolate the political solely within the domain of the individual; rather, it reveals how the political cannot be so easily contained in that specific site while examining a multitude of systems that shape the individual-as-individual (including those discursive and ideological ones that foreground the individual).

The traumas that birthed diasporic communities play an integral role in identity formation for these communities. They are firmly woven into the warp and woof of the communities' understandings of themselves in relation to the past and the present, the global and the local. These violent acts provide an essential context for reading diasporic texts. Yet, much current research into diasporic writing and diasporas almost completely elides this violence, or relegates it to "backdrop", not even context, much less text. Following a general trend in recent humanities and social sciences research, diasporic inquiry has privileged the concepts of the individual and identity formation (at the individual level) over and above the military, economic, technological and ideological apparatuses (that is, the insignia of the military) in the shaping of diasporic experience. Ignoring the relation of technē to poesis, though, is fraught with risk, for it can lead to institutional overseeing and scopic targeting of what does and does not fall within the domain of a discipline. In this manner, diasporic studies, unwittingly, replicates the trauma of the cut or mark that constitutes diasporic communities from the outset. What operates as the domain of the political in much contemporary humanities and social sciences research is, in fact, a containment of the political subject in the image of the individual and individual identity.

Again, diasporic studies is by no means unique in this delimiting of the political, but it seems a particularly odd, unnecessary and even dangerous narrowing of the objects of inquiry – an abbreviation of inquiry itself – when one is concerned with diasporas (as our all-too-brief list above reveals). If diasporic writing contests the optimistic assumptions of cosmopolitanism, exclusively under the rubric of individual identity politics, then it displaces the larger forces found in the insignia of the military that actually shape political identity, and it abandons these for an inquiry into subjectivity motivated by the struggle for recognition. If diasporic writing is to have the kind of political purchase that is often claimed for it, it should perhaps consider the more elusive horizons around which diasporic experience is nevertheless played out.

Containing Diaspora in the Humanities: The Law, the Text and the State

Diaspora would always have been a curse. In its current sense, originating in *Deuteronomy*, diaspora itself (from the Greek translation of *za'avah* in the Hebrew scroll) is one among the catalogue of curses that would befall the chosen people if they did not submit to the commandments: "thou shalt be a diaspora (or dispersion) in all kingdoms of the earth" (xxviii: 25). And in a rare moment of humour in *John*, when Jesus proposes to disappear to join "the Father who sent me", the response of the Jews is to assume that he intends to go "into the diaspora among the gentiles" (vii: 35). The humour can help lessen the sense of what is at stake here. One purpose of the Testament of John is to demonstrate how Jesus fulfils the conditions set out in *Deuteronomy*: to show that this man was not a false prophet but the real thing. The pertinent sign must strictly be neither a sign nor a wonder but it must make itself apparent in the absolute disappearance of Jesus from the temporal sphere. The relative disappearance of the diaspora, in contrast, would be the sign only of a curse. This is what resolves the difference between the Old and New Testaments. Jesus's disappearance must be absolute both apparently (as a sign of absence in the absence of a sign) and conspicuously (as a wonder). In this way the dichotomies of *Deuteronomy* between the law and its disobedience are resolved only in their repetition – the absolute alterity of the atemporal divine in dichotomy with the mortal dislocations of law, sovereignty and identity in time.

It is probably no accident that this pattern, inscribed in the deep historicity of the Judaic and Christian traditions, seems to be replicated in the patterns of diaspora that we are calling Asian. The curses described in *Deuteronomy*, recognisable in contemporary contexts as the direct consequences of disasters like war (poverty, famine, displacement, separation, criminality, death, dispersion and a host of other consequences), are formulated as a kind of deterrent. The curses will not only have been a verbal deterrent against erring from the commandments but they also would be, in their actuality, the promise of their fulfillment in advance – they would make examples of their victims: "they shall be upon thee for a sign and for a wonder [*mopheth*, that is, something conspicuous], and upon thy seed for ever" (xxviii: 46).

So the law that outlines this horrific catalogue of consequences for disobeying it is always and everywhere made evident by a sleight of hand that identifies existing woes as evidence for the power of the Father to visit them upon disobedient victims. Thus the curses of war, plague, famine and drought become the signs for the powerful wrath of an almighty authority. In the phrase coined by Franco Moretti, these signs and wonders might just as well be the "signs *taken* for wonders" that ground the mystical foundations of authority that Moretti examines in his book of that title. Alluding to Moretti, Homi Bhabha addresses the issue of the ambivalence of authority in his "Signs Taken for Wonders", in which he analyses three moments when texts of the civilising mission meet with their own dislocation – the printed bible distributed and dispersed among the colonised people of Delhi in 1817, Joseph Conrad's Marlowe coming across Towson's *Inquiry into some Points of Seamanship*, and V. S. Naipaul's discovery of the same text in "Conrad's Darkness":

> Written as they are in the name of the father and the author, these texts of the civilizing mission immediately suggest the triumph of the colonialist movement in early English Evangelism and modern English literature. The discovery of the book installs the sign of appropriate representation: the word of God, truth, art creates conditions for a beginning, a practice of history and narrative. But the institution of the Word in the wilds is also an *Entstellung*, a process of displacement, distortion, dislocation, repetition – the dazzling light of literature sheds only areas of darkness.[3]

One interesting aspect for us in Bhabha's analysis is the way he shows how the authorised colonial text – the word of the law itself – becomes subject to its own curse in diaspora. In this case the distortions, displacements and dislocations are revealed to be functions of the law itself – its repeatability and the inevitable difference in each repetition as it disperses into the future of its legislations. *Deuteronomy* is already the embodiment of its own curse in this sense, as the literal meaning of "Deuteronomy" is "second law", but is based on a misinterpretation at a crucial stage of the translation process. The *Devarim* (or Words) identifies itself as a repetition by Moses of his original law. The possibility of repetition can be seen, then, as both blessing and curse because it gives the law its legislative possibility while simultaneously exposing it to dislocations as it disperses into the wild.

The pattern of Bhabha's analysis turns up again in a later essay, "Dissemination", this time locating the force of *dis*location no longer in the structural repeatability of the law but now – much more problematically – in the figures of the various diasporic peoples of the contemporary world:

> At this point I must give way to the *vox populi*: to a relatively unspoken tradition of the people of the pagus – colonials, postcolonials, migrants, minorities – wandering peoples who will not be contained within the *Heim* of the national culture and its unisonant discourse, but are themselves marks of a shifting boundary that alienates the frontiers of the modern nation. (*Location*, 164)

And here we raise a flag of caution. This attempt to shift from a structural phenomenon to a subjectivity resultant from it – which throughout Bhabha's work runs alongside his more meticulous analyses of the paradoxes of law under colonialism – works like a kind of hallucination of alterity in the figure of the diasporic wanderer. Just as the Jews thought that Jesus was going to disappear into the diaspora, Bhabha locates the law's own ambivalent alterity in the figure of diasporic people. But diasporic peoples are hardly ever marks of a shifting boundary. Diaspora more often marks the steadfastness of modern national boundaries as well as the fecund reproducibility of boundaries as these boundaries re-emerge like high fences around refugee camps. We draw attention to this only to show that the valorisation of alterity in contemporary work on hybridity, multiculturalism, diaspora, and so on, runs the risk of attempting in all the traditional ways to separate the blessing from the curse.

Returning briefly to the curse, what we find in *Deuteronomy* is an account of alienation:

> The stranger within thee shall get up above thee very high; and thou shalt come down very low [*ger qereb 'alah ma'al ma'al yarad mattah mattah*]. He shall lend to thee, and thou shalt not lend to him: he shall be the head, and thou shalt be the tail. (xxviii: 43–4)

What this passage makes clear (despite some peculiar but interesting translation decisions among the recent Anglo-American texts) is that the question of identity can be grasped as a struggle of sovereignty, in which the force of a relative alterity plays against the force of a relative identity. The very high (*ma'al ma'al*) and the very low (*mattah mattah*) constitute a topology, which corresponds to an economic system (lending and borrowing) and a dynamic (heads and tails). What is at stake is the relation between sovereign and subject, which can thrive when the stranger within (*ger qereb*) is subordinate (as the borrower and the tail). The curse manifests in the stranger becoming the lender. The ascendance of the stranger within – this relative alterity – would be the curse of those dispossessed of their sovereignty – the wandering peoples identified in the citation from Bhabha – forever in debt to their own foreignness. The thing to underscore here would be that the stranger cannot be separated from its opposite – *our identity*. The blessings and curses are so constructed to reveal these alternatives as belonging to each other. For each blessing there corresponds a curse, and each correspondence follows the form of an inversion. Diaspora would thus have always been the inversion of sovereignty. And in the dialectic of the inverted world the inversion is revealed as a repetition of the same from a different viewpoint.

The *hallucination* of alterity in the figure of the diasporic wanderer, therefore, finds analogous form in the *image* of the individual that passes for the political subject in some recent writing. That is, the diasporic sign of relative alterity is taken for the wonder of radical, absolute alterity and, thus, mirrors and repeats the containment of the political in individual identity politics, as if alterity could be made conspicuous in the sign of hybrid identity. Diasporic communities do not necessarily and inherently challenge the insignia of the military or the sovereignty of the nation; in fact, they do just the opposite. *They are the necessary result of state sovereignty and prove its power through their existence.* They are the cursed that prove the blessings of the state's sovereignty, as well as the curses of disobedience. Just as importantly, they are the potential existential condition of the blessed. How their lives and horizons have been abbreviated – cut out and cut short – serves as warning to those still in the sovereign's good graces. The unstated relationship between the state and its severed diasporic populations does not therefore come to light as a boundary dividing, say, an inside from an outside. Rather it reveals a division no less *within* the state than *outside* it, a division excessive to the state in three respects: it is its waste, its condition and, as Excess 3, its other. Both a property of the state and an impropriety, this excess of a third kind nonetheless disappears from view if one fixes on either the state or on its diasporas. Bhabha therefore probably does not go far enough in his valorisation of diasporic individuals as challenging in and of themselves the "unisonant discourse" of the nation and its narrative of sovereignty. He unintentionally risks valorising the effects of structural and systemic forces that in fact reveal state sovereignty. The valorisation of the effects diverts attention from the structural and systemic forces – the insignia of the military – and, therefore, contains and abbreviates the political subject within the domain of the individual. Such a theoretical move is itself a sign taken for a wonder because it reads the relative alterity of diaspora as a blessing rather than a curse. The state's sovereignty is not undermined by such an interpretation, only repeated – as the repetition of the law already enacted in the translation of *Devarim* as *Deuteronomy* suggests. Such readings, however, risk converting diasporic research into thaumatology, the study of wonders.

The sheer conspicuousness of diaspora leads writers like Bhabha to what seems to us to be a hasty valorisation of the symptom as an alternative to, rather than as a consequence of, structural and historical conditions that also account for the generalisable global phenomena of sovereign states at war with each other. Global war is conducted in many ways (and at a range of temperatures between cold and hot) that include those conditions that we sometimes call "peace". For this reason it would be a mistake to neglect Bhabha's motivation – which in line with a number of political theorists today provokes his attempt to rethink political philosophy and political community beyond the historical precedence of sovereignty, identity (of whatever kind) and state. But it is also a mistake to allow the mark of the state on the cursed, disobedient individual to be interpreted as resistant to the power that provides that mark.

Political frontiers expose communities to their others – undoubtedly – but the radical structural condition of the *frontier* itself is rarely considered to take precedence over the communities bounded by it, despite the fact that sovereignty is dependent upon the defining, policing and defence of frontiers. Communities who are dispossessed of their sovereignty of the frontier might well be taken as signs for the inadequacy of current thinking and current international practice (as in Bhabha's argument), but they probably should not be mistaken as the marks of the frontier itself. What is so enigmatic and powerful about political frontiers is that they resist such identifications. So long as there is a frontier, there is an "other" – whether any particular other shows itself or not, whence the perpetual "othering" of neighbours. But the alterity of the frontier is not itself the identity of others on the other side, though it does provide the grounds of identity for diasporic groups either actual or potential. Here we have an a priori condition, an irreducible structural condition that, without being identifiable as such, gives us identities in contrast with others. The relative alterity of being in-contrast-with – simultaneously a relative difference and a relative identity – simply serves the thought of the sovereign over and above the stranger inside you: the subaltern in the service of the sovereign.

The extent of the problem can be indicated if we look at a short "Postscript" to an essay, "Against the Lures of Diaspora", by Rey Chow. Chow's work is relevant here because it represents a sustained attempt to address the problems of cultural displacement on a globe marked by the multiple legacies of imperialism. Chow's work often draws attention to the continued and often paradoxical imbalances produced in interactions between the west and the east: the role of western critical discourses and the way that role changes with the subject of enunciation; the role of western technologies in enabling non-western cultural development but along the lines of the technicities we delineate in this book; the postmodernist replication of orientalism, and so on. She too argues against the valorisation of minority positions, especially those of intellectuals in diaspora, because, as she sees it, the valorisation masks a number of hegemonic relations that contain and domesticate any significant cultural contestations. Chow articulates, in conclusion, a statement that at first sight would be entirely in support of our own critical position. She writes that:

> Any attempt to deal with "women" or the "oppressed classes" in the "third world" that does not at the same time come to terms with the historical conditions of its own articulation is bound to repeat the exploitativeness that used to and still characterizes most "exchanges" between "West" and "East."[4]

The marked terms here indicate the way the mask works: women, oppressed classes, third world, exchanges, east and west. In their valorisation, these terms operate as "intangible goods", values that intellectuals trade in, a form of exchange and hegemonic oppression that simply repeats those of imperial and colonial power. And Chow accurately identifies how these diasporic signs can be taken for wonders:

> Like "the people," "real people," "the populace," "the peasant," "the poor," "the homeless," and all such names, these signifiers *work* insofar as they gesture towards another place (the lack in discourse-construction) that is "authentic" but that cannot be admitted into the circuit of exchange. ("Against the Lures", 118)

In Chow's account, then, these *relative* alterities give rise to the hallucination of an *absolute* alterity. But, like the alterity of the political frontier, this "other place" outside the circuit of exchange is just *not there*.

So how does Chow reconcile this admirable critical vigilance against what she calls "the lures of diaspora" with her position as a Chinese diasporic intellectual? She would seem to be taking almost exactly the contrary position to Bhabha. Bhabha's critique of the law and its dislocation in repetition certainly corresponds with Chow's critique of the hegemonic repetition of imperial force in the figure of the diasporic intellectual. But where Bhabha locates an irreducible dissonance in the figure of the homeless wanderer, in the irreducible hybridity of hybrid identity, in what he calls the "third space", Chow comes down on the side of political identity. Her counter to charges of essentialist identity politics is to affirm and avow a political identity grounded in historical materialism. It is not by chance that she can ground her position with an appeal to Hegel's dialectic:

> If we describe the postcolonial space in Hegelian terms, we can say that it is a space in which the object (women, minorities, other peoples) encounters its Notion [i.e., *Concept*] (criterion for testing object), or in which the "being-in-itself" encounters the "being-for-an-other. ('Against the Lures', 115)

In Hegel's dialectic of experience, consciousness eventually must come to terms with itself. For Chow, third-world intellectuals in diaspora must achieve the status of conscious subjects of knowledge at the cost of the discovery of their long-term historical object-hood: "Third world intellectuals acquire and affirm their own 'consciousness' only to find, continually, that it is a 'consciousness' laden with the history of their objecthood" ("Against the Lures", 115).

When they also have to come to terms with the fact that, in the "first world", they continue to be "beheld as other", the lure of diaspora no longer beckons:

> For "third world" intellectuals especially, this means that recourse to alterity – the other culture, nation, sex, or body in another historical time and geographical space – no longer suffices as a means of intervention simply because alterity as such is still the old pure "object" (the being-in-itself) that has not been dialectically grasped. Such recourse to alterity is repeatedly trapped within the lures of

a "self"-image – a nativism – that is, precisely, imperialism's other. ("Against the Lures", 116)

This is an ingenious explanation, the old object now valorised as interventionist diasporic subject (and thus objectified all over again).

But Chow now takes it one step further. The diasporic intellectual, lured by her own objectivity, now reproduces the hegemonic relation between orientalist discourses and the east by disguising the oppression that continues unabated in the so called "native" lands; that is, by supporting the myth of the Chinese *zuguo*, the glorious native homeland. In other words, as we have been arguing, the hallucination of alterity in diaspora has many ways of masking wide ranging political conditions. For this reason Chow recommends an unmasking policy:

> We need to unmask ourselves through a scrupulous declaration of self-interest. Such declaration does not clean our hands, but it prevents the continuance of a tendency, rather strong among "third world" intellectuals in diaspora as well as researchers of non-western cultures in "first world" nations, to sentimentalize precisely those day-to-day realities from which they are distanced. ("Against the Lures", 116)

Here, however, it is difficult to see how Chow has escaped her own charge of essentialist identity politics. Beneath the mask (hybrid identity contributing to the sentimental image of the minority third-world subject) lies a more authentic version of Chinese diasporic identity: the one she is arguing for. (Chow's habit of putting words like "authentic" in demystifying quotation marks lends its own force to the sense of truth beneath the mask.) Unmasking and demystification are both essential components of a critical vigilance against the lures of diaspora but what now is the ground of the unmasking identity? This revelatory unmasking remains the action of the identifiable agent of identity politics. Critical and ingenious as the circuit might be, it remains circular, beginning with valorised diasporic Asian identity, passing through the revelation of unmasking before returning that agency back to its original identity (diasporic Asian). For it would seem that no other has access to this critique. Similarly, Chow's moves to separate herself from the essentialised otherness she delineates as institutional practice ironically reveal the sovereignty of the university to incorporate and domesticate dissent, in much the same way that the state displays its sovereignty through the existence of diasporas. There would seem to be no end to the power of the law to repeat itself through its dichotomies and no end to the number of shapes taken by the oscillation between sovereignty and diaspora. The canonical New Testament attempt to separate out an absolute atemporal alterity from the relative forces of the contingent temporal world emerges in a number of ways in contemporary discourses. Bhabha's hallucination of alterity in the wandering peoples of the earth and Chow's attempt to unmask the diasporic intellectual are but two such ways. Chow takes the side of contingent forces, which at least has the advantage of rendering the insignia of the military conspicuous, but which leads her to a strategy of unmasking that simply recreates the objectivity found in the Cartesian subject. Bhabha takes the side of irreducible alterity, which has the advantage of locating the irreducible condition of the law in repetition, but which moves the focus of analysis from the structural, historical and systemic forces that shape subjectivity to their effects.

In each case an identity politics threatens to draw attention away from the powerful processes played out between the state and the war machine that are materialised in and realised through the insignia of the military, processes that will turn out to have little to do with individual identities but which nonetheless ground the politics of national as well as transnational identity in simultaneously diachronic and synchronic ways – in the historical progress of diasporic histories and the systemic conditions of globally over-determined social relations. We are not arguing the irrelevance of individual identity in diasporic research, but rather pointing toward what is elided by an overemphasis on it and what is risked in the process of unduly and unnecessarily delimiting the diasporic research enterprise. Diasporic communities require a widened reading of their experience if the utopian discourse of cosmopolitanism that operates within globalisation is to be substantively challenged. If diasporic research is not so widened, and if the political remains contained in the image of the individual, diasporic communities will not only remain, as they always have, the tragic and cursed results of violence that proves the power of sovereignty, they will suffer a similar fate at the hands of our own academic research community that examines so narrowly, that so abbreviates, their situation. Any political potential in this research will have been, therefore, successfully contained.

The Hinge

A. The Hinge of Genius

As we have shown in previous chapters, Loy's peculiar mimesis cannot be reduced to the conventional notion – the imitation by art of some event, feeling, object or action – unless we acknowledge that the action (object, feeling, event) in question was already only to be understood on the model of this art. We might think about the way Loy uses the article (from *articulus*, little joint) *as* to get an idea of how this mimesis might work. We read "Der Blinde Junge" *as* a blind person sees – meaning both – *in the way that* and *like*, a combination of literal and figurative aspects. The poetry operates each time in a kind of self-hinging way *as* its topic or object. Another poem, "Apology of Genius," shows what is at stake in the hinge, represented by the little article *as*, and reveals something of its somewhat unpredictable and uncertain power. Loy's satirical appropriation and condensation of two related literary forms, the *apologia* (a formal statement of justification or defence) and the *apologue* (appeasing and persuading the rude and ignorant through comparisons made in the form of a fable), remain one of her most cunning and complex poetic statements. Here are the three opening lines:

> Ostracized as we are with God
> The watchers of the civilized wastes
> reverse their signals on our track.

The ambiguity of the phrase "ostracized as" demands a decision. Are we ostracised – put outside, banished, expelled, excluded from society, favour or privilege – *because* we are with God or are we ostracised *like* God, in the same way that God too is ostracised, expelled: *ostracised as we are . . . oh yes we are certainly ostracised, and with God, who is ostracised too*. Or perhaps it just means ostracised *while* we are with God, *as* as *while*, duration. However, a more firmly grounded sense underpins this ambiguity of sense and reference of the "as". We artists, the poem implies, are ostracised in the same way that God is *in or by modern urbanism* as its divine waste. We artists have been ostracised because of our ambiguous association with the divine. We are ostracised while we are with God. The waste, or whatever it is that is left over after the death of God, that other divine otherness also put outside as a kind of waste, *that's us.*

There follows a dense and again very unclearly drawn metaphor: "The watchers of the civilised wastes/reverse their signals on our track" (Loy, *Lunar*, 77). Who are the watchers of these civilized wastes? As the *Lunar Baedeker* collection will confirm, the wastes of Rome, Paris, London, New York are condensed in the phrase "the civilized wastes". Who are the watchers? Observers like us? Is the plural subject "we" implicated with watching? The "We" seems to turn on the relation between the signals and the track (their signals; our track) and sets up a new relation, them and us. They reverse their signals, the cityscape watchers, when they are on our track. The outside-ness ostracised as the "we" now plays an active causal role. It has an effect on the signals. So it is the watchers who act. They reverse their signals. But they reverse their signals on our track.

"Apology of Genius" at once satirises the two related literary forms, the *apologia* and the *apologue*, and puts them to work. The apology dimension, implicating not only Plato's celebrated *Apology of Socrates* but also the great tradition of literary apologies, particularly those of Sir Philip Sidney and Percy Shelley, helps to maintain a certain ironic distance between the text and the speaker's plural pronoun without eradicating all sense of the statement's intent – its powerful defence of the poetic in an urbanised world. Sidney, for instance, argues that poetry has qualities that place it above other activities because it encompasses and includes many of the objectives of various disciplines. It seems he primarily responds to the charge that history and philosophy are more important, or in some way more valid, than poetry. He sets out to prove this false and to show how poetry incorporates and surpasses both. So Shelley's apology in his "Defence of Poetry" already serves something of Loy's objective in its subtle repetition of Sidney. "Apology of Genius" is in some respects a clever précis repeating again, yet subtly also subverting, many of the points made by Shelley. The fabulous dimension of the apologue, however, now grafted onto the apologia, subverts both forms by taking the defence as its main message and moral (in a sort of fabulated defence, or apology apologised). The second stanza presents the genius in terms consistent with Loy's other poems of this period, hinging images of disease, leprosy and lunacy to values of innocence, magic and luminosity:

> Lepers of the moon
> all magically diseased
> we come among you
> innocent
> of our luminous sores
>
> unknowing
> how perturbing lights
> our spirit
> on the passion of Man (*Lunar*, 77)

The comparisons drawn are between speaker and addressees, making explicit the implication of the fabulous form, that the addressees are too ignorant and foolish to understand a more subtle presentation: "you turn on us your smooth fools' faces/like buttocks bared in aboriginal mockeries" (*Lunar*, 77). So the apology itself can be read in terms of its own self-identification, as luminous and clearly feminised sore, innocently appearing on the diseased flesh of modernity. The pattern is consistent, to an extent, with the message of Shelley's defence, in which he affirms poetry's relative freedom from the accidents of historical period and asserts its connection with divinity. But Loy's version (fabulously) recasts Shelley's distinctions. Shelley had written:

> A poet considers the vices of his contemporaries as the temporary dress in which his creations must be arrayed, and which cover without concealing the eternal proportions of their beauty . . . The beauty of the internal nature cannot be so far concealed by its accidental vesture, but that the spirit of its form shall communicate itself to the very disguise, and indicate the shape it hides from the manner in which it is worn.

Loy's satire nicely communicates the underlying scorn implied by Shelley's rhetoric of feeble disguise and inner beauty but, in turning the rhetoric inside out and adding to it the tones of feminine disease, she manages to rescue a remarkable political point. Shelley's image (no less fabulous in its own way) has an eternal and essential inner nature cunningly adopt the disguise of current fashion in order to reveal itself, in this much rehearsed rhetoric of concealing/revealing, veiling/unveiling. It thus falls into the pattern, typical of Romanticism, according to which a distinction is made between some thing (as it is in itself) and its external representation (as it appears to us). Loy's version has genius no more governed by current fashions than Shelley's inner beauty was supposed to have been, but operating otherwise: the rhetoric of excess takes over from the dialectic of Romanticism:

> Our wills are formed
> by curious disciplines
> beyond your laws
>
> You may give birth to us
> or marry us
> the chances of your flesh
> are not our destiny – (*Lunar*, 77)

In the fable, luminous disease replaces inner beauty and, in the defence, the poet begins to form an incalculable excess over and above the contingent legality of blood and marriage ties. In this sense the eternal (and frankly neo-Platonic) truth of Shelley's vision, which he opposes to the accidents of transient temporality, can now be read as the radically accidental products of curious disciplines – more accidental than "the chances of your flesh" and thus less tied to anything that could be pinned down as their proper moment. In this we begin to follow the emergence of an excess that precedes and eludes the notions of waste (Excess 1) that are said to fall out of economics (institutions, families, nations) as well as the seductive notions of excess (Excess 2) that underlie the radical polemics of everyone from Bataille to Bhabha. The echo of Shelley's "Beauty" now resounds as a kind of criminality beyond crime – no less beautiful but outside all laws:

> we forge the dusk of chaos
> to that imperious jewellery of the Universe
>   – the Beautiful –
>
> While to your eyes
>   A delicate crop
> of criminal mystic immortelles
> stands to the censor's scythe (*Lunar*, 78).

This fabulous criminality links Loy's urbanism to that of Edgar Allan Poe, especially to his "The Man of the Crowd", in which Poe's narrator, evoking an ungainly composite of La Bruyère and Dickens, finds an apparently mysterious outsider to be nothing but the empty mockery of the inside, the man of the crowd, "the type and genius of deep crime".[5]

The function of the connective "as", in the first line, now looks both more complex and more disciplined. The little hinge, "*as*", operates simultaneously as the vehicle of the fable and the claim of the defence itself. We are *as* ostracised and *as* divine, by virtue of the *as*. The apology defends the power of the *as*, as the power of fabulation itself, and simultaneously ostracises it beyond laws, beyond all urban rationality. How, then, does the *as* operate in relation to the military?

B. Targeting the Hinge

The hinge is an indispensable element of the military body, allowing it to perform its operations of attaching and detaching, but the military body cannot control it. The hinge operates as an excess of a third kind (Excess 3), providing the military body with all of its potential permutations and relations to parts of itself and parts outside itself. At the same time, its entire connective potential reveals what must always lie outside of the military body: the condition that makes attaching and detaching possible. As military personnel and materiel become more dispersed from command centres, and as military operations become more reliant on increasingly complicated and networked weapons and intelligence gathering technologies, so the operation of the hinge becomes more evident as a condition without which the military body would not be able to function at all. When the military body shifted to being a global spectral entity during the Cold War, material and immaterial hinges linking and detaching the nation from its military body/machine, as well as the military to its battery of technological software and hardware, required an innumerable range of hinges. The military's task (in our senses simultaneously scopic and episcopal) became one of surveying and controlling the entire globe, targeting it, watching it and overseeing it.

Containment operated as the key goal of the US military geo-political policy and technicity during the Cold War, in those technologies of global surveillance that were put into place by the US and its allies during the second half of the twentieth century and directed toward containing the spread of communism. These have only been further intensified with the emergence of another abstract war, the one waged on terror. The emphasis has shifted, however, from containment to explicit targeting and pre-emptive action. The military's scopic role is linked explicitly to the episcopal function of the nation-state in the war on terror, with the need for marking citizen from terrorist. The division between overseeing and targeting, in fact, has been effectively foregrounded as the state now not only watches over but must also target, as in the case of diaspora, while the military also watches and draws crosshairs. Increasingly both functions (scopic and episcopal) rely on technology. These kinds of reliance and the divisions wrought by them are displayed in several ads for military suppliers.

A series of ads by Lockheed Martin in the form of mini-video clips ran on the websites for major US newspapers in the first decade of the twenty-first century. Each one displays a terrain – one a general view of a city, another a crowded city street scene, another rural, another nautical, and another from space. The spaces in the ads depict theatres of surveillance and engagement: earth, sea, air and outer space, the space of human action and its future. Each ad follows a similar pattern: a phrase appears, "bad guys" or "terrorists", and a line points to a space in the image in which there is no visible enemy, only a blurry spot or a building no different from any surrounding it. Another line appears, marking the now marked person. Then a third identifies "friend-lies" or "citizen". A question appears, asking what allows us to make the distinction – a question that is prompted by the fact that the distinction is asserted in each instance in the form of a declarative phrase. The divisions in the ads are certain and known. Information, we are told, is the answer. Then the slogan appears, "Turning data into knowledge, and knowledge into action". This can be unfolded as a simplified form of the shift from marking to eliminating, from episcopal (watching over, protecting) to scopic (target-ing, striking). Other variations of the ads include a cityscape in which the ads identify an apartment complex, a market, and then a missile launch pad. Each is invisible to the naked eye. The technology of surveillance reveals what the organic eye cannot so that the state via its attachment to the military can act against the target.

These ads have run on websites of newspapers like *The Washington Post*. They are therefore not merely intended to persuade governments to bestow contracts on Lockheed Martin but perhaps more importantly to influence investors to buy Lockheed Martin shares, intimately linking the economy with a military technology that can have "dual use" value. The dual use value, though, also further blurs the lines between citizen and suspect, citizen and target that the technology is meant to delineate, especially with the perpetual war conditions that mark the Cold War and War on Terror eras. But the animated online ads too obviously deliver their message about technology's power and the military use of it in the dual episcopal (watching over, pro-tecting) and scopic (targeting, striking) modalities. The various technologies required for coordinating streams of information and data required by the military to perform its targeting tasks (surveillance, decision-making and striking) are the same technologies displaying the ads. The simplified inter-net version (touting technological power and profitability) thus folds back onto the complex system that it attempts to represent, a self-hinging effect unintentionally satirisinsg the situation by revealing its circular logic. This narrative of ease and mastery (achieved through the appropriation and exten-sion of the senses by techno-science in the service of the state) also displays the in-appearance of the hinge attaching the technology to its object (as to itself). The ads recall obliquely H. G. Wells's story "The Case of Davidson's Eyes" (which concerns the unhinged vision of a London doctor) in their expression of a desire to have the body politic prosthetically extended into global surveillance and action, the eye again as weapon.

Unmanning the Homeland

To survive terrorism, according to the logic of the jungle, you *become terrorism*. This becoming terrorism haunts the army as an institution and the military class as a whole, in the East and the West, in the North and the South – whence this year's [1985] spate of summit meetings, in Rome, Bonn and Washinton. (Paul Virilio)[6]

Today, if it is no longer politically necessary to opt for war or its conduct in the field, this is because "pure war" has long ago been declared, *with deterrence*, in the field of knowledge at the heart of heart of military-industrial and scientific design. (Paul Virilio, *Landscape*, 94)

The eye is accurate but the hand is not . . . Eye-only aiming is certainly possible with emerging technologies. (US National Research Council report *Star 21*)

A report in February 2002 on CNN's very popular business program "Moneyline" featured the next step in attack planes: the Unmanned Combat Air Vehicle (UCAV). The brief report, aimed at potential defence industry investors, claimed that the new planes, although long in the planning, development and testing stages, were the perfect weapon for fighting the (un)declared "War on Terror". Further, the CNN reporter said, the aircraft would have "Homeland Security" applications that allowed for the planes to not only detect terrorist activity but to act against it – the shift from surveillance to armed engagement, from episcopy to scopic action. The reporter's statement echoed those of a Northrop Grumman spokesman, who said his company's role "is supplying the command, control, communications and intelligence to find the bad guys and bop them in the head."[7] Unmanned Aerial Vehicles (UAVs) are already used for mechanical targeting by the US and Israeli governments, but they are still programmed and guided regarding their strikes, not making autonomous "intelligent" decisions. In other words, the UCAVs soon will seek strategically to unman the homeland. The power and the technicity of the military and the state to divide terrorist from citizen, and legal citizen from illegal, is becoming fully automated. The sovereign right to kill or dispossess (render one diasporic) meets its extended power in the military technology that ended in the nuclear dawn in New Mexico. The state's power to protect its citizens derives from its power to kill them or banish them. Additionally, the citizen serves the state and the military through a series of hinges, attaching and detaching senses from the citizen in order to police, control and, if need be, target the citizen. The appropriated senses of the corporeal citizen now are automated by the body politic and turned within the nation while also tracing its borders: circumscribing, excluding and including. UVACs are yet another hinge of the military body, attaching themselves to the terrain and sovereignty of the nation by detaching targeted humans from the same.

   US military technology from World War II to the present has pursued two simultaneous but somewhat antithetical desires: one is embodied in MANPRINT (Manpower and Personnel Integration), which is the human-machine integration system to make soldiers part of the overall weapons system design and implementation (including business and logistics practices); the other one finds form in taking "the human element" out of the decision-making and activation of weapons system loop, an essential dimension to the implementation of failproof nuclear strategies. Both operate, however, with the assumptions that drove C^3I underpinning the Cold War: that is, the increased demands on systems, the speed of decision-making, and the chance of human or machine error within these systems. The essence of and justification for both MANPRINT and fully automated systems is, of course, speed. Machine speed clearly outstrips human speed, but it does so for and in response to clearly human aims: the advantage and danger of surprise. Speed is the answer to defending oneself against a surprise attack as well as the answer to how to surprise the enemy. During the Cold War and now with the "War on Terror", surprise demands speed, a point we will address more thoroughly later in the chapter.

Once a move from automated systems, which simply perform a series of pre-programmed functions, to "intelligent" weapons systems occurs, the possibility of mechanical, digital or robotic error enters the system. The intelligence system in "smart" weapons is intended to eliminate the chance of human error – owing to "slow" reaction times – while also removing the attacking military's personnel from the battle scene (hence, the emergence of so-called "humane weapons"). But the smart weapons must be able to discern an actual target from a false one, or the correct target from the myriad of wrong ones, so the potential for error is inherent in the system; choosing error must be part of how the weapon can choose. It cannot be otherwise; if it were, then the weapon would not have to choose and would not, therefore, be "smart".

Beginning in the Cold War, the general trajectory of militarisation models implemented has been the inevitability of cybernetic processes controlling not only battlefield decisions and actions but political decision-making and actions. The move to employ such models in "Homeland Security" is but the next step in a process begun in the middle part of the twentieth century, imagined in the first year of the past century (with the Serbian scientist Nikolai Tesla envisioning robotic warfare in his 1900 article "The Problem of Increasing Human Energy"), and yet passed along to the US public as the latest "vision" of warfare. The programme manager of UCAV, Colonel Michael Leahy, told ABC news in the US, "because we are in a research and development environment, we want to make the future".[8] Making the future means, evidently, replicating the past now. Be this as it may, MANPRINT, in light of events that transpired during the Gulf War, added a new domain to its training and operations system in 1994 to reduce "friendly fire" (also called "fratricide" by the US military). With unmanned and armed aircraft patrolling the skies for "Homeland Security" at some future moment in the war on terror, such a domain might need to enter the completely cybernetic processes involved in machine-controlled weapons systems.

An increase in virtual villages and "smart" communities would seem to make such checks necessary. The technotopia urban space of the virtual village implies its being policed by and under surveillance by the UAVs circling above it and possibly targeted by UCAVs. The technology of the virtual village results from the military research and development that results in "smart" systems, and they cannot fail but to co-exist interdependently. The virtual village with its vigilant protector drones is a wireless, gateless version of the "gated communities", which are already the ideal of some well-off but fearful US suburban dwellers. One of the many advantages of the UCAV, according to a *Jane's Defense Weekly* analyst, is that it attacks coordinates, thus not requiring routing commands. (Rowell, "A New Idea", 1) But when the future of warfare – for example, the UCAV – meets a potential future for urban dwelling – for example, Helsinki's Virtual Village – then some serious problems could well emerge. (Helskinki's Virtual Village is an attempt to provide a state-of-the-art wireless infrastructure and wireless servers for all living within the village. The goal is to conflate all IT services to just a cell phone, dispensing with the PC altogether.) One of the essential dimensions of a "smart" community is its reliance on Global Position Satellite (GPS) systems. But GPS, depending on context, in military abbreviation can stand for either Global Position Satellite or Gunner's Primary Sight. In either case, vision is used to target, and the implication is that any surveillance is also potentially a move toward targeting and firing on the target. The mobile phones that allow the citizens of Helsinki's Virtual Village to access and browse broadband domains, as well as track each other inside the virtual village, also render each and every one of them a recognisable coordinate that a UCAV can pinpoint, target and eliminate.

The military technological link between the virtual village, or the virtual village as "smart" gated community, and the UCAV is made explicit by the role of DARPA (Defense Advanced Research Project Agency) in the creation of the internet (originally called DARPAnet), cellular phones and GPS, as well as the UCAV. The "smart" gated community and UCAV both carry the insignia of the military through the very technologies that make them possible. But with armed, si(gh)ted UCAVs circling high above "Homeland Security" protected homes, one is reminded of Virilio's warning about all technologies: that the creation of every invention is also the creation of its accident – the accident that is structurally necessary for the invention to function at all, just as the possibility of choosing the wrong target is structurally necessary for a smart weapon.

Intelligent systems, of course, rely on intelligence, and it is this sector of the defence industry that has seen and will continue to see the greatest increase in spending on R&D in the US. Intelligence systems will play a very large role in the war on terror, especially as it was the failure of intelligence (technological, systemic and human failure) that allowed the 9/11 attacks to happen in the first place. Rather than reconsidering the over-reliance on such systems, the US government's response has been to pour even more money into electronic surveillance and analysis of intelligence related to command and control models inherited from the Cold War. The problem was not over-reliance, evidently, but under-funding. Such a response is already paying huge dividends for specific US companies (for example, Northrop Grumman's stock rose 16 per cent when the New York Stock Exchange was closed briefly owing to the 9/11 attacks in 2001 and it reached a three-year high two days into the first bombings of Afghanistan in 2001). Lockheed Martin landed the US$200 billion contract for the next generation fighter (itself with UCAV potential) because of the "intelligent" weapons systems it built for nuclear weapons and ballistic missile defence, including its "combat Internet system" that will put "a dot-com face on the modern battlefield" (Berrigan, *War Profiteers*, 2). With a stagnant economy and global recession in 2001, the 9/11 attacks and Washington's fiscal response to them shaped the economic terrain for the years following, and could well do so for possibly decades to come. In response to the massive increase in US defence spending (in the 2009 budget this spending was over US$512 billion as base military spending, with an additional US$66 billion for operations in Iraq and Afghanistan, which accounts for over half of the discretionary spending of the US government) some stock exchanges now list a Defence Index.

The X-45A UCAV, manufactured by Boeing, was in the works long before the World Trade Center attacks of September 2001 and has been touted as the most likely weapons system to be pressed into "Homeland Security" service. Conveniently, the military side of Boeing prospered as the civilian side suffered immediately following the September 2001 attacks, as a result of reduced air travel following the military (terrorist) application of Boeing's civilian aircraft. But what is worth considering is that built into the R&D process is the fact that an event will cause the demand for the planned technological innovation to emerge. The momentum operative within technicity anticipates and creates the need. And such an event need not ever manifest itself for such things to generate profits, as stock market gain is based upon speculation. This is an extension of the inevitable increase in the automated and cybernetic dimensions of military technologies and civilian technologies, as well as the economies predicated upon them. The human is taken out of the loop, remaining only in the design phase (and even then it is driven by a mechanistic application of R&D to the supply and demand of market economies).

Perhaps, once again, Yugoslavia will show the future of urban dwelling embedded in military engagement, as it did throughout almost the entire twentieth century. Perhaps Belgrade being hit by graphite bombs that knocked out power supplies, and the US setting up a mobile TV station that took over the broadcast airwaves of the city and the nation under siege, signal the urban fate during the manufactured state of constant emergency in the war on terror and whatever awaits beyond it. What the NATO military forces claimed to have achieved in Belgrade might be considered the anti-neutron bomb. Whereas the neutron bomb wiped out a population leaving an urban centre's infrastructure intact, the current technology targets the infrastructure without "significant" loss of civilian lives.[9]

Against this we may assess the claims represented for and by the development, manufacture and implementation of intelligent precision munitions, which would speculatively show the future of military engagement embedded cleanly amongst urban dwellings. Once again, the state turns to the military to perform both episcopal and scopic functions. This seductive promise manifests a cynical vision of a fantasy future when small unmanned aircraft are capable of recognising and taking out hidden enemies secreted in public or private amongst legitimate citizens going about their business. How, exactly, is the future manifested? If there is anything to the rhetoric of *making* the future other than the covert replication of the past, then this would, as always, have to do with the R&D struggle for the control of the clichéed element of surprise. One way to understand responses to the World Trade Center attacks would be to focus on the economics of surprise, according to which a certain retrospective inevitability (intelligence would always have been able to predict attacks that would not anyway have been unprecedented) reveals all the more clearly the temporal and spatial indeterminacy – literally speaking, blindness – against which the war on terror operates.

If terrorism involves control over the difference between the visible and the invisible – in both their temporal and spatial relations – then the effective war against terrorism implies, in Virilio's terms, *becoming terrorism* (*Landscape*, 76). And this is indeed how the future is manifested today. The future is, as we have shown, already quite old. The conditions that make this kind of war possible were already manifested by the US in the Persian Gulf War, based on refinements of experiments conducted in the Vietnam War. Here precision weapons (operational since at least World War II) are swiftly eclipsed by so called *intelligent* precision weapons, which allow the human agent to operate at a significant distance from the range of the field of action. "The UCAV weapon system," explains a defense website hosted by the Federation of American Scientists, "will exploit the design and operational freedoms of relocating the pilot outside of the vehicle to enable a new paradigm in aircraft affordability while maintaining the rationale, judgment, and moral qualities of the human operator."[10] The projectile no longer requires a support, which would have to be piloted dangerously close to the action, but it now assumes the burden of piloting itself to its target, recognising the target when it arrives and then guiding itself for the assault. The "moral qualities" of human pilot as agent outside the aircraft remain intact through the perpetuation of the myth of control and the unhinging of the ultimate responsibility on the part of any individual actor for the action taken by the craft. The hinge of the military operates here as that which simultaneously attaches and detaches human agency to technological weapons systems, allowing selective control and relinquishing of control, thus dividing agency in strategic ways. The intelligent munitions system is so called because it relieves the human agent of the need to observe the action, operating therefore in the clearest way as an exemplary visual prosthetic in a tradition that constitutes one of the central trends of modern technoscience.

The surprise attack, then, manifests what can be understood as the face of a need – the unacceptable face of terrorism as the unacceptable face of surprise – and thus the need for control of the surprise. The face operates as the visible aspect of an essential duplicity – a disguise, a masquerade or a decoy. We might easily be distracted by the attacks, the need they represent (on the face of it) and the US response in putting intelligent urban projectiles into production. These productions can, on the contrary, be seen as the face of a larger, invisible but no less existent future whose conditions are manifested in widespread ways. The US Navy's cruise missile program in 1972 included the following instructions to potential contractors: "design a device able to be fired from a submerged submarine under way off San Diego, fly cross-country so low it has to pull up over mountains, and upon reaching Chicago, navigate to a point that puts it inside the base paths of Wrigley Field".[11] The technology that allows production of these kinds of intelligent projectiles already, only thirty years later, feels relatively archaic. But the need it responds to follows an unmistakably futural logic.

The unmanning of urban projectiles can be seen as one of a series of projects that often involve the collaborative efforts of air forces and space programmes. Cities remain the model target and the combined technologies of speed, intelligence and precision allow the development of projectiles capable of travelling several thousand miles in a few minutes, isolating discrete targets and striking them accurately. What makes this a realistic possibility is the technology of the Space Plane. George Friedman, in his *The Future of War*, informs us that a projectile built on the combination of current cruise missile technology and that of the Space Plane "would have an intercontinental range of 10,000 miles and a sustained speed of Mach 30 or about 30,000 miles an hour, or 8.5 miles per second" (*Future*, 341). There are a number of possible sites from which such a projectile can receive its instructions, including remote ground stations, aircraft or, most efficiently, space-based craft.

The Janus-faced entity constituted by the division between the projectile and its satellite reconnaissance platform is the logical successor of the manned aircraft. This is not, as it might seem, simply science fiction. US Air Force Hypersonic Technology ("HyTech") has developed a hydrocarbon-powered scramjet-based missile (that is, an extremely fast projectile capable of generating and surviving severe temperatures and accessing high altitudes), which can be adapted to incorporate NASA's Hyper-X technology, which by drawing on hydrogen fuel rather than hydrocarbons, can attain even higher speeds and (unlimited) altitudes. This technology transforms the geo-political field of action because it makes it possible to operate unmanned aircraft at hypersonic speeds and over intercontinental distances from the remote and difficult-to-detect vantage of the space beyond the earth's atmosphere.

The unmanned urban projectile loitering over inner-city spaces cannot be abstracted from the logic of this intractable move into outer space. The unmanned projectile masquerading perhaps as benevolent satellite – the acceptable face of the war against terror and general global episcopy – can appear, on the contrary, as the visible face of an "invisible order", which is the phrase that Friedman uses for what he calls the "topography of space" (*Future*, 342). This topography is determined fundamentally by the peculiar relationship between the two planets – earth and moon – which constitute the local planetary system. The mythical or cosmic aspects of Friedman's speculations, we should remember, are underpinned in concrete ways by an actually realised struggle for control over the invisible vantage: the dark side of the moon. The moon, as Friedman labours to remind us, keeps half its surface secret from the earth, which in its complex rotations cannot help presenting the whole of its surface to its more coy satellite. The analogy (moon is to earth as unmanned craft is to city/target) should not distract from the concrete conditions it represents. As Friedman says:

> Military forces on the moon could monitor activities on the earth continually using more advanced optics than currently exist (during dark phases, infrared and other means would have to be used), while weapons, logistics and command facilities could be hidden out of sight of earth forces, on the moon's far side. (*Future*, 343)

The unmanned aircraft would play the same function – placing the whole of an urban environment under observation and at risk while limiting the ability of elements in that environment to mount a surprise attack. The speculative element – hypothesising technologies that do not yet exist – provides a clue as to the fantastic aspect of the claims made for technologies that do in fact exist. The ancient fantasy of a hidden vantage point from which to observe and to act capriciously – limiting the power of the observed to do the same and limiting their power of surprise – remains a fantasy, even if it is increasingly well supported by technologies of surveillance and attack. As we have shown, it can be very powerful in itself.

Against the claims made on behalf of these technologies – many of which are underscored in Friedman's impeccably informed and apparently sober though basically utopian book – it would be worth extrapolating from them the logic that is actually at work. The key claim about the precision of intelligent munitions would perhaps be for their ability to distinguish accurately between military and non-military personnel. After a century of "total war" we are often astonished to read claims for the end of collateral damage and a return to the clean distinctions between civilian and military and between friend and enemy. However the logic of surprise – whether in its spatial or temporal dimensions – militates permanently against these claims. The struggle will never be anything but the struggle for control over the element of surprise, which in its essential form embodies the Janus-faced dichotomy according to which *any* distinction might at any unpredictable moment be overturned or revealed as a lie. The actual logic of the unmanned aircraft informs a reversal and repetition of the event to which it masquerades as a response – the logic of prosthetic control of the surprise, an uncanny human face.

To conclude, we can pose the following question: what will unmanned aircraft do to the landscape of urban sites? We have hinted at some possible answers, not the least troubling of which is the immediate conversion of all mobile phones into coordinates of attack. But the logic behind the unmanned aircraft, as we have intimated, marks the urban landscape as a field of action in ways both new and remarkably old – invoking old strategies/technologies/logics as new and bringing clichéed scenarios and descriptions into active use again. Perhaps, as recent US administrations continue their steadfast intensification of unilateralism, shedding treaties left and right, a potential victim will be the 1967 Treaty on Principles Governing the Activities of States in the Exploration and Use of Outer Space, Including the Moon and Other Celestial Bodies, which rendered the moon a site free from any military activity. Such action is already figured in Friedman's analyses and assumed by US Department of Defense strategic plans. Then, perhaps, the dark side of the moon will become the platform from which militaries can convert urban centres (targets) into mirror images of the munitions lift-off sites: the clichéed wasteland of the lunar landscape.

Notes

1. Paul Virilio, *The Strategy of Deception*, trans. Chris Turner (London: Verso, 2001) p. 62.
2. Mina Loy, *The Lost Lunar Baedeker: Poems*, ed. Roger Conover (New York: Farrar, Straus and Giroux, 1996) p. 77.
3. Homi Bhabha *The Location of Culture* (London: Routledge, 1994) p. 104.
4. Rey Chow, *Writing Diaspora: Tactics of Intervention in Contemporary Cultural Studies*, (Bloomington and Indianapolis: Indiana University Press, 1993) p. 119.
5. Edgar Allan Poe, *Tales of Mystery and Imagination* (London: Everyman, 1984) pp. 107–16.
6. Paul Virilio, *A Landscape of Events*, trans. Julie Rose (Cambridge, MA: MIT Press, [1985] 2000) p. 76.
7. F. Berrigan, "The War Profiteers: How are Weapons Manufacturers Faring in the War?" www.worldpolicy.org/projects/arms/updateds/profiteers121701.htm (2001).
8. E. Rowell, "A New Idea Takes Off: Air Warfare Machines Heading Toward Next Generation", http://abcnews.go.com/sec. . .ech/CuttingEdge/cuttingedge001215.htm (2001).
9. See Steve Graham, "Switching Cities Off: Urban Infrastructure and US Air Power". *City*, 2005; 9:2, 169–94.
10. http://www.fas.org/man/dod-101/sys/ac/ucav.htm
11. George and Meredith Friedman, *The Future of War: Power, Technology and American World Dominance in the Twenty-First Century*, (New York: St Martin's Griffin, 1996) p. 27.

Chapter 10

Scoping Out

... it is easy to miss the target (*skopos*) and hard to hit it (Aristotle)[1]

Then shall the right aiming thunderbolts go abroad; and from the clouds, as from a well drawn bow, shall they fly to the mark [*epi skopon alountai*] (Wisdom of Solomon 5. 21)

Ready: Targeting the Source

In one episode of the popular TV show *CSI* ("Crime Scene Investigation") the team is called out to a leafy residential area to investigate a fatal shooting. A woman lies dead outside her new home with a bullet lodged in her heart. She had been in the process of moving in. Although there are several immediate witnesses who saw her fall, they neither saw nor heard the shooter, whose action has dramatically interrupted a domestic squabble between the victim's ex and current husbands. Once the team goes to work, all witnesses are systematically eliminated as suspects. The main action of the show, as always, involves meticulous analysis of available evidence. The exact position of the victim when she was shot, combined with the position, calibre and size of the bullet, once it has been painstakingly removed from the dead woman's heart, provide the information that leads the team to the source of the shot. Bullets of the same calibre must be fired from the correct kind of gun at increasing distances into several firm jellies matching the density of the woman's heart. They must then take the angle (descending) into account, in order to determine the arc of the bullet's trajectory. It turns out that the bullet must have been fired at an angle into the air from more than two blocks away. The shooter is at length discovered and the action recreated for the viewers: someone enjoying target practice in his back garden is distracted by the angry shouts of a neighbour and, misfiring one of his bullets in the air over several houses, thus unknowingly finds an accidental target. As he is handcuffed and arrested, he protests, "I was just having a little target practice". "Yes, well," replies the investigator, "that's why firing live rounds is illegal in built-up areas, stupid".

The show and its narrative touch on some key factors of urban targeting. One function of crime fiction (which includes thrillers, mysteries, police procedurals and detective stories of all kinds) would be a kind of consolation. Edgar Allan Poe, who wrote what are plausibly the first texts of their kind ("The Murders in the Rue Morgue", "The Mystery of Marie Roget", and "The Purloined Letter") had already written a satire on the kind of impulse to which the mystery narrative responds, "The Man of the Crowd", which notoriously leaves the mystery not only unsolved but structurally insoluble. In that context the conventional crime narrative may be regarded as a fantasy of the impossible set against a backdrop of rapid urban intensification.[2] It takes the form of the double narrative. The narrative of solution leads to a narrative reconstruction of the crime (or accident), implanting a kind of narrative pre-history behind the main narrative. *CSI* emphasises the consoling function of the crime story. Delving about in the ruined remains of diverse victims, blood-spattered walls, shot-up civic environments, and so on, the CSI team exploits a technology of investigation against which no mystery remains unsolved – everything is calculable. In the episode described above the victim turns out to have been an accidental target. The narrative logic thus equates the accident with crime. The two can signify together in shorthand the capricious anxious-making conditions of urban life in general. For CSI, however, the sources of many urban anxieties and often personal ruin in turn become the targets of an (as it were) reverse targeting, the benevolent eye of the city police augmented by advanced investigative technologies.

Aim: Skopos

The *skopos* in early times was a watcher or watchman, someone stationed on the *skopia* (the high ground) as a lookout.[3] So the *skopos*, first of all, is one who watches out for and looks after a community as its guardian – a kind of *epi-scopus* or over-seer.[4] The term *episcopy* was used for a variety of civic duties crucial to the administration of early urban communities. Later, *skopos* will become the name for the speculator more generally, the one who seeks out and marks the object of some game or quest. The *skopos* hides out and marks the game. In a military idiom he is a spy or scout. At the same time, the *skopos* is also the object on which one fixes one's eye, the mark itself, the target. Plato and Aristotle both use *skopos* in this sense, as synonymous with *telos*, the object or aim of an action or passion as well as the process that leads to the goal.

Skopos thus functions as a kind of hinge that joins and at the same time separates the marker from the mark. It is attached both to the one who aims and to what is aimed at, detaching them at the same time and then moving to another mark. It therefore connects the watcher not just to something watched but to the conditions of his watching per se, where watching becomes an act with an end that at once belongs to it (that is, to watching) yet does not belong to it.

By an oblique process (and so not a direct teleology) the term for watchfulness ends up also as the term for target. That is, "target" is the target term for watchfulness – the silent teleology of the vigilant gaze. Aristotle, for instance, repeatedly uses the notion of *skopos* as an analogue for the aims of ethical action (*praxis*) in the *Nicomachean Ethics*. Combining the doctrine of the *telos* with that of the *mean*, Aristotle outlines the conditions necessary for ethical conduct. The *telos* of *praxis* must be understood in analogy with the notion of *skopos*: "In all the conditions for ethics," he argues "there is a target [*skopos*] which the reasoning person focuses on and so tightens or relaxes" (*Nicomachean*, 1138b). This moving target only ever has analogical status because, in contrast to all other virtues (including *techne*, *episteme*, *phronesis*, *sophia* and *nous*), *praxis* has no aim outside itself. The aim of just action is just action. One must watch over one's passions, aiming for neither too little nor too much but for the so-called *mesotes*, the intermediate state, arrived at in a process reminiscent (supposedly) of the actions of tightening and relaxing the strings of the bow. Unlike the archer, however, the ethical agent has no target outside himself. The aim is to achieve the condition from which it is possible to aim correctly (the aim of just action is to be able to act justly).

St Paul's second epistle to the Corinthians demonstrates the special character of targeting logic: "We look not at the things which are seen, but at the things which are not seen: for the things which are seen [are] temporal; but the things which are not seen [are] eternal" (2 Cor. iv: 18). The use here, as with other instances in late classical Greek writing, of the term *skopounton*, "we look at" (again from *skopeo*, "to look") shows us that what the text implies (in this classical defence of the *hidden* glory of Paul's gospel) involves more than just taking notice of or paying attention to what is seen or, as the analogy implies, assenting to or accepting that these things exist. *Skopeo*, rather, implies seeking out or making designs upon, hunting out with an appropriative eye. The target must be marked out – *scoped* – for it is not just waiting around to be discovered. Paul's metaphysical doctrine, which explicitly distinguishes an empirical and finite visible from a transcendental and eternal invisible, locates the target beyond reach, out of sight. As always, the metaphysics recaptures itself in its iterations but fails to lock on to what cannot be seen. The target in the case of Aristotle as well as in the case of Paul's letter cannot be distinguished from what makes targeting possible, which in the tautology of metaphysics just is the state of ethical and/or divine grace.

The analogical status of the target of conditions like ethical action or religious faith might provoke a suspicion here, suggesting perhaps that such conditions have been derived from the technological apparatus that makes the targeting possible in the first place; for example, were it not for bows and arrows there would be no ethics or religion. However, both the metaphysical and the empirical target seem derived from the same (hidden) source, which in itself already conditions the distinction between the metaphysical and the empirical as that between watching and targeting, repeating one in the other and deforming it in the same movement. To progress from watching to targeting would be a matter of focusing on what in the field of vision cannot be seen, thus bringing it into view nonetheless, which is the primary role of analogy, after all. In this complexity the possibility of the oblique and perhaps accidental target emerges as a necessary condition for accurate targeting per se.

The complications inherent in the notion of target both precede and continue to haunt standard notions of targeting, where it becomes increasingly imperative, as we observe in even the earliest of military targeting technologies, not only to separate the marking from the mark but also to separate the marking from its fulfillment in a strike. Especially with the rise of aerial bombing, the targeting of urban sites, where targets are likely to be located in politically sensitive areas, particularly demands the ability to identify precise targets and to launch precision guided munitions quickly. To this end, devices like the *Viper* can be used; the *Viper* is a small, portable system comprised of a laser range finder, digital map display and GPS receiver that can derive target coordinates, which can then be relayed to an airborne crew. Such crews are able to change targets or upload entire new missions en route with a data-link system called Combat Track II.[5] This technology has been described as an e-mail connection between mission planners and the air crews, to relay up-to-date satellite-generated information on the target area, forming a series of hinges linking the target to the munitions carrier and the munitions carrier to the marker, in order to conflate as much as possible the act of marking and striking the target.

What has happened here, at a fundamental level, can be grasped as a determinate dissociation of *skopos* in the first sense (vigilant watchfulness) from *skopos* in the second sense (target, goal, aim), where the system nonetheless depends upon a *skopos* in both senses (impossibly) combined. The attempt to combine them always produces a blind spot necessitating further separations, in exactly the manner of the conscious intentional act. One can be conscious of an object but one can only be conscious of one's consciousness through objectifying it in the delay between thoughts, that is, in a repetition. In this delay watchfulness (like consciousness) is born(e). Targeting, which watchfulness makes possible, would thus be the attempt to shorten (ideally to zero) the extent of this delay, and military targeting technology seems designed to stop time altogether, which is to say, to altogether reduce the length of the period between marking the mark and hitting the mark. The target is thus not just the binary opposite of the marker (the object-subject chestnut) but its betrayal in a *marking* that brings vigilant watchfulness to a hasty end or at least casting it in another place immediately.

Targeting technology like the *Viper* device detaches the role of targeting from the role of launching the projectile in a way that seems attendant on the diversification of the role of the *episcopus* through vast and various urban infrastructures. In the most obvious instance, once the role of the watchman (aided by a few constables) in cities is no longer adequate for the overseeing of an increasingly unruly populace, there emerges a series of intensive transformations in policing techniques. In London, for instance, Henry Fielding's Bow Street Runners were organised and ruthless enough to establish for the criminal community a shocking precedent, thus inspiring a new sense of awe towards the *epi-scopal* role, not replacing the role of the Church by any means, but nonetheless deploying its force otherwise, making explicit the shared vocabulary of military and religious institutions but distancing them both and distinguishing at the same time a relatively new power: the city police.[6] The "awe", of course, is accompanied by virulent resentment and counteraggression. Succeeding the runners, the Bow Street Horse Patrol, armed with truncheon, cutlass and pistol, patrolled London in striking blue uniforms (with leather hats, brass buttons and blue boots). The imperative at moments like this would be to underline the differences (rather than the always more obvious similarities) not only between police and thieves but perhaps more fundamentally between police and military. When the so-called Gordon Riots broke out, lasting a week, the military were sent in to quell the trouble, killing or wounding over 450 citizens, and so on the model of the Bow Street constabulary a more powerfully organised police force was formed.

Episcopal development accompanies every aspect of urban development – which is actually the same thing. With the increase in trade in and out of ports, as an early instance, marine police are formed to watch over the river. Perhaps the somewhat oxymoronic *watchful targeting* is emblematic of the urban episcopacy generally, which, as we have suggested, occupies various urban institutions: the police force itself is divided up into several technical offices, of which CSI is only the most popular, incorporating every surveillance technology in existence for after-the-fact crime scene investigation.

Fire: Marks of Woe

Both senses of *Skopos* are preserved in William Blake's "London", written at an early stage of transformations typical of modern urbanism (the poem was first published in 1794, when urban plans resulting from the conflagration of 1666 had become fairly well established). The poem systematically observes the problems that would provoke the same episcopal transformations we are charting. But both the city's targets and the one who targets them are put explicitly into view by the poem. It places enunciation and statement disjunctively side by side, with the speaker condemning the failures of civic guardianship:

London

I wander through each chartered street,
Near where the chartered Thames does flow,

And mark in every face I meet
Marks of weakness, marks of woe.

In every cry of every man,
In every Infant's cry of fear,
In every voice, in every ban,
The mind-forged manacles I hear.

How the Chimney-sweeper's cry
Every black'ning Church appalls;
And the hapless Soldier's sigh
Runs in blood down Palace walls.

But most through midnight streets I hear
How the youthful Harlot's curse
Blasts the new-born Infant's tear,
And blights with plagues the Marriage hearse.

The various ways in which the city is targeted by disaster (including economics, poverty, hypocrisy, corruption, war and sexually transmitted disease) are themselves targeted by a speaker whose scopic drive seems to have produced a desire for the woe that he marks (truly a marksman in the most ordinary sense) wherever he looks in the hunt for it. That the word "chartered" appears twice in the first two lines indicates further an interest on the part of the marker in official urban overseeing (oversight) and its effects, which demand yet more scopic patrolling. Similarly the repetition of "mark" as verb and noun foregrounds early in the poem the effects of oversight (the marks it leaves which the persona marks) as well as the channelling function of *skopos*. The marker insists on his position as "watchful targeter" and therefore as a hinge within the urban epi-scopal project.

The key to modern urban policing lies, after all, in the notion of the mark (or *skopos*). From the victims and clients of frauds, scams, stings and prostitutes to the criminals and prostitutes themselves: each are in some way marked and each is known as "*the* mark". Starting with the discovery of fingerprints in the nineteenth century, the history of modern law enforcement agencies is also the history of the creation and expansion of huge databases, archives containing information on crime, criminals and victims. Such archives provide the means of identifying both the mark (victim) and the culprit. Where fingerprints are not available (and fingerprints can now be retrieved from very old bodies), or dental records, it is possible to identify victims using forensic anthropology (identification of victims by bones). Archives like the FBI federal database (and the one for London's Metropolitan Police) add up to a network of potential super-national police cooperation.

The aim is to find a match (which thus helps to form the series: *skopos, telos*, target, mark, match). In the television series *CSI*, this is made clear when the camera looks at a mark on a dead body, a wound or a piece of debris for instance, then the camera zooms down on it and sometimes into it, marking out all its little details so it can be identified. Investigators try to identify the criminal, marking in their turn the criminal in the database, or his modus operandi, for the purposes of elimination (in all senses). The modus operandi is the way in which the criminal leaves his mark on the scene. Technology for matching includes not only carbon dating in forensic anthropology, but also DNA and mitochondrial DNA (DNA recovered from bone marrow through the female line), now functioning as a legal and binding technique for suspect confirmation and elimination. Direction, size and shape of blood splashes at the scene of a crime can, with computer graphics, be used in a reconstruction of the scene. The same technology (which constitutes this archive) can also be used to take what remains of a crime scene in order to reconstruct the crime itself: it can remake what the face looks like from a skull; it can run time sequences in badly burnt-out arson cases, showing when and where the fire started; and it can reveal the direction, velocity and power of shots. These computer databases, which constitute what might be termed a *new* archive of knowledge, represent the state of watchfulness today and form an essential complement to the police armouries and their weapons training. Snipers in SWAT teams now duplicate the role of investigators on computers.[7]

The aim of targeting theory is to improve the speed, accuracy and force of the projectile (the scope of weaponry) but the same technology makes the reverse possible too, as criminal investigation, journalism and popular crime fiction, each in a different way, demonstrate. The epi-scopal function is multiplied too in prisons and clinics of all kinds, as well as in schools and universities. The media (often explicitly serving the "Guardian" or "Watchman" function) reach into every section of urban life, only apparently inverting the role so that the populace becomes a vast community of watchers interacting each with their own personal medium. Urban episcopal diversification almost reaches its apotheosis, of course, with the Strategic Defence Initiative (Star Wars) programme, which combines watchful vigilance with targeting in exemplary ways, yet remains at a stage of fanciful projection, the technological application of a science fiction promise. The combination of technologies involved in SDI – extraterrestrial optics, satellites, laser, nuclear weapons, and so on – as well as the projective planning involved in their potential deployment (the anticipated need) – embodies proleptic episcopy on a galactic scale. In a bid to be the guardian of all US cities, and an update of Cold War goals, not to mention technologies, it will have to keep watchful vigilance over the entire planet at all times.

From Jerusalem's Mount Skopos to the Eiffel Tower in Paris, every city, it seems, has a *Skopia* of its own (a high place from which one can look down over a city) not just emblematic of height (which certainly serves an iconic function for the urban value of verticality) but also in many cases serving explicitly episcopal functions too (including world trade, hoteliery, communications, broadcast media and government).

Thus Blake's speaker wanders the city but his is no aimless wandering.[8]

The speaker serves something of the function of the watchman. The poem ironically echoes contemporary journalistic trends and thus satirises the function – before its historical development – of crime scene investigation. The complaints, which will gather in force throughout the early stages of modern global urbanism, are typical, but what is most striking is perhaps how the city is targeted by its enlightened and otherwise untouched citizen. The "I" is no stranger but the appalled voice of a moral conscience that is also in every way a function of the problems he identifies. The temptation, when reading this poem, is to grasp it as Blake's own appalled expression at the state of the city in which he lives and works. However the function of the "I" and his "mark" would contest this, revealing not an expression but a sly characterisation. Wandering, as perhaps will always have been the case, has a purpose. As is the case with so many trajectories in modern, as well as contemporary, narratives explaining how we have arrived at any present moment, the target can often be found in urbanism.

Wandering

In the introduction to their illustrated book for children, *Man Must Move: The Story of Transport* (published in 1960), Laurie Lee and David Lambert propose three broad generalisations, authorised by the established scientific knowledge of the time. They offer a minor premise first, the Darwinian commonplace: "The Story of Transport began when man's ape-like ancestors descended from the trees and took their first upright steps on the ground."[9] The motif of wandering begins here, at the origin of the species, according to this generally accepted (though still controversial) fact. They then follow this with a major one: "All life is a wanderer. There is nothing still in the universe. The earth itself is in constant motion. It spins, revolves around the sun and, with its family of planets in the Milky Way, journeys a gigantic pathway through space" (*Man Must Move*, 10). The motif of wandering begins, then, not with the origin of species but with the origin of the universe itself. Having tucked the minor premise safely inside the major one, they return to it, establishing an inevitable conclusion: "Man is also a wanderer, and has been since his beginnings. There is a natural instinct in most living things to escape from their birthplace, to spread out. Only thus can they find space to breed" (*Man Must Move*, 10). In this way the story of transport is grounded on an inalienable and universal need for humans to track their way through space, in search of more space to create more wanderers who will need even more space to create even more wanderers. All life is a wanderer; man is a wanderer; therefore, man must move: the itinerant imperative.

Inalienable and universal: this itinerant imperative rules out the political role of the stranger, as if from before the foundation of legitimate organised societies. If everyone is a stranger then no one is a stranger (or at least no stranger than anyone else). Thus any organised society for whom the notion of stranger has meaning already transgresses the itinerant imperative. A policed boundary would always have been a transgression in this sense, in which case human prehistory – insofar as this can be reported – would be the history of such transgressions. It may not be absurd to think of political boundaries as transgressions ipso facto. The act of foundation must institute a boundary without prior consent of law or nature, and must thus oppose itself to a supposed natural law (that is, the physical and ontological law of wandering). Staking claims, marking out territories, building walls: all transgress this itinerant imperative, by preventing, impeding or slowing down movement. But, on the contrary, the very notion of transgression – the step beyond – includes in its concept the exceeding of limits and boundaries that man's movement has always implied. The stranger would only be strange in transgression of identifiable limits.

Thus according to a familiar dialectical process, settlements (and later cities and states) set themselves up as kinds of institution against transgression per se, each time in contradistinction to this itinerant imperative. Where would mankind be without its limits? "An instinct in all of us," Lee and Lambert continue, "makes us want to search and discover the world" (*Man Must Move*, 12). Again, this wandering is not, exactly, aimless. There are reasons for it. "Originally, no doubt," they speculate, "the reason was hunger" (*Man Must Move*, 12). The targets, the *scopi* of prehistoric wandering, were thus always either food or space. The narrative quickly takes on familiar geo-political coordinates as the story become colonial:

> In time, early man colonized the earth, moving first in families and later in tribes, searching always for food and space. Little by little he fanned across Asia, seeking new lands before him, and crossed into America from Siberia to Alaska by a land bridge or shallow sea. Down America, Africa and the pacific islands, the strong drove the weaker before them, until the earliest wanderers were pushed to the edges of the world." (*Man Must Move*, 12)

But settlement no less than wandering is an essential component of the story told by Lee and Lambert. Here the twin aims of wandering (food and space) are extended via a strange regression into those of trade and war: "Another reason, even older than trade, was man's baser instinct for war". The illustration in the book represents a supposedly pre-historical scene that nonetheless readily recalls (in 1960) more recent depictions of World War II engagements and their consequent urban destruction – though in the mock woodprint illustration, it is unclear what the nature and cause of the conflagration at the city's edge are. In fact the whole story of wandering and the itinerant imperative can be easily related to the previous 200 years of massive colonial expansion, the overriding imperatives of international trade, more or less constant world war and its consequent urban destruction on vastly increasing scales. Images in the dominant idiom of conflict photography saturate the world press as a kind of prosthetic memory. Lee and Lambert, on the contrary, choose to update man's imperative to wander with an image of elderly tourists clasping a map with camera ready. They thus wind up with what on the surface is a reassuring version of historical progress which nevertheless communicates a covert, underlying unease that is typical of its time. This book – and many others like it – served an episcopal function for a generation growing up.

Men, Missiles and Machines

Lancelot Hogben's *Men, Missiles and Machines: The Wonderful World of Power* (1957), published in the same series as *Man Must Move*, treats the same generation of young readers (boys for the most part, of course) making up the target market of the series to Hogben's pedagogical clarity, while subtly implanting a more politically nuanced thesis.[10] Each chapter of *Men, Missiles and Machines* charts the development of a specific mode of power (man-power, gravity, heat, electricity and atoms, with a final section on harnessing natural power sources). Two striking features are worth remarking: first, each chapter tells roughly the same story, with mechanical history suddenly gaining pace after the seventeenth century and culminating in the fully functioning modern city; and, second, the middle term – the *missile* – acts (again) as the hinge between man and the technology of his civilised comforts, yet culminates in devastated cities of fused glass. Sophisticated children may well have identified these two apparently separate strong narrative threads and the paradox clearly implied. We learn, then, that the city is the target of modern technology in two senses (the end of technology *is* the end of technology). The first introductory chapter deals quickly with thousands of years of mildly enhanced practical labour before the book settles down to its main topic in chapter 2, "Getting to Grips with Gravity". As Europe emerges out of barbarism (falsely identified as a renaissance), by harvesting the knowledge of Moslems, Hindus, Greeks and Chinese, a warlike trajectory is established. Hogben here identifies the two forces that will have long-term consequences: time-measurement (adapted from Moslem technology) and propulsion (now enhanced by Chinese fireworks). He writes:

> In China, whence it had come, gunpowder for crackers had been a harmless plaything. In Europe it was now the sinews of war. A new branch of military science was growing up: how to track the path of the cannon-ball. This new interest in the study of matter in motion thus coincided with the emergence of a new instrument for measuring time in short intervals. (Hogben, *Men*, 12)

So Hogben's basic (and uncontroversial) argument is that the study of matter in motion gains a theoretical impetus in the seventeenth century as a function of military science.[11]

And so the study of gravity – especially after Galileo had begun to analyse the motion of a cannonball in terms of archery – blends the practical knowledge of the savage with the science of modernity. If a mounted archer knows how to take account of the speed and direction of his horse and the seventeenth century gunner can take into account the pull of gravity on a cannonball (all colourfully illustrated in Hogben's book), then modern naval gunnery, we learn, "takes account of ship's roll, wind direction, speed of target, *as well as* gravity" (*Men*, 15). Hogben's calculations are of two kinds. The first provides the general scientific knowledge (including the relations between mass and acceleration, the effects of gravity, the inner workings of bombs, how dynamos work); the second includes the *fact* of scientific knowledge in a general historical trajectory that equates means and ends with social forces and their consequences. Savage know-how + scientific theory = powerful and accurate projectiles.

The tone of Hogben's teaching – bolstered by a cool facility with his topic (fulfilling the promise of the subtitle's "Wonderful World of Power") but not quite untouched by its political implications – helps to prepare a generation for the pervasively reassuring register of popular science, which broadens out considerably when considered as one more function of a general episcopacy.[12] Both *Man Must Move* and *Men, Missiles and Machines* provide uncontroversial accounts of the progress of technology but neither entirely wards off a growing sense of doubt. *Man Must Move* represents an affirmation of itinerancy but tells a tale of widespread settlement. In *Men, Missiles and Machines*, the invention of the dynamo can be represented as having transformed for the better the domestic life of the city, yet a few pages further on the same power has been harnessed in a technology that destroys cities absolutely. Something of the inescapable and paradoxical basis of targeting technology has infected these documents of targeting culture. The two functions of aiming and watching over (the *scopic* and the *episcopal*) can be neither entirely separated nor brought neatly together. A hinge of some kind is always either required or presupposed. So it emerges that what the technology cannot control of its marvellous capabilities is the hinge itself, that is, the condition of its marvellous capabilities.

The Secret Future

> L'invisible ennemi plaie d'argent au soleil
> Et l'avenir secret que la fusée élucide
> (The Invisible enemy a silver wound in the sunlight
> And the secret future a flare illuminates) (Guillame Apollinaire)[13]

The hinge that provides the conditions of technology's enactment is often confused with technology itself. The end of World War II created an ineluctable anxiety about these trajectories, parabolic and otherwise, as cities were turned to sand and glass as well as humming dynamos of futuristic change. As a result we have the many narratives delineated in the children's knowledge books, such as Hogben and Lee and Lambert, about the ways in which technology will deliver a brighter, better tomorrow filled with control and mastery over time and space, as best manifested in cities. The episcopal function of these children's books clearly attempts to ameliorate these anxieties, much as the series *CSI* is meant to ameliorate the anxiety of individual random violence that stalks our city streets. In the process, the confusion of technology with its hinge leads to a breakdown of the teleologies leading to urban targeting. The enthusiasm of technological, urban targeting and the confusion of hinge and technology, however, was not new to the post World War II era, and is clearly manifest at the onset of World War I in a wide range of artistic works, including the poetry of Guillaume Apollinaire.

Apollinaire's *La petite auto* tracks the common narrative trajectories delineated in Hogben, and with many of the same ambivalent concerns. The poem narrates a car trip from Versailles to Paris on the night of the call-up for the war in August 1914. Technology (the auto) moves the persona from village to city, while also moving him from what he believes is a past/present about to be irrevocably transformed (as will he be) in a new future/present. The auto (self, automatic and car) is meant to deliver a promise at individual, national and grand historical levels (with the progress of the race). The itinerant imperative is pushed into high gear with the call-up, and the persona is anxious to move and play his role in the delivery of that promise. The auto serves as the hinge between the rural and the urban, and the past/present and future/present. But Apollinaire's poem exposes the incalculable future that the technologies and narratives are meant to overcome. Wedged into the middle of the poem, wedged into the middle of the narrative of the move toward a more promising urban future, is the auto itself, not as delivering technology but as the hinge revealing what technology cannot control.

As the persona drives toward Paris and waxes enthusiastic about the adventure of the future ahead, in some of the same euphoric tones of Hogben and others ("Je sentais en moi des êtres neufs pleins de dexterité / Bâtir et aussi agencer un univers nouveau" – "I felt within me skillful new beings / Build and even arrange a new universe"), the trip is delayed and badly fractured by the auto itself (Apollinaire, *Calligrammes*, 107). Similarly, Apollinaire's traditional poetic line print layout runs head on into the 'concrete' poetry, or visual mimesis, of the car. In the auto is the delay of the future and its promise, as "the nocturnal journey" becomes "an afternoon in Fountainbleu" owing to numerous technological failures: "our three headlights died" on "the tender night before the war" amongst the "villages". Underscoring his point, Apollinaire draws a line beneath the concrete, word-formed auto, with the line "et trois fois nous nous arrêtâmes pour changer un pneu qui avait éclaté" ("and three times we stopped to change a flat tire") (*Calligrammes*, 109).

Arriving in Paris much later than planned, just as the draft postings were going up, the drivers believe "the little car had driven [them] into a New era" ("Que la petite auto nous avait conduits dans une époque Nouvelle") (*Calligrammes*, 111). Their belief in being so delivered is belied by increasing ironies found in their current state, the most obvious of which being their late arrival in the new era. Apollinaire, at this juncture, also returns to the traditional poetic line, so the typesetting reinforces the state of things (village, past, rural) they have supposedly left. With the technological break-down of the auto – the punctures and blackouts – the telos of the city and/ as future has been derailed and deflated. The great dawn they had expected to greet them in the city has become an afternoon like many others, with a nation-state lining up its citizens for mass slaughter and inadvertently con-verting its capital into a target yet again. The vehicle we are meant to arrive in (the telos of the urban future and the technology that will link us to it) has been undone by what could not be calculated in the technology itself.

Paul Virilio identifies in Apollinaire's poems of war an accurate descrip-tion of how in the 1914–18 war all visible trace of the target disappears for soldiers in the new battle zone, where everything previously visible has either been razed or lies bedded down into trenches. The poem "Désir" (from the collection *Lueurs des Tirs*) evokes a soldier's imagination of targets identifiable only by name or position but not actually seen. Virilio explains, "Numerous veterans from the 1914–18 war have said to me that although they killed enemy soldiers, at least they did not see who they were killing, since others had now taken responsibility for seeing in their stead."[14] What Apollinaire's poem describes is, in Virilio's words, "a kind of telescopic tensing towards an imagined encounter" (Virilio, *War*, 15). The poem does indeed evoke a series of non-visible yet actual positions, before, behind, beyond, beneath the immediate zone of engagement *to come*, and presents with an increasingly severe humour (or is it an increasingly humorous severity?) the simultaneous absurdity and seriousness of the soldier's desire to grasp the actuality of the otherwise abstracted target:

> Butte du Mesnil je t'imagine en vain
> Des fils de fer des mitrailleuses des ennemis trop sûrs d'eux
> Trop enfoncés sous terre déjà enterrés[15]

The iron wire of the machine guns – the enemy, too sure of them and now too sunken underground, lies already buried: the inability of the speaker to evoke an image of the Butte du Mesnil is also the certainty that it will become the site of "violent and dark" struggle nonetheless; it already in principle has.

The *names* of targets can perform their own peculiar provocations:

> Je désir
> Te serrer dans ma main Main de Massiges
> Si décharnée sur la carte
>
> Le boyau Goethe où j'ai tiré
> J'ai tiré même sur le boyau Nietzsche[16]

Desire is focused with intensity upon targets that reveal themselves only as words on a map, projected targets provoking responses that satirically (re)

Visée

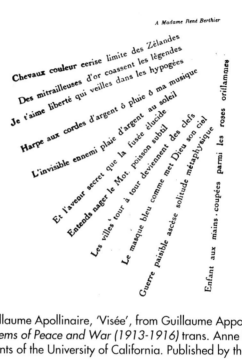

Figure 10.1   Guillaume Apollinaire, 'Visée', from Guillaume Appollinaire, *Calligrammes: Poems of Peace and War (1913-1916)* trans. Anne Hyde Greet, © 1980 by the Regents of the University of California. Published by the University of California Press

incarnate them through fierce disseminations, in preparation for a violent night. The violent determination of future event repeats the logic of targeting according to which time itself (which at the other extreme calls on eternal vigilance) must be brought up short, brought to its end.

If "Désir" evokes the soldier's aiming at invisible targets then a poem from the same year, "Visée" from *Case d'Armons*, evokes the other position, one with "responsibility for seeing". The "triangle de Visée," (or aiming triangle), a device for discovering the position of enemy artillery, has been taken over by the poem itself, which reproduces the movement of aiming upwards and downwards. The lines offer at best suggestive images but lightly avoid coherence, thus producing a war poem that refuses to distance itself from the technology of war. In this identification, however, a basic aim of the technology is made manifest. If targeting is designed to call an abrupt halt to the vagaries, the inconsistencies and the anxieties provoked by what cannot be known, let alone calculated, of the future, then this poem seems specially designed, on the contrary, to multiply these. The device aims in several directions; and in each direction the visual line (explicitly not, of course, the line of fire) performs a startling dispersion of its sense, suggesting at once the eternal vigilance of the watcher and yet a singular spotlight on its future target. The singular target would be one of the many possibilities of targeting per se, which include the accidental target, the target of misdirection, the indiscriminate target and the merely convenient target.

Notes

1. Aristotle, *Nicomachean Ethics*, trans. H. Rackham (Cambridge, MA: Harvard University Press, 1926).
2. Arthur Conan Doyle's Sherlock Holmes stories borrow directly from Poe the specifically targeted/targeting knowledge of the investigator, Holmes, who knows all, but only what he needs to know to solve crimes.
3. Σκοπια: "*a lookout-place, a mountain-peak*, Homer: of the Trojan acropolis, Euripides: cf. *Skopelos*. 2. metaphor, *the height* or *highest point* of anything, Pindar. II. *a watchtower*, Latin *specula*, Herodotus, Plato III. *a lookout, watch*, σκοπειν εχηειν, to keep *watch*", Liddell and Scott.
4. The Greek *episcopos* was of course translated as "Bishop" (via the Latin deformation *ebiscopus*) in the New Testament versions (OED: OE. *biscop* (also in North. *biscob*), *bisceop*, *biscep*, an early adopted word (cf. OS. *biskop*, MDu. *bisscop*, Du. *bisschop*), OHG. *biscof*, *piscof* (MHG., mod.G. *bischof*), ON. *biskup* (Sw. *biscop*, Da. *bisp*), a. Romanic **biscopo* or vulgar L. (*e*)*biscopus*:—L. *episcopus*, a. Gr. ἐπίσκοπος overlooker, overseer, f. ἐπί on + -σκοπος looking, σκοπός watcher; used in Greek, and to some extent also in Latin, both in the general sense, and as the title of various civil officers; with the rise of Christianity it gradually received a specific sense in the Church, with which it passed into Slavonic, Teutonic, and Celtic. With the form *biscopo*, *biscobo*, which passed into Teutonic, cf. also It. *vescovo*, OF. *vesque*, Pg. *bispo*, Pr. *vesque*, *bisbe*.).
5. *National Defence Magazine*, April 2002, http://www.nationaldefencemagazine. org/article.cfm?Id=755
6. Eagleton's claim that English Literature (and the Aesthetic Ideology) replaced the waning authority of the Church neglects the wide range (the scope in fact) of this epi-scopal diversification.
7. Thanks to Chrissie Tan for her expertise on investigative technologies.
8. Blake's wandering reporter of urban scenes call to mind that common urban literary figure, the *flâneur*, who crops up in Poe, Dickens, Baudelaire, Benjamin and many others. In this instance, the peregrinating persona embodies a bifocality regarding the urban events s/he encounters. Clearly there is social and political commentary about explicit and implicit forms of violence, but the epi-scopal nature of the reportage participates in the very means of surveillance the state deploys for different ends. Thus the persona is complicit in the formations and technologies of episcopy while condoning the violence and privilege resultant from them despite the fact that they indeed allow her/him to write the poem in this manner and about these concerns.

9. Laurie Lee and David Lambert, *Man Must Move: The Story of Transport* (London: Rathbone Books, 1960) p. 10.

10. Lancelot Hogben, *Men, Missiles and Machines: The Wonderful World of Power* (London: Rathbone Books, 1957).

11. Hogben's earlier and vastly influential *Mathematics for the Million* makes a similar case for mathematics, addressing a larger readership of adult pupils hungry for what at the time was largely perceived as inaccessible and esoteric knowledge (mathematics). The basic premise is that theoretical science follows the historical and political demands of patterns of social relation.

12. The fact that popular science is as capable of deepest alarm as calm reassurance makes little difference; the *image repertoire* of science, whether hard, social or popular, always includes both the calculative and probing values of insight and expertise. The target is exposure.

13. Guillame Apollinaire, "Visée", in *Caligrammes: Poems of Peace and War (1913–1916)*, trans. Anne Hyde Greet (Berkeley: University of California Press, 2004) p. 151. Greet translates the title as "Aim".

14. Paul Virilio, *War and Cinema*, trans. P. Camiler (London: Verso, 1989) p. 14.

15. In Anne Hyde Greet's translation:

    > Butte of Mesnil vainly I evoke you
    > Iron wire machine guns brazen enemies
    > Sunken too far underground already buried. (*Caligrammes*, 243)

16. Greet translates the lines:

    > I long
    > To grasp you in my hand Main de Massiges
    > So fleshless on the map
    >
    > Goethe's trench I have fired at
    > I have even fired at the guts of Nietzsche. (*Caligrammes*, 245)

Chapter 11

Satellites of Love and War

We have attempted to find analytic material in the traces of underlying conditions, the historicity of current state-of-the-art technologies and technological doctrines, which can be discovered playing decisive roles in global affairs. The modernist treatment of these conditions yields a particularly fecund source, reaching beyond the narrow frameworks of modern logic, that is, the mythical self identification of a logical foundation new since the seventeenth century, whether regarded as empiricist or rational. Modernist aesthetics mobilises, rather, the estranged, sometimes archaic, rhetorical and prosodic resources that can be discovered in texts and practices that lie outside the idioms of post-romantic art, like Mina Loy's experiments combining the courtly love tradition with turn-of-the-century science or Marcel Duchamp's planning and execution of the *Large Glass*, which took years of application, as if it was the work of some quattrocento craftsman meticulously applying precious metals in wood panels or on stained glass.

In these ways modernist aesthetics activates the irrationality implied by what remains excessive to calculative, pragmatic or positivist doctrines. These resources remain powerful enough, in their subterranean ways, to allow an engagement with present conditions, as well as with what lies beyond them. The phrase "present conditions" never designated anything, of course, but *crisis*; and contemporary technologies have been developed simultaneously to produce and yet solve critical conditions. A consistent pattern therefore emerges according to which the statement of the solution is rigorously, yet never successfully, divorced from the statement of the problem, a grounding division, nonetheless, according to which division, the crisis itself, must increasingly be contained, excluded, domesticated, tamed, or otherwise made safe and harnessed for its uncontainable power – on the performative level. In this way a kind of closure is produced as the theme of a narrative, separating the act (solution) from its conditions (the problematic) in the several modes of problem identification: for example, the machines do not yet see enough or respond quickly enough; they are too slow, too blind.

The novel discourse of novelty evokes an imaginary world that has become rapidly more transparent, more efficient. The problematic itself, however, is old. John Locke's *Essay Concerning Human Understanding*, for instance, evokes in 1689 this same world in its apparently neonatal state. Apologetic, Locke introduces his speculation in the register of a slightly stretched hyperbole. The extravagant conjecture begins with the unproven yet suggestive possibility that "sprits can assume to themselves bodies of different bulk, figure, and conformation of parts".[1] As we have observed, writers like H. G. Wells (Wells in his singular, also slightly fictional, register) would later speculate on these powers of unseen spirits, as would a generally disseminated military technicity, emerging too in its neo-nascent state after the seventeenth century. Locke's interest lies obviously not in the possibility of spirits but in the more forceful conjectures concerning the senses that the hyperbole allows. The advantage such spirits would have over normal seventeenth-century humans would lie in their ability to "so frame, and shape to themselves organs of sensation or perception, as to suit them to their present design, and the circumstances of the object they would consider" (Locke, *Essay*, 275). The ability, then, to transcend the limitations of the organs of perception, would – if such a thing were possible – allow an unimaginably greater level of knowledge:

> For how much would that man exceed all others in knowledge, who had but the faculty to so alter the structure of his eyes, that one sense, as to make it capable of all the several degrees of vision, which the assistance of glasses (casually at first light on) has taught us to conceive? What wonders would he discover, who could so fit his eye to all sorts of objects, as to see, when he pleased, the figure and the motion of the minute particles in the blood, and other juices of animals as distinctly as he does, at other times, the shape and motion of the animals themselves. (Locke, *Essay*, 275)

The hyperbole serves two slightly different rhetorical purposes. First, it helps to bolster Locke's main preoccupation, which is to establish beyond doubt the empirical basis of knowledge: all we know as well as all we can guess at depends entirely on "the ideas received from our sensation and reflection" (Locke, *Essay*, 276). We might imagine what complete freedom of sensate manipulation can allow only on the basis of those limitations the senses presently impose, that is, by analogy. Secondly, though, the floodgates of empiricist experimentation are open. Three centuries increasingly rich with attempts ultimately to alter the structure of the eye bear testimony to the possibility suggested, undoubtedly without intention, by Locke. His point is complete with the observation that, "in our present state", such organs would be to no advantage: "God has fitted us for the neighbourhood of the bodies that surround us, and we have to do with" (Locke, *Essay*, 275). We cannot in our present state achieve perfection in knowledge; rather, our faculties serve us well enough for our present needs. Nevertheless, the rhetoric itself escapes its conservative purposes. The speculation – however fanciful it may be (and Locke apologises for this) – is grounded on an assumption that is so rigorously empiricist that it sunders itself, opening onto an abyss that cannot be contained. The contingency of the "present state" would in historical terms be the guiding theme of modern logic and technology, the promise of altered states its inevitable consequence, now unhooked from the idea of this all-seeing God and his inscrutable purposes. If one alters the conditions of perception, it follows then that our needs may also be changed as well as our surroundings: the (multiplying) neighbourhoods of other bodies and the ways in which we relate to them. The human through his technological prosthetics can perhaps, the narratives suggest, become all-seeing himself. The operations of vision – deep internal vision, vision at a distance, vision of the invisible, global vision – can be infinitely extended through technological prosthesis; therefore human knowledge too can be infinitely extended through technological prosthesis.

The now obvious and yet intricate objections to the historical heritage of both empiricism and logical rationalism (which are merely counterparts) nevertheless remain more or less contained within fields regarded as aesthetic: another key closure of the problematic itself. The closure occurs in two steps. First, the key objection to an empirical basis for human knowledge, which remains at all times inherent in the covert logic of the empiricist approach, follows from the contingent, nomadic, heart of empiricism itself, according to which the grounds of knowledge remain forever unknowable and thus knowledge is contingent entirely on whatever state prevails of the organs of sensation and the faculties of reflection. Moreover, the rationalist basis of knowledge is tethered contingently like its partner, dependent entirely on calculations grounded on whatever state of the calculable prevails. The empirical and the calculable together form the basis of modern technology. Considerations produced late in the eighteenth century by German philosophy and romantic poetry provide, in this first step, an enclosure for the excessive questions of origin that would otherwise perpetually trouble the techno-logical grounds of modern life; the transcendental imagination, the sublime and its several analytics maintain a mythological currency within the space opened by Kant in the *Critique of Judgment*, but made in the centuries that follow somehow reducible through ignorance or negligence to an aesthetic criticism. A second step adopts the *effects* of the laws of art, the rules of judgement, as a kind of aesthetic surface for modern life, paintings and the plastic arts now supplemented by often moving images and the swift turnaround of edifices and engines of all kinds as they spread to the sky and beyond.

With the emergence of a specifically modernist aesthetics – dry with wit but fierce in its intent – the separated, mythologised, fragmented elements of modern history begin to collide with a violence to match the escalating technological violence of the milieu. The determinate divisions that produce the separated spheres of technology, scientific experimentation, art and the organic body are now stripped bare. These alienating separations, normally maintained, disguised and rewritten in terms of the distinction between scopic aims and episcopal intentions (or the military and the civic/public spheres) are returned to their source in disturbing images, counter-narratives and actions. We conclude this study with an exemplary comparison: two bold failures. The first of these, late on the scene, promises to encircle the globe. Its rings around the world promise the episcopal dream of total control in network-centric defence and warfare systems. The promise, however, is fulfilled in a way more evocative of the second exhibit, one of the twentieth century's most complex constructions, Marcel Duchamp's mechanical manifestation of the functional collapse of modern life, *The Bride Stripped Bare by her Bachelors, Even* (*The Large Glass*).

Satellites of War

> The SBIRS program addresses critical warfighter needs in the areas of missile warning, missile defence and battlespace characterisation. SBIRS is a program in which we have worked to balance requirements with affordability. It promises to provide an effective transition from DSP to an improved system that meets a wide range of theater and national needs. (General Joseph Ashy, US Air Force)[2]

A long, complex, history connects broadcast media, as an integral apparatus serving episcopal functions, to the often contested or negotiated public spheres of cities and states. The incorporation of satellite systems into broadcast media and telecommunications helps to further blur the boundaries between entertainment, industry and the military. The fascinating possibility, forecast by H. G. Wells in "Davidson's Eyes", of being able to "live visually in one part of the world, while one lives bodily in another part of the world" is realised through numerous tele-technologies, most notably television and the internet, but they can carry out episcopal functions in specific surveillance, weapons and intelligence systems too. Recently, the US Nation Reconnaissance Office (NRO) has extended the possibility further with the stakes raised in its massive, top-secret project Future Imagery Architecture (FIA), which replaces the large Defence Support Program (DSP), put into place for the Cold War. FIA began in the late 1990s and received increased funding in 2001 even prior to the attacks on the World Trade Center and Washington DC, making it the most expensive project in the history of intelligence gathering, and it has subsequently become the centrepiece for the US-led War on Terror. It drives the network-centric warfare the US military and government wish to provide for this war, if not for absolute US-global control. Despite numerous serious problems with the system, the episcopal dream it represents for current, state-of-the-art military planning and execution remains firmly in place, representing the projected future of the armed forces.[3] Owing to its exceptionally high security status, the actual scale and details of the programme are not available, but the overall shape and intention of the project is.

 The Defence Support Program initially set up for Cold War surveillance and upgraded over the years includes a range of satellites with varying degrees of accuracy, resolution and ability to "hover", or closely examine a specific site for an extended period of time.[4] These satellites currently travel at Mach 25, and can cover any part of the earth twice a day. "Visible light" satellites, also called "Keyhole-class" satellites, have a resolution of five to six inches, which means they can distinguish between objects on the ground of that size or larger. Other satellites are radar-imaging, and have a resolution of about three feet.[5] The Space Based Infrared System (SBIRS) that provides the satellite component of FIA and network-centric warfare will be a constellation of high- and low-altitude satellites. In addition to replacing the old Defence Support Program and providing the backbone of network-centric warfare, FIA and SBIRS constitute an important dimension of the National Missile Defence System, also known as "Star Wars", intended to intercept and destroy Inter Continental Ballistic Missiles by means of space-based lasers. The ultimate aim of this network of systems is to provide global infra-red coverage in such a way that the fourfold requirements of a total defence system are adequately met: missile warning, missile defence, technical intelligence and characterisation of the battle space.

Where the latter two dimensions ("technical intelligence" and "battle-space characterisation") are concerned, however, a need has not yet been met for adequate imaging. As a result, one of the oldest visual tricks is retained: "For a long time, U.S. satellites have been taking pictures in stereo-optic pairs," Robert Windrem writes, "meaning side-by-side images taken at slightly different angles. That permits intelligence analysts to get a 3-D view, like you would through a child's stereopticon" (Windrem, "Spy Satellites"). The optical and visual effects of the past, as in the stereopticon Keystone postcard (see Chapter 1), continue to operate in the present as well as indicating directions for the future. The visual trick of overlapping images magnified to create the illusion of 3D, rudimentary and explicitly illusory as it was, led directly to state and military decision-making and policy formation. The desire for more and better artificially-generated 3D animations has led to one of the most recent developments in FIA, known as "envisions".

A host of software applications, some of which are military-directed though many are not, feature the conversion of two-dimensional images into the illusion of 3D. The most obvious application in both military and civilian use is in computer gaming, an area of the market economy that is complicated by deep interconnections between capital, digital technology, the military and entertainment. But this technology replicates and intensifies the desires for the kind of visual effects that predominate in the nineteenth century. The invention of the pixel image has not altered the basic power to have the reproduction (or simply production) trick the eye into believing that what has been represented is the real. The mother sitting at home viewing her son through the stereoscope at the front in France during World War I also engaged in a sleight-of-eye technological trickery that rendered two-dimensional images as three-dimensional. The images and modelling have become more sophisticated. So the narrative of targeting, and its increasing intelligence and specificity, reinforces the sense that the technology has allowed a more secure distinction between citizen and enemy.

By simply doing what it does well, the visualising technology that the military uses always indicates how much better the lamentably inefficient targeting and sighting technology could be. The machines need to be faster, smarter, better sighted, and so on, if they are to match the operational fluency projected by the visual simulations. The self-reproducing effect of a technicity projected into its own future operates by revealing to military theorists and their civilian counterparts possibilities yet to be realised. Although the technology of vision simultaneously inspires and disappoints, it remains a vast improvement, to those who depend on it, over technologies past, not to mention the naked biological organ. This quantitative documentation of improvement presents the other face of the narrative separating the problem from its solution, with the grounding division locked into the technology itself. Technology thus divides a past (less accurate or detailed targeting and sighting) from a future (increasingly accurate and detailed targeting and sighting) in a presentation based on the operative superiority of visual simulation as opposed to visual capture. The inexistent past of visual simulation no less than its future grounds the technicity of military R&D on an impressive fiction.

In lectures given to pilots at US Air Force bases about the history of aerial reconnaissance and targeting, the narrative of unhinging the senses from the body, technologically enhancing them and then returning them in their improved form, culminates with this type of image manipulation and enhancement. Ending the instruction with 3D image-enhancement technology makes chronological sense as it represents "the state of the art", and in this way captures the teleology of technicity itself. "Perhaps the greatest capability of EO (electro-optical) images is you can manipulate it using digital techniques. The human eye," the Air Force lecture notes remind us, "can detect about 30 shades of gray. An EO system can detect 256 shades of gray. If an object was parked in the shadow of a building you could change the individual pixel value of the image to identify targets that otherwise could not be seen by the human eye."[6] The shift from analogue technologies to digital has given the pixel a special status. The image can henceforth be manipulated at the level of the pixel or even sub-pixel in order to perform various targeting functions, which the seventeenth-century optic nerve would never have been able to accomplish. With the reading and scanning of digital images by computers, the grounds of perception and the expansion of knowledge become accessible solely by machines; the neighbourhood of organic perception would still thus be restricted to the twenty-five odd yards of real space but opening onto targeted space by virtue of the stereoscopic image.

These machinic readings of machinic signatures not only support the imperative that drives weapon technology, according to which mastery, control and manipulation of conditions be maintained at a safe distance, but they also manifest the patterns that characterise the relationship between the technological imagination and the machinic object itself. The focus on the pixel and its sub-pixilation, which allows a more sophisticated kind of multispectral imaging, reveals a pattern of operation where drawbacks in one kind of imaging technology turn out to be resources for another kind. The Federation of American Scientists website explains the advantages of multispectral imaging:

> The utility of subdividing the ultraviolet, visible and infrared spectra into distinct bins for imaging has long been known. In Multispectral Imaging (MSI), multiple images of a scene or object are created using light from different parts of the spectrum. If the proper wavelengths are selected, multispectral images can be used to detect many militarily important items such as camouflage, thermal emissions and hazardous wastes to name a few. A primary goal of using multispectral/ hyperspectral remote sensing image data is to discriminate, classify, identify as well as quantify materials present in the image.[7]

In this evocation of the scopic ideal (the increasing purity of target discrimination) we also find an interesting and interested play of promises and detours under the guise of disinterested machinic modification of the image. The subdivision of pixels and multispectral imaging, said to serve the purposes of calculation and division, serves also a less obvious role in the imaginary relation between viewer and image. First, the explanation elides how the aesthetics of the image, as projection, as simulacrum, has become a justification for the ends of targeting, ideally and perhaps transcendentally removed from the world. The relationship of intelligence to targeting, of calculation to destruction, is obscured. The possibility of error too receives less attention than might be expected of a technology that depends so much on vagary, given that spectral, pixel and sub-pixel imaging produces the possibility of images outside, beneath or other than the image elements that generate them. But secondly, it avoids how the aesthetics of the image implies an element of pleasure in this relationship whose end, which may nonetheless be destruction, remains in fact beyond a horizon that will not be outstripped.

There is necessarily play in the pixel; the pixel plays. The final lines of this brief explanation provide an insight into the anxieties and desires that lurk at the heart of the enterprise:

> Another important applications [sic] are subpixel target detection, which allows one to detect targets of interest with sizes smaller than the pixel resolution, and abundance estimation, which allows one to detect concentrations of different signature spectra present in pixels. In remote sensing image analysis, the difficulty arises in the fact that a scene pixel is mixed linearly or nonlinearly by different materials resident in the pixel where direct applications of commonly used image analysis techniques generally do not work well. (Federation of America Scientists, Hyperspectral Imaging webpage)

The imaging technology that proceeds according to the manipulability of elements of a picture (moving freely between digital, analogue, spectral or sub-pixel aspects) promises imaging of the most sophisticated and technologically stunning capacities, yet at the same time confounds any attempt to achieve the scopic ideal: total calculability of the target via the image. This last insight leads to a curious discovery. In some ways the target resides in the pixel itself, as if targeting in the traditional military sense was simply a ruse for pursuing an image beyond the image (analogous in some ways to the discovery of a sub-atomic universe). The image, after all, is broken down into its picture elements (pixels) in a way that is analogous to how intelligence breaks the theatre of conflict down into its distinct components. But with the pixel, one can go further, and a kind of "pixilation" occurs (pixilation was the technique used in theatrical and early cinematographic productions, whereby human characters move or appear to move as if artificially animated). The effect produced by pixilation is obviously fake, even corny, which leads to the idea of someone being *pixilated*: mildly insane, fey, whimsical, bewildered, confused, intoxicated, tipsy. The intoxication of the pixel operates according to a nonetheless quite sober programme. The new technology promises a speed and transparency hitherto unheard of, yet immediately reneges on its promise, pulling back at the last minute, playing easy but hard to get.

The value of envisioning technology for network-centric warfare emerges in the confluence of targeting and episcopy. Selecting targets from central commands or from in-the-field situations, whether in helicopters, planes or on foot in urban settings, is essential to the implementation of military technicity at every level. Multispectral imaging plays an integral role in the Future Imagery Architecture as the National Reconnaissance Office in the US seeks to fulfill its "vision" as "Freedom's Sentinel in Space" and "Revolutionizing Global Reconnaissance". This mission represents the state at its most explicitly episcopal, overseeing the entire globe from space, converting the earth's sphere into a flat two-dimensional object/image without horizon that can then be manipulated and selectively reconverted back to an artificially enhanced three-dimensional image when and where the state needs it to be fleshed out. In network-centric warfare, the digital enhancement of any bit of satellite imagery would be available at any time, and in "real time" to anyone in the state apparatus: government, military or private contractor to the military. The National Imaging and Mapping Agency in the US has undertaken a massive image archiving project that would allow this online, real-time accessing to have current as well as past images available for targeting and intelligence purposes at any time from any electronic access point. Pilots operating in inclement weather can access past images and programme their flights according to stored images of the terrain. Commanders can visualise with digitally enhanced 3D capacity from afar the terrain that ground and air troops must negotiate. They move from one-dimensional vision to stereoscopic vision through the pixel and its manipulations, through machinic readings and renderings.

The problem with the dream of network-centric warfare, and the various independent yet complementary systems it relies upon, is that it just does not work very well, according to its own standards and evaluators. A 2003 detailed report was prepared by the Defence Science Board and The Air Force Scientific Advisory Board Joint Task Force delineating the problems that the FIA programme has encountered. The report states that "SBIRS High has been a troubled program that could be considered a case study for how not to execute a space program" and that "the task force believes this FIA program is not executable".[8] Despite this report and its blunt conclusions, huge funding remains in place for its perpetuation and repair. A critical situation, which couples less than ideal present conditions with the inherent momentum of technicity, dictates that the solution to the problem be found in the problem itself. Networks and netwar reveal the state of the art of military planning and technology, and their capacities, as military theorists Arquilla and Ronfeldt argue, is maintained by narratives of their efficacy.[9] Lawmakers and military advisors caught in the technology of narrative cannot but allow these various technologies to speak through them.

Satellites of Love

The Bride Stripped bare by her bachelors even.
To separate *the mass-produced readymade* from the *readyfound* – The separation is an operation – (Marcel Duchamp, *The Green Box*)[10]

As we have noted, Duchamp's *Large Glass*, which he classifies as a "delay", seems to implant in experience a sense of delay that is not necessarily related to anything that one could say has been delayed – unless it be the delay itself. Duchamp embeds this obscure delay in three dimensions, thus immediately suggesting the essential fourth.[11] *The Large Glass* invokes by way of the inexistent fourth dimension the inevitably untouchable temporality of a supersensible *beyond*, towards which its mechanical histrionics systematically yet vainly tend.

The title, *The Bride Stripped Bare by her Bachelors, Even* (*La mariée mise à nu par ses célibataires*), designates not a work as such but a constellation of elements and events to which *The Large Glass* (*La mariée mise à nu par ses célibataires, meme* / known as *The Large Glass*) belongs. *The 1914 Box* and *The Green Box* (which currently resides near the *Glass* in Philadelphia), as well as several other collections, composed of notes, plans and comments related to *The Bride*, were regarded by Duchamp as no less important to the concept than the *Glass* itself (Duchamp, *Writings*, 26–71). And the series of paintings, drawings and plans produced in the lead-up to and during the execution of the *Glass*, as well as in its wake, presents a yet wider and no less pertinent frame of reference. Even the *Etant donnés* (1946–66), already proposed in *The Green Box*, seems to offer a recreation, in alternative operations, of the

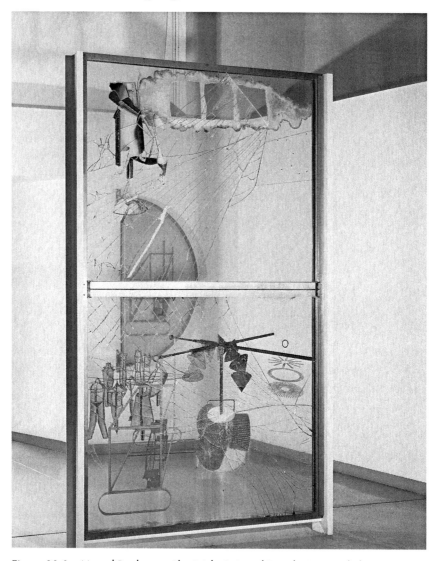

Figure 11.1   Marcel Duchamp, *The Bride Stripped Bare by Her Bachelors, Even (The Large Glass)* (1915–23). Permission by Adagp, © Succession Marcel Duchamp/ADAGP, Paris 2010; image provided by the Philadelphia Museum of Art

basic dynamic of the *Glass*, although *Fountain* with its mocking qualification, "original lost", perhaps presents the purest schematic.

A "horizon" separates the bride's space (above) from that of her nine bachelors (below). The bachelors themselves perform, as the notes of the *Green Box* explain, nine roles that together constitute an obvious satire on the partly declining apparatuses of what we can identify in our own terms as an urban episcopacy: the priest, the department store delivery boy, the gendarme, the cuirassier, the flunky (or liveried servant), the undertaker, the stationmaster, the busboy (or waiter's assistant), and the policeman. From their position below the horizon on the left, the nine malic moulds then proceed to take aim along a series of apparatuses that include a glider containing a watermill wheel, capillary tubes, a chocolate grinder ("The Bachelor Grinds his own Chocolate", a contemporary department store advertisement had declared), through bayonet and scissors and other contraptions and regions, until arriving, above the horizon on the right, at the nine shots: "bullet" holes in the glass that have missed their target, the bride's so-called "draft pistons".

With *The Large Glass* we face something quite exacting. The embedding of the visible in the invisible and vice versa is partly tangible in the transparency of the glass and the opacity of the sculptural elements affixed to it. Furthermore the relation between divisions (the division between the upper and lower sections – the horizon – is also internally divided) and the hinges and joints that more or less connect the elements (more to the glass and less to each other) force the observer into following the unveiling *ad infinitum*, for there can be no stripping beyond the horizon that lies between, dividing the bride and her bachelors. The absurd urgency of the processes evoked through the contrast between the stillness of the work itself and busy machinations stripped bare by it corresponds to the increasing urgency of technological processes that continue to intensify throughout the modern period, adumbrating many years in advance projects like the Space Based Infrared System Defence Program.

In *The Green Box* Duchamp provides a note on his use of glass, which in conventional terms replaces the more traditional canvas as the support or medium for the work. The work itself, now on glass, would no longer be a "picture" but it would become in this way a delay:

> *Kind of Subtitle*
> **Delay in Glass**
> *Use 'delay' instead of picture or painting; picture on glass becomes delay in glass – but delay in glass does not mean picture on glass –*
>   *It's merely a way of succeeding in no longer thinking that the thing in question is a picture . . . a delay in glass as you would say a poem in prose or a spittoon in silver*
> (Duchamp, *Writings*, 26)

Also noting that "the transparency of the glass plays for you", Duchamp identifies a key characteristic of the new support. It has two facilitating qualities: first its transparency allows the artist to dispense with background, setting or landscape and thus to focus on the figures themselves; and secondly it allows the artist and/or viewer to change the background at will, just by changing their position or the position of the *Glass*. *The Large Glass* thus operates like a kind of moveable window with figures. The *Glass* complicates the window effect (a transparent support through which one views an outside object) by inscribing on it an allegory of viewing (sighting, scoping and targeting) as a kind of absurd and failed movement of machination. (Its current installation in Philadelphia, however, means that it has been embedded in the same spot for many years and so the background depends first on where the spectator stands and second on the current state of the immediate environment and the position of passers-by at a given moment.) The transparency of the support and the delay effect of the iconic figures inscribed upon it together provide a kind of lens through which the world may seem transfigured.

The "bride" occupies the left third of the upper panel of the *Glass*, by convention perhaps the first element upon which one lays one's eyes. Duchamp had experimented by attempting to transfer a photograph of the painting *Bride* (1912) directly. In practice he painted on a meticulous counterfeit in monochrome: a painted copy of a photograph of a painting, and one of many evident *trompe l'oeil* effects of the *Glass*. The significance of the series of counterfeits becomes clearer still when we consider *Bride*'s gestation and its emergence as a further abstraction from *Passage from Virgin to Bride* (1912). The ritualised passage symbolised by weddings (the goddess Hymen hitching together or hinging separated elements, and the hymen broken in the passage) undergoes exhaustive examination in the period leading up to the planning and execution of the *Glass*. The double counterfeit of virgin in bride and of bride in virgin utilises, under cover of these topics of religious and artistic obsession, the crude metaphor of the sexual relation in order to once again figure the impossibility of figuring art outside the elusive operations of its own transfiguration.

The explicit connection between photographic technologies and the *Glass* implicates art and its operations in the technological sphere but where art implants delay in its pure state, the technological sphere seems mobilised to eradicate it (we might recall this effect in relation to the photographic reproduction of *Fountain*'s replica in *The Blind Man* from 1917). Delay in its pure state (whatever that might be) can only be pictured as negativity in relation to some positive process subjected contingently or accidentally to delay. The idea of a pure state of delay must thus be somehow subtracted from the conventional economies where one normally encounters it. *The Large Glass* mobilises a repertoire of conventional economies available from several dramatic spheres of operation, including the visible sphere of art and aesthetics, a multitude of noisy popular culture idioms, the intricate dramas of the game of chess, a developing and always militarised techno-science, Cartesian metaphysics, and an iconography that is simultaneously religious and sexual, which animates all these other spheres. In what at first might seem like a simple reversal, the *Glass* organises these economies so that they operate as both subverted by delay, and, as such, subversions of the delay.

By calling the *Glass* a "delay", and by situating upon it the confounded dynamics of these several economies, Duchamp invites us to follow innumerable operations by which delay itself becomes subject to delays. *The Large Glass* must come to embody the operation according to which it delays its own completion. It must embody in its completed form the essential quality of incompleteness (and Duchamp only after many years of dust and accidents declared the *Glass* "definitively unfinished"). The conventional economies inscribed in various ways upon it thus form the embodied remains of its own idea; and their respective failures serve as the condensed metaphor for the great underlying failure, which can be expressed in two ways: the failure of art to become a work, or the failure of the work to become art. Those who gaze on and through *The Large Glass* expecting to find there an object of aesthetics find instead that its own operational aesthetics has gathered the objectifying gaze into its machinery and set it too on the passage to failure.

The new arrangement involves a situation according to which both a fundamental and a phenomenal (in Joyce's word, "funnaminal") principle (in our rubric modernist aesthetics) fends off a challenge from two opposed kinds of aesthetic order: a conventional aesthetics that objectifies art as a privileged and separated sphere from which unique works express evanescent truths to be protected in their ineffable beauty; and a counter-aesthetics that would objectify art, render its evanescent truth explicable, visible, containable and controllable. The *Glass* mocks the aesthetics of beauty and the ideals of representation while parodying the desperation of an objectifying aesthetic that strips its objects bare to reveal the mechanisms by which they operate. By standing apart from both, while combining them in its absurd schematic, the *Glass* implicates the essential complicity of techno-science with a supposedly older metaphysics of beauty.

If by its peculiar operations *The Large Glass* belongs to a century that in the sphere of art it more or less defines, then the development of techno-science remains quite unaffected (now as then) by its intervention. But as soon as we give up the prejudice that art implies "works" (or inversely that the work implies art) we stand to learn from the peculiar events it produces in its abyssal commentary on the sphere that has been designated for it: aesthetics. *The Large Glass*, particularly, in combining the motifs that we have consistently identified as the operational themes of weapons technology, suggests a sustained engagement not only with the deepest provocations of military research and development but also, more destructively, with the regimes that foster the demand for military technicity. *The Large Glass* offers itself as a sign of things to come in its meticulous hinging of remnants from modes of life that at that time were passing away.

A certain hinge-logic emerges particularly clearly. In *The Green Box* Duchamp had written:

> Perhaps make a *hinge picture*. (Folding yardstick, book . . .) develop *the principle of the hinge* in the displacements 1st in the plane 2nd in space.
>
> Find an *automatic description* of the hinge.
>
> Perhaps introduce it in the Pendu femelle. (Duchamp, *Writings*, 27).

"Automatic description", auto-machinic or motorised self-description, entails that the hinged figures describe the abstract figure of the hinge (hence the "4dim'l" requirement). The bride and its parts evidently compose a series of hinges: the *pendu femelle* itself (apparently hanging on a *tromp l'oeil* hook from the frame at the upper left); the "wasp or sex cylinder" that hangs from it; and "the milky way or top inscription" that floats along the top of the upper panel surrounding its three "draft pistons" hanging, again from *trompē l'oeil* hooks, from the top frame ("Kind of milky way *flesh color* surrounding unevenly densely the 3 pistons" (Duchamp, *Writings*, 36) The pistons themselves, empty but formed from the outlines of photographic stills of gauze netting (reminiscent of a wedding or funeral veil) agitated gently by a draft from an open window, function according to a less visible but nonetheless evident hinge principle that attaches them to their transfigured yet absent source. The hooks operate like quotation marks (hence the "top inscription") or as a satire on the pegs from which developing photographic images hang, another symbol of delay.

The inscription, locked further into the inescapable logic of the *Glass*, connects with the motif of targeting: "This flesh-like milky way to be used as a support for the inscription which is concerned with the cannon shots" (Duchamp, *Writings*, 36). The nine shots also mark obscurely the procedures by which they arrived: nine matchsticks dipped in red paint and fired from a toy gun in an arrangement to the right of the inscription, and then holes carefully drilled through the glass at the points marked. In these ways, the *Glass* performs the narrative of how it comes to be, as the event of itself in the metaphor of failed sexual relations. The process, which is circular yet incomplete, operates (like the several spirals inscribed onto the glass) in a way similar to that of the mathematical moebius strip. A two-sided object, given a twist in its circular arrangement, now only has one endless side. Whether one regards the two sides in terms of the back and the front of the glass, or in terms of the upper and lower panels, the mode in which they are affixed as conceptual elements maintains them both apart and yet endlessly intertwined, as simultaneously detached and attached.

One final unintentional *coup d'art* occurred when both panels of the *Glass* shattered whilst in transit. Duchamp patiently – echoes again of the quattrocento craftsman – repaired the glass and encased each shattered panel between two further glass panels, mounting the whole in its frame of steel and wood.

This "chance completion", as Duchamp called it (critics have speculated on this stoic response to what by almost any standards must be regarded as a catastrophic event), incorporates the evidence of the accident (thus enshrining it ironically as exemplar of the accidental) in patterns of fracture that uncannily resemble the original drawings for the capillary tubes, and which were themselves based upon the standard stoppages. It is as if Duchamp had anticipated what Fredrick Kiesler describes as "the outburst of broken glass streaks which now veins the whole picture".[12] Kiesler, writing one year after this final chance completion, captures much of what remains effective in *The Large Glass*, relating it back to the brush-painted glass of the Middle Ages and to the then current industrial and military developments in transparent materials designed to withstand force and to prevent breakage. He says:

The *Large Glass* is nothing short of being the masterpiece of the first quarter of twentieth century painting. It is architecture, sculpture, and painting in ONE. To create such an X-ray painting of space, materiae and psychic, one needs as a lens (a) oneself, well focused and dusted off, (b) the subconscious as camera obscura, (c) a super-consciousness as sensitizer, and (d) the clash of this trinity to illuminate the scene. The glass plate cracked in 1931 [actually it had been broken in 1927], cutting strokes across the plane that would have broken any other composition, but not this singular masterpiece of tectonic integration. (Kiesler, "Design", 54)

The architectural imagination, as one might expect, is piqued by the use of the foremost building and design material of the era. As "the only material that expresses surface-and-space at the same time," he notes, glass "satisfies what we need as designers and builders: an inclosure that is space in itself, an inclosure that divides and at the same time links" (Kiesler, "Design", 55). As we have noted too, glass is by no means the only hinge material of a work that is composed more or less solely of hinges. But perhaps the cracked glass evokes the hinge that most consistently describes the divisions and relations we have been charting throughout this book.

Notes

1. John Locke, *An Essay in Human Understanding* (London: Penguin, 1997) p. 275.
2. Quoted on the website for Joint Interoperability Test Command, http://jitc.fhu. disa.mil/sbirs/sbirs.htm
3. Adam J. Hebert, senior editor of *Air Force Magazine*, writing in November 2003 (v.86:11), reveals that an additional $7 billion was acquired to help the troubled programmes. He also notes that the announcement of the funding acquisition was unusual given the highly classified nature of the project, which rarely reveals any information about number or type of satellites, or even funding issues (http://www.afa.org/magazine/nov2003/1103world.html).
   A copy of a detailed report by the Defense Science Board and the Air Force Scientific Advisory Board Joint Task Force delineating the problems the programme has encountered was written in 2003 and is available at http://www.spaceref.com/news/viewsr.html?pid=10285
   The report states that "SBIRS High has been a troubled program that could be considered a case study for how not to execute a space program" and that "the task force believes this FIA program is not executable".
4. General information about The Defense Support Program (DSP) is available at http://www.losangeles.af.mil/SMC/PA/Fact_Sheets/dsp_fs.htm
5. Robert Windrem, "Spy Satellites Enter New Dimension", http://msnbc.msn.com/id/3077885/
6. http://www.fas.org/irp/doddir/army/tacimlp.htm
7. See the Hyperspectral Imaging webpage, http://fas.org/irp/imint/hyper.htm
8. http://www.spaceref.com/news/viewsr.html?pid=10285

9. John Arquilla and David Ronfeldt, *Networks and Netwars*, (Santa Monica, CA: RAND, 2001) p. 327.
10. Marcel Duchamp, *Salt Seller: The Writings of Marcel Duchamp*, ed. Michel Sanouillet and Elmer Peterson (Oxford: Oxford University Press, 1973) p. 26.
11. As Lynda Dalrymple-Henderson shows, two sources for Duchamp's thoughts on a fourth dimension are likely: Alain Jouffret's *Géométries à 4 dimensions* and Poincaré's "n-dimensional" geometry. These experiments in physics that galvanised not only modern aesthetics but also military R&D help to further fragment previous notions of an ultimate homogeneity in space and time.
12. Frederick Kiesler, "Design – Correlation: Marcel Duchamp's *Large Glass*", *The Architectural Record* May 1937, 81:5, p. 54.

Index

Note: Page numbers in **bold** refer to illustrations.

absolute monarchy, 122–3
abstract art, 72
the absurd, 68
achresis, 104, 109, 112, 113, 114, 171
action, and thought, 147–8
Ades, Dawn, 160
Adorno, Theodor, 4
Adrian, E. D., 147, 156
advertising
  Bell Helicopter, 50–2, **51**, 54, 57
  Comanche helicopter, 62–3
  Stereopticon images, 3–4
aerodynamics, link with neurology, 156
aesthetics
  broadcast technologies, 98
  connection with military technology, 4, 5,
    15–16, 43, 51, 82, 98, 150, 159
  critical discourses, 4–5
  Marinetti's manifesto, 61
  marketing of Bell Helicopter, 50–1, 52
  Nietzsche's view, 149–50
  Romanticism, 52–4
  separation from functionality, 6–7, 14
  see also modernist aesthetics
Afghanistan, 192
Agamben, Giorgio, 145
Air Force Scientific Advisory Board, 221
air power, 22, 137
aircraft
  in Ellard and Johnstone installation, 5–6
  "penetration" technology, 100
  programming of flights, 220
  role of *Viper* device, 200–1
  slow-motion shot in films, 6, 58
  see also Apache helicopter; Unmanned
    Combat Air Vehicle (UCAV)
alba (song at dawn), 32–3
Albania, 137
allegory
  story of sirens, 141
  in Wells's stories, 151
alterity
  of frontier, 180
  hallucination of, 143, 178, 181, 182
  see also the Other
Antheil, George, 41, 42–3

anxiety, 82
Apocalypse Now (film), 49
Apollinaire, Guillaume, 207, 208–10
  "Désir" 209–10
  La petite auto, 208–9
  "Visée", 207, 210–11, **210**
Apollodorus, 140
apologia/apology
  literary tradition, 184–5
  Loy's "Apology of Genius", 171, 184,
    186–7
architecture, Duchamp's *Glass*, 227
Aristotle, 111, 140
  on *achresis*, 104, 113, 171
  on *skopos*, 197, 198, 199
  on *techne*, 7
armament, Heidegger's reflections on, 88
armoured land vehicles, 28
Arquilla, John, 16, 221
art for art's sake, 6
Ashy, General Joseph, 216
Asian diasporic communities, 172–3
atomic bomb, 86, 197
automation/automatism, 68
  in Barnes's *Nightwood*, 73, 78, 79, 80–1, 161
autonomy, 128
avant-garde, 6, 9, 73–4
aviation, use of camera obscura, 28

Ballet mécanique (film), 41–2
Barnes, Djuna, 70
  Nightwood, 68, 77–81, 88, 110, 114, 161
Barrett, William, *Irrational Man*, 86
battle space characterisation, 217
battlefield, 49–50
Baudelaire, Charles, 55, 61, 66n, 100, 211n
Baudrillard, Jean, 4, 33
Baumgarten, Alexander, 54
beauty, 18, 53
  in marketing campaign for Bell Helicopter,
    49, 50–1, 52
Beckett, Samuel, 69
Being, Heidegger's metaphysics, 87–8
Belgrade, 192
Bell Helicopter Textron, 49–52, **51**
Benjamin, Walter, 4, 160, 211n

Bennington, Geoff, 140
Bergson, Henri, 74, 75
Berman, Art, 68–9, 86
Bhabha, Homi, 171, 177–8, 178, 179–80, 181, 182
Bierce, Ambrose, 173
Bion, Wilfred, 148, 150
Bishop, John, 99, 108, 112, 113
black light, 40–1
Blake, William, "London", 201–2, 203–4
The Blind Man, **40**, 158–9, 224
blindness
    black light of optical effect, 40–1
    in Conrad's *The End of the Tether*, 120, 157
    in Duchamp's aesthetics, 158
    effect of increased field of vision for combat, 162
    in Loy's "Der Blinde Junge", 35–7, 39–40
    postcolonial, 124
    in Wells's *Country of the Blind*, 156–8
Boccioni, Umberto, 38, 39, 71
body *see* human body
body politic
    in absolute monarchy, 122–3
    appropriation of citizens' senses by, 189
Boeing, 192
Bosnia, 135–6
Botticelli, Sandro, 56
boundaries, shifting of, diaspora, 171, 178
Bow Street Runners, 201
Bozzolla, Angelo, 38
Bragaglia, Anton Giulio, 60, 61
Braque, Georges, 77
Breton, André, 83
British Empire, 117
British Petroleum, 132, 133
broadcast technologies, 73
    in Barnes's *Nightwood*, 78
    connections with public sphere, 216
    connections with systems and institutions, 98
    in *Finnegans Wake*, 106–9, 109, 113–14
    link with ventriloquism and narrative, 96–7
Buñuel, Luis, 111
    on filmmaking and visual technology, 44–5
    Un chien andalou, 43–4
Burke, Carolyn, 47n
Burma (Myanmar), 122, 123, 129, 131–2
Burmah Oil, 132–3

C3I (containment, control, communications and information), 98, 114, 123, 150–1, 159, 190
Cagniard de la Tour, Charles, 138
California, 172
Cambodia, 122, 123, 124–5, 172
camera
    in *Ballet mécanique*, 42
    revealment of casualties in *Three Kings*, 34–5
camera obscura
    classic representation by, 27–8
    resemblance of Apache cockpit to, 25, 26
Cameron, James, 45

camouflage, 162
capabilities, 127–9, 132
Capra, Frank, 44
cartography, 28
catharsis, 140–1
cell phones, 191
Chambers's *Miscellany of Useful and Entertaining Tracts*, 102
Chaplin, Charlie, 44
China
    foreign policy in South East Asia, 123–4
    gunpowder, 206
    huge migrations in mid-nineteenth century, 172
    transfer of Hong Kong to, 174–5
Chow, Rey, "Against the Lures of Diaspora", 180–3
Chrysler, siren advert, **139**
CIA (Central Intelligence Agency), 134n
cinema
    Buñuel on "segmentation", 44
    montage, 44
    pixilation technique in early productions, 220
    slow motion airplane lift-off shot, 5–6
cities
    episcopic functions in, 200–1, 203, 208
    targeted by unmanned urban projectiles, 194
    see also urbanism
civil defence, 137, 138
classical aesthetics, distinction with modern aesthetics, 63
CNN (Cable News Network), 34, 35, 189
Cold War
    C3I (containment, control, communications and information), 98, 114, 159
    Defense Support program (DSP), 216–17
    and formation of Asian diasporic groups, 172
    and formation of postcolonial states, 122, 123, 123–5
    importance of military technologies, 48n, 187, 188, 190
    sirens, 137, 141
    under Reagan, 126
collages, Picasso, 13
colonialism
    attached to Cold War, 122
    as capital growth, 131–2
    in Conrad's *The End of the Tether*, 119–20, 121–2
    law under, 178
    in Lee and Lambert's *Man Must Move*, 205
"combat Internet system", 192
command, 96
communications technology
    broadcast technologies, 96–7
    in Jarry's idea for time machine, 75–6
Communism, 150, 187
Compton-Hall, Richard, 107
computer gaming, 217
Connor, Steven, 102, 138–9

Conrad, Joseph, 177
  The End of the Tether, 118–22, 129, 157
consumer goods, technologies, 4, 106
containment, in US Cold War policy, 187
Corinthians, 199
Coventry, 137
Crary, Jonathan, 27
crime, technologies for identifying criminals,
  202–3
crime fiction, 198
cruise missiles, 194
CSI (TV show), 197–8, 202–3, 208
Cuba, 48n
cubism, 9, 12
cultural displacement, in Chow's account of
  diaspora, 181–3
cultural studies, 170
cybernetic processes, 190
cyborgs
  qualities of soldier of the future, 126
  The Terminator, 45

Dali, Salvador, 111
  Invisible Man, 82–3
  Un chien andalou, 43–4
darkling
  modernist aesthetics and techno-science,
    106, 112
  text of *Finnegans Wake*, 98–9, 100, 109–11,
    112
DARPA (Defense Advanced Research Project
  Agency), 191
decoys, 162–3, **163**
Defence Science Board, 221
Defense Support program (DSP), 216–17
Deleuze, Gilles, 145
Delhi, 177
Derrida, Jacques, 115n, 135
  aporia of the perhaps, 141, 143–4
  reading of Kant's *Third Critique*, 19–20
Descartes, René, 41, 85, 99, 103
detachment, 117–18
Deuteronomy, 176–7, 177, 178, 179
diasporic communities, 171–6
  Bhabha's analysis, 177–8
  Chow's arguments against valorisation of,
    180–3
  in *Deuteronomy*, 176–7
  figure of intellectual, 181–2
  and hallucination of alterity, 178, 179, 181,
    182
  identity formation, 178–9
  power of sovereignty over, 122, 125,
    179
  rendered as useless, 169–70, 170–1
  role of military in forming, 171, 174
  role in postcolonial currencies, 130, 132
  valorisation of, 171, 179–80
  see also migrant communities
diasporic studies, 175–6
Dickens, Charles, 211n
digital technology, 217–20
dirty money, 129–31, 132
disappearance, aesthetics of, 63–4, 66
discipline, 174

division
  in Barnes's *Nightwood*, 79, 79–80
  between aesthetic and technological,
    15–16, 114
  between visual technology and aesthetics,
    26, 35
  evoked in Duchamp's "ready-mades", 159
  in military technology, 82, 159
  in modernist aesthetics, 6–7, 7–8, 14, 69,
    81, 213, 215–16
  power of intelligent weaponry, 162
  in Saussurean linguistics, 12–13
DNA, 203
Doyle, Sir Arthur Conan, 211n
dream
  aesthetic of *Finnegans Wake*, 109, 110, 112,
    113, 114
  state of pilot of Apache helicopter, 111–12
Dresden, 137
drugs trade, illegal capital, 129–30
Duchamp, Marcel, 5, 16, 35, 68, 70, 74, 76–7,
    81, 91n
  The Bride, **62**
  *The Bride Stripped Bare by Her Bachelors,
    Even (The Large Glass)*, 61, **64**, 78, 108,
    159, 163, 213, 216, 221–7, **222**
  *Etant donnés: la chute de l'eau et le gaz
    d'éclairage*, 159–61, **161**, 163, 221–2
  Fountain, 222, 224
  The Green Box, 221–3, 223, 225–6
  Network of Stoppages, 16–18, **17**
  Nude Descending a Staircase, **59**, 61–2, 158
  Passage from Virgin to Bride, 77
  "ready-mades", 159
Duck Soup (film), 25
Duras, Marguerite, 34

Eagleton, Terry, 211n
East Timor, 133
economics
  in Conrad's *The End of the Tether*, 119–20
  dirty money, 129–32
Einstein, Albert, 38
Eisenstein, Sergei, 44
electro-optical images, 218
electromagnetic technologies, 8, 35, 39
Ellard, Graham, installation *The Geneva
  Express* (with Johnstone), 5–6
emergency, state of
  emblem of siren, 138, 145
  in Kusturica's *Underground*, 137, 138, 143
  presence of Gospa in Bosnia, 136, 145
empiricism, 31, 215
  conflict with rationalism, 157
  Locke's speculations on, 214–15
Enlightenment, and modernity, 27, 31
episcopic functions, 20–2, 187, 193, 207
  in civic and urban environments, 20, 198,
    201, 203
  and targeting, 220
  tele-technologies, 216
episcopy, 20, 198
ethics
  Aristotle, 7
  concerns of modernist writers, 68, 69

ethics (*cont.*)
  and division between technology and
    aesthetics, 7–8
  history and relation to the other, 105,
    106
  and *praxis* (ethical action), 7, 16, 199
Europe, Heidegger's characterisation, 87
excess, 103–5, 170
  operation of military hinge as, 187
  represented by diasporic movements,
    169–70, 170–1, 179
exile, 173
existentialism
  elements in Barnes's *Nightwood*, 80
  in Sartre's *La Nausée*, 84–5
eyes
  in Loy's "Der Blinde Junge", 38–9
  metaphor on in Conrad's *The End of the
    Tether*, 120
  projection in IHADSS, 111–12
  in surrealism, 43–4

fascism, 68–9
Federation of American Scientists, 193,
  219
FIA (Future Imagery Architecture), 216, 220,
  221
Fielding, Henry, 201
fingerprinting, 202
Fliegende Blätter, 83
flying machines, in Wells's "Argonauts of the
  Air", 152, 154–5
forensic anthropology, 202, 203
Foucault, Michel, 4, 122, 127–8
Freud, Sigmund, 147–8, 150
Friedman, George, 194, 195, 196
friendship, Derrida on politics of, 143–4
frontiers, 180
Fuhrmann, August, 30
functionality
  separation from aesthetics, 6–7, 14
  in weapons technology, 65
Future, 194, 195
futurism
  Boccioni's "Technical Manifesto", 38
  and Bragaglia's photodynamism, 60
  engagement with technology, 42–3, 70
  manifesto for radio, 98
  Marinetti, 60–1
  in music, 42–3
  and synaesthesia, 100

La Gaceta literaria, 44–5
Galileo, 206
Gange, John, 6
"gated communities", 191
gender
  as division in modernist aesthetics, 81
  theme in *Les Demoiselles d'Avignon*, 9
German Romantics, 68–9
gliders, 152, 153
Global Position Satellite, 191
global war, 179
globalisation, 123, 175
Glosson, General "Buster", 100

gramophone, in *Finnegans Wake*, 113
gravity, in Hogben's *Men, Missiles and
  Machines*, 206–7
Greek mythology, sirens, 140–1
Greet, Anne Hyde, 212n
Guam, 172
Guattari, Felix, 145
guided missiles, 45, 193
Gulf War, 100, 190, 193
  in *Three Kings*, 33–5
Gunn, Thom, 47n

Habermas, Jürgen, 4
Halim, Tunku, *Vermillion Eye*, 132–3
Hasbro toys, 125
Hawaii, 172
Hebert, Adam J., 227n
Hegel, G. W. F., 31–2, 39, 99, 181
Heidegger, Martin, 4, 84–5, 150
  Introduction to Metaphysics, 86–9
helicopters
  AH-IZ Super Cobra, 49–52, 54, 57, 162
  Apache **51**, **63**, 65, **65**; cockpit 25–6, **26**,
    29–31; "fire-and-forget" missile 45;
    pilot, 111–12, 114, 160
  Comanche, 62–3, 64, 65, 65–6
Helsinki, Virtual Village, 191
Hemingway, Ernest, 46n
hinge/*tache*
  of body and body politic, 124–5
  in Duchamp's ideas for picture in *The
    Green Box*, 225–6
  and military body, 22, 117–18, 122, 125,
    126, 187, 189, 193
  in networks and narrative, 16
  in perception of art, 9
Hiroshima Mon Amour (Duras), 34
history, in Joyce's *Ulysses*, 105
Hobson-Jobson, 108
Hogben, Lancelot, *Men, Missiles and
  Machines*, 206–7, 207–8, 208
Homeland Security, 189, 190, 191, 192
Homer, 21
  The Odyssey, 138, 140–1
Honeywell (military systems manufacturer),
  29
Hong Kong, 130, 174–5
Horkheimer, Max, 4
Hoxha, Enver, 137
human body
  as excess, 103
  and narrative in *Three Kings*, 34–5
  in Picasso's art, 11–12, 13
human evolution, Vico's version, 99, 104
Husserl, Edmund, 103
Hutton, Edward, 71
Huxley, Aldous, 105
hybrid identity, 181

identity formation, diasporic communities,
  175–6, 178–9
identity politics, 170
  in diasporic writing, 176, 181–3
IHADSS (integrated helmet and display sight
  system), 29–31, 35, 111–12, **111**

illegal goods, production and trade in
postcolonial countries, 129–32
illusion
capabilities of military technology, 100
in ventriloquism, 95, 96, 101, 102
images
digital technologies, 218–20
effect of optoelectronic war, 30
Indonesia, 122, 124, 132
information explosion, 102
infrared decoys, 162–3
insignia of the military, 124, 125, 132, 170,
172–5, 183, 191
instrumentality, 6
division with aesthetic, 51
pilot of Apache helicopter, 25
rendering diasporic communities as
worthless, 169
intelligence, 96
role in war on terror, 191
and targeting, 18–19, 219
technical, 217
intelligence community, notion of target, 19
intelligent weapons systems, 162, 190, 192,
193–4, 195, 216
Inter Continental Ballistic Missiles, 217
International Labour Organization (ILO),
132
internet, 191, 216
invisibility
military technologies, 100
see also visibility
Iraq, 137, 192
see also Gulf War
Israel, 189

Jane's Defense Weekly, 191
Japan, 123, 172, 174
Jarry, Alfred, 75–6
Jaspers, Karl, 86
Jastrow, Joseph, 83
John (Gospel), 176
Johnstone, Stephen, installation *The Geneva
Express* (with Ellard), 5–6
Joselit, David, 11–12, 13
Jouffret, Alain, 228n
Joyce, James
Finnegans Wake, 32, 41, 45, 95, 98–101,
104–5, 106–9, 109–11, 112, 112–14, 162,
225
Ulysses, 105
Judovitz, Dalia, 159, 161
Juvenal, 36

Kafka, Franz, *The Castle*, 97, 103, 108
Kahn, Douglas, 100
Kaiserpanorama, 30
Kandinsky, Vasily, 72, 73, 75, 100
Kant, Immanuel, 148, 149, 150, 155
on beauty, 18, 19, 19–20, 54, 103
transcendental subject, 20, 56, 76
Keaton, Buster, 44
Keats, John, "Ode on Melancholy", 52–4, 63
Kelvin, William Thomson, 1st Baron, 75
Kettering, Charles F., 48n

Keystone View Company, postcard, **3**, 4, 12,
22, 217
Kiesler, Frederick, 226–7
Kiki (actress/model), 42
Klee, Paul, 8
Klein, Melanie, 148–9, 150
knowledge
Locke's speculations, 214–15
techne, 7, 95, 102
Korea, 172, 174
Kosovo, 174, 175
Krauss, Rosalind, 11, 13
Kusturica, Emir, *Underground*, 136–7, 138,
140, 141, 142–3

Lacan, Jacques, 4
Lamarr, Hedy, 48n
Lambert, David, *Man Must Move* (with Lee),
204–6, 207–8
landmines, Cambodia, 124–5
Langdon, Harry, 44
Langley Air Base, 28
language
division with body, 12–13
Joyce's multilingual puns in *Finnegans
Wake*, 99, 101
phonocentrism, 102–3
role in dividing of senses, 109
Laos, 172
law
in *Deuteronomy*, 177
and sovereignty, 145
under colonialism, 178
Leahy, Colonel Michael, 190
Lee, Laurie, *Man Must Move* (with Lambert),
204–6, 207–8
Léger, Fernand, 41–2
LeMay, General Curtis, 46–7n
Lilienthal, Otto, 152, 153, 154, 155
linguistics, Saussure, 12–13
Locke, John, *Essay Concerning Human
Understanding*, 213–15
Lockheed Martin, 50, 163, 187–8
London, Jack, 137
London
in Blake's "London", 201–2
Metropolitan Police, 202
origins of police force, 201
Loy, Mina, 68, 70, 75, 77, 81, 158, 213
"The Apology of Genius", 169, 171, 183–7
"Der Blinde Junge", 35–40, 41, 183
"Songs to Joannes", 70–3
Lucas, Keith, 156
Luria, A. R., 100
Lyotard, Jean-François, 4

MacBeth, George, 140
Macedonia, 174
Mach, Ernst, 58
Machiavelli, Niccolò, 144
machination, Heidegger's reflections on,
88–9
machinic modification, 218–19
McKim, Colonel Michael, 83–4
magic lanterns, 40, 161

Mairet, Philip, 85, 86
Malaysia, 122, 129, 133
Mallarmé, Stéphane, 55–7, 60, 69–70, 76
Mandal, Fritz, 48n
MANPRINT (manpower and integration)
    cockpit, 29–31, 44–5, 189, 190
Marcos, Ferdinand, 131
Marey, Etienne-Jules, 28, 58, 60, 61–2, 158
Marinetti, F. T., 36, 37, 60–1, 108
marketing
    Bell AH-IZ Helicopter campaign, 49,
        50–2, **51**, 57
    information for naval decoys, 162
    Lockheed Martin material on naval decoys,
        163
Marx, Karl, 99
Maxim, Hiram, 152, 153–4, 154
mechanisation, in Duchamp's *Etant donnés*,
    161
"mechanisms of power", 128
media
    broadcasting, 109, 113–14, 216
    "guardian" function in urban life, 203
Medugorje, Bosnia, 135–6
migrant communities
    dominant idea and alternative perspective,
        169–70
    role in postcolonial currencies, 131, 133
    see also diasporic communities
military body
    attachable and detachable parts, 125
    and colonialism in *The End of the Tether*,
        119–20
    in governance, 22
    hinge/*tache*, 16, 22, 117–18, 125, 171, 187,
        189, 193
    manifested in transformer, 125–6
    in South East Asia, 131
    and state sovereignty, 124
military technology
    and aesthetics, 4, 5, 15–16, 43, 50–1, 82, 98,
        150, 159
    appropriation of consumer hardware, 106
    command centre and field of action, 118
    exploitation of one-way transmission, 96
    and *Finnegans Wake*, 100, 109
    hinge linking divided regions, 15–16
    and invisibility, 64–5
    manufacture of deceptions, 85
    prosthetic extension, 26–7, 27–8, 35,
        111–12
    R&D, 192, 193, 218
    shift towards networks, 16
    struggle to eradicate excess, 170
    in Wells's tale about tanks, 28–9
mimesis
    in Loy's poetry, 39–40, 183
    in Picasso's early experimental studies, 9
miracles, apparition of Gospa, 135–6
missile warning and defence, 217
modernism
    and gap in visual technology/aesthetics,
        26, 35
    Picasso's art and rise of postmodernism,
        11–12

the subject, 13–15
    treatment of technologies in global world,
        213
    writers influencing discourses on, 4–5
modernist aesthetics, 5
    and collision of history with technology,
        215–16
    conceptualisation of communications
        technologies, 96–7
    connections with technology, 4, 5, 213
    darkling, 98–100, 106, 109–12, 114
    distinction with classical aesthetics, 63
    division with technology, 15–16, 114
    and history's collision with technology,
        215–16
    ideas forming heritage of, 61
    and the incalculable space, 104–5
    and the invisible, 64–5
    mobilising of archaic resources, 213
    and optical effect, 41
    and optoelectronics, 9, 30, 156
    and poetics, 27, 35
    and Romanticism, 54–5
    struggle to represent excess, 170
    subversion of idea of sexual relations, 61–2
    synaesthesia, 8, 72–3, 100
    and transcendentalism/universalisation,
        68–9
    and urbanisation processes, 22
modernity
    division of aesthetic and functional, 6–7,
        14
    division between *praxis* and *poiesis*, 7–8
    economic conditions of production and
        reproduction, 105–6
    Enlightenment aspect, 27, 31
    field of vision, 27
    Heidegger on abandonment of Being in,
        87–8
    as phantom dawn, 31–2
    role of the city, 22
    writers influencing discourses on, 4–5
moon, dark side of, 196
Moretti, Franco, 177
mourning, relationship to responsibility, 69
movement, experimentation and
    documentation of, 57–8, **59**, 158
Multispectral Imaging (MSI), 219, 220
Murphy, Dudley, 41–2
Musée Picasso, 9, 23n
museum, Duchamp's commentary on, 160
music
    futurism, 42–3
    Kandinsky's ideas, 72, 73
Muybridge, Eadweard, 58, 60, 61–2, 158
    Nude Descending a Staircase, **59**
Myanmar *see* Burma

Naipaul, V. S., 177
narratives
    technics, 16, 150
    technologies in *Finnegans Wake*, 106–7,
        114
NASA (National Aeronautics and Space
    Administration), 194

nation-states
connection of military with, 21
necessary engagement with excess, 170
in postcolonial South East Asia, 122–5
National Imaging and Mapping Agency, 220
National Reconnaissance Office (NRO), 216, 220
National Socialism, 87
NATO (North Atlantic Treaty Organisation), 192
Network-Centric Warfare, **18**, 216, 217, 220–1
networks, 16, 221
neurology, 150, 156
neutron bomb, 192
New Mexico, 189
New Testament, 176, 182
New York, Chinatown, 172
Nicholls, Peter, 60–1
Nietzsche, Friedrich, 135, 147, 150, 155
Bion's debt to, 148, 149–50
Human All Too Human, 143–4
9/11 attacks, 191, 192
Northrop Grumann, 189, 192
nuclear power, 137, 138, 189

objet d'art, 6
the occult, in Wells's short stories, 151–2
oil companies, South East Asia, 312–13
operations community, notion of target, 19
optical science, 40–1
optoelectronics, 8
connection with modernist aesthetics, 9, 30, 156
Duchamp's commentary on technics of, 160
technologies for targeting and surveillance, 150–1
ordinance, and use of camera obscura in seventeenth century, 28
the Other
ethical relation to, 105, 106
in Sartre's *La Nausée*, 85
see also alterity

Pakistan, 173
paranoia, in Dali's *Invisible Man*, 82–3
Patriot missile system, 126
Paul, St, 199
Paz, Octavio, 158
Pearl Harbor, 138
Pepper's ghost, 40, 163
perception
gap created by modernity, 12–13, 27, 35, 88
Locke's speculations on, 214–15
in MANPRINT cockpit, 29, 31
"reframing", 83–4
types of organs, 147
performance, in technological representation, 6, 58–60
Perry, W. J., 25
perspective (in visual space), 158
Philippines, 122, 124, 132, 172

philosophy
eighteenth-century considerations on question of origin, 215
Nietzsche on transformation of, 149
phonocentrism, 102–3
photodynamism, 70
Bragaglia, 60, 61
photography
and aesthetics of disappearance, 63
experiments with movement, 58
in Picasso's work, 13
Picasso, Pablo
on beauty, 18, 19
early experimental studies, 9, 77
supposed "return to order", 11, 12, 13
works: *Les Demoiselles d'Avignon* 9–11, **10**, 12, 77; *Portrait of Igor Stravinsky* **15**; *Portrait of Olga in an Armchair*, **14**
Pilot Night Vision System (PNVS), 31
pixels, 217, 218, 219–20
Plato, 56, 103, 140, 156, 184, 198
Poe, Edgar Allen, 55, 114, 115n, 186, 198, 211n
poetry, Loy's definition, 73
poiesis, 7, 14–15
Poincaré, Henri, 228n
police
investigative technologies, 198, 202
origins of, 201
politics
account of catastrophic times in *Nightwood*, 81
attitudes depicted in *Underground*, 142–3
in Chow's account of cultural displacement, 181, 182
delimitation by diasporic studies, 175–6
Schmitt's thinking, 143
polyphony
in *Finnegans Wake*, 106–7
in ventriloquism, 101
popular science, Hogben's *Men, Missiles and Machines*, 207
post-Enlightenment, visual culture, 27
postcolonial criticism/studies, 123, 124, 170
postcolonial world
in Conrad's *The End of the Tether*, 119–20, 122
localised military bodies, 128–9
nation building in South East Asia, 122–5
production and trade in illegal goods, 129–31
postmodernism
"drift" of thought, 170
Picasso and development from modernism, 11–12
writers influencing discourses on, 4–5
Pound, Ezra, 32–3
power relations, Foucault's thinking, 128–9
pre-emptive action, 187
production
economic conditions of, 105–6
and uselessness of diasporic communities, 169
projective/projectile identification, 150
propulsion, 206

prosopopoeia (personification)
  Bell Helicopter, 50
  in Keats's "Ode on Melancholy", 53
prosthetics
  in *Ballet mécanique*, 42–3
  broadcast media, 109, 113
  extension of senses, 3–4, 215
  and gap between visible text and remote
    object, 41
  and landmines, 124
  in military technology, 26–7, 27–8, 35, 193
  narrative of Duchamp's *Network of
    Stoppages*, 18
  soldier of the future, 126–7
  visual culture in Apache helicopter cockpit,
    25–6, 29
psychoanalysis, 150
  Bion on thought and action, 148
  elements in Barnes's *Nightwood*, 80
  readings of Picasso's art, 11–12
psychology
  constructivist, 85
  idioms used by Dali in *Invisible Man*, 82–3

radar technology, 100, 101
  decoys, 162–3
radio technology, 95–6, 103
  in *Finnegans Wake*, 107–8
  futurists' glorification of, 98
RAND Corporation, 16
rationalism, conflict with empiricism, 157
Ray, Man, 42
recording technologies, 90–1
  in Barnes's *Nightwood*, 78
Renaissance music
  love song adopted by Loy, 70–1
  suggested in Kafka's telephone passage, 97
Rimbaud, Arthur, 100
Romance literature, 32–3
Romanticism
  aesthetics, 52–4
  considerations about question of origin,
    215
  distinction between essence and
    representation of a thing, 185–6
  and universalisation of spirit, 68–9
Ronfeldt, David, 16, 221
Russell, David, *Three Kings*, 33–5
Russia, in Heidegger's characterisation of
    Europe, 87
Russolo, Luigi, 42

San Francisco, Chinatown, 172
Sartre, Jean-Paul, *La Nausée*, 84–5, 89–90
satellite technology
  in broadcast media and
    telecommunications, 216
  in US military strategy, 48n, 98, 216–17
satire
  in Barnes's *Nightwood*, 77
  in Blake's "London", 204
  Loy's "Apology of Genius", 171, 183–4
  Poe's "The Man of the Crowd", 198
  in *Underground*, 141
Saussure, Ferdinand de, 12–13, 91n

SBIRS (Space Based Infrared System), 216,
    217, 221, 223
Schiller, Friedrich, 54
Schmitt, Carl, 143, 144
Schoenberg, Arnold, 72
Schopenhauer, Arthur, 148, 149
Schwarzenegger, Arnold, 45
science fiction, 155
scopic functions, *see also skopos*
Seckel, Hélène, 9
sensation
  receptors, 147
  technics, 148–9
senses
  appropriated and automated by body
    politic, 189
  confusion by broadcast media, 113–14
  control by IHADSS, 111–12
  and control of mind, 156
  sensory information in *Finnegans Wake*,
    100–1, 109–10
  synaesthetic experience, 8
  technologies as prosthetic extensions of,
    3–4, 113–14
  see also synaesthesia
Serbians, 165n
sexual difference, metaphors, 53–4
sexual relations
  modernist attempts to subvert, 61–2
  theme in *Les Demoiselles d'Avignon*, 9
Shell, 312–13
Shelley, Percy Bysshe, 184, 185–6
ships, steam-driven engines in Conrad's *The
    End of the Tether*, 119–20, 120–1
short stories, 151
Sidney, Sir Philip, 184–5
sight, prosthetic extension in military
    technology, 26
Singapore, 125, 129, 130, 131, 132
Sino-Japanese war, 172, 174
sirens, 96, 137–8, 138–41
  "Big Joe" advert, **139**
  in *Underground*, 137–8, 145
skopos
  in Blake's "London", 201–2
  meanings, 20–1, 198–9, 200
  scopic functions, 20, 187, 193, 207, 219
Sloterdijk, Peter, 144
"smart" weapons, 190, 191
soldier
  and civilians, 173–4
  of the future, 126, **127**
sound, prosthetic application, 108–9
South East Asia
  economic crash (1997), 175
  postcolonial states, 122, 123, 123–5, 125
sovereignty
  and the law, 145
  power over communities, 122, 125, 174
  state's loss of, 123
Soviet Union, 124
Space Plane, 194
speed
  connection with modernist aesthetics, 9,
    73–4

as essence of US military technology, 190
technologies, 6, 8, 57–8, 58–60, 65
time machine, 74–5
spirit, Heidegger's concern for, 87, 89
spirits, in Locke's speculations on perception, 214
the spiritual, 210
Spitfires, 49
Stalinism, 87
Star Wars programme, 203, 217
Starling, Ernest, 156
state
    and citizens, 170, 189
    loss of sovereignty, 123
    narrative of diaspora, 170–1, 173, 179
    use of military body, 125
Stendhal, 144
stereoscopy
    Keystone images, **3**, 4, 22, 152, 217
    satellite images, 217–18
Stravinsky, Igor, 13
Suharto, Thojib N. J., 123, 132, 133
Sukarno, Ahmed, 123–4
surrealism, 85
    use of the eye, 43–4
surveillance
    and globalisation, 175
    Lockheed Martin ads, 187–8
    technologies, 90, 150–1, 188, 195, 216
    US Cold War policy, 98, 187
    in virtual village, 190–1
SWAT (Special Weapons and Tactics), 203
Swedenborg, Emanuel, 100
Sylvania Electronics Division, 48n
synaesthesia
    in *Finnegans Wake*, 110
    in modernist aesthetics, 8, 72–3, 100, 101
    pilot of Apache helicopter, 112

tache see hinge/*tache*
Taiping Rebellion, 174
Takara toys, 125
talking machines, 89
tanks *see* armoured land vehicles
target, metaphysical and empirical notions, 199–200
targeting
    in Apollinaire's poetry, 209–11
    and digital images, 217–18
    Lockheed Martin system, 50
    military technologies, 28–9, 150–1, 162–3, 188, 200–1
    in network-centric warfare, 220
    relationship of intelligence to, 18–19, 219
    scopic and episcopic functions, 20–2, 198–9
    state's emphasis on, 187
    technologies for criminal investigation, 203
    use of Unmanned Aerial Vehicles (UAV), 189
techne, 7, 14, 15–16, 95
technicity, 105–6, 218, 221
    air raid siren, 137, 145

technology
    account of progress in children's knowledge books, 207–8
    auto in Apollinaire's *La petite auto*, 208–9
    connections with modern aesthetics, 4, 5, 15, 51, 70, 106, 114, 213, 215–16
    functionality, 6, 14
    and Heidegger on emptiness of Being, 88
    operations, 5
    and power relations, 128–9
telecommunications
    coverage of war, 34
    satellite systems, 216
    and text in *Finnegans Wake*, 106
telephony, 4, 103
    in *Finnegans Wake*, 108
tele-technologies, 216
    and Duchamp's *Étant donnés*, 160
    stereoscopic images, 22
Tennyson, Alfred, 1st Baron Tennyson, 135
The Terminator (film), 45
terrorism, 188–9, 193
Tesla, Nikolai, 125, 190
THAAD (Theater High Altitude Area Defense), 125
Thailand, 122, 130, 132
Thompson, J. J., 76
thought, and action, 147–8
Three Kings (Russell, film), 33–5
time
    "real-time" technologies, 27, 29, 98, 150
    and speed technologies, 8
time machine, 74–6
Tirana, 137
Tokyo, 137
"total war", 174, 195
the transcendental, Kant, 20, 56
transcendentalism, Berman's ideas, 68–9
transformers, 125–7, **127**, 133
Treaty on Principles Governing the Activities of States in the Exploration and Use of Outer Space (1967), 196
Truffaut, François, 31
Turner, J. M. W., 163

Un chien andalou (Buñuel and Dali, film), 43–4
Underground (Kusturica, film), 136–7, 138, 140, 141, 142–3
United States
    Chinese émigrés, 172
    civil war, 28
    Cold War policy, 98, 123–4, 187
    defence spending, 191–2
    episcopic aims of Star Wars programme, 203
    geo-political policy, 150
    in Heidegger's characterisation of Europe, 87
    intensification of unilateralism, 196
    pilgrims to Bosnian site of miracles, 135–6
    sponsorship of South East Asian corrupt regimes, 123, 124
    see also US National Research Council; US navy; USAF

universalisation, Berman's ideas, 68–9
unmanned urban projectiles, 194–6
unmanned vehicles, 171
    UAVs and UCAVs, 189, 190–1, 192, 193
Unocal, 131
urbanism, 6, 87
    and Blake's "London", 201–2
    and history of targeting, 21
    and modern policing, 202
    and separation of scopic and episcopic
        services, 22
    as target in modern narratives, 204, 206
    see also cities
US National Research Council, 189
US navy, 194
USAF (United States Air Force), 216, 218
    Hypersonic Technology ("Hy Tech"), 194
    Intelligence Targeting Guide, 18–19

Vaihinger, Hans, 155
Valéry, Paul, 25
ventriloquism, 95–6, 101–2, 114
Vertov, Dziga, 44
Vico, Giambattista, 99, 100, 104, 105
Vietnam, 122, 172
    war, 126, 165n, 174
Viper device, 200–1
Virilio, Paul, 4, 25
    on aesthetics of appearance and
        disappearance, 63, 64, 65, 66, 162
    on Apollinaire's poems, 207
    concern with electromagnetic
        technologies, 8
    on diasporic movements, 169, 170
    Open Sky, 33
    on surviving terrorism and deterrence,
        188–9
    warning about all technologies, 191
virtual village, 190–1
visibility
    and the invisible, 57, 63–4, 65–6, 111, 122,
        132, 162, 193
    and role of art, 8–9
    role of optoelectronic technology, 8
visual culture
    cockpit of Apache helicopter, 25–6
    and division with visual technology, 8–9,
        26, 35
    perception and prosthesis, 11, 215
    and perspective, 158
    post-Enlightenment, 27
    in *Three Kings*, 35
    in Wells's tale about tanks, 28–9
visual mass media, 26
visual technologies, 6
    Apache cockpit, 26, 29
    black light, 40–1
    Buñuel's hopes for, 44–5

in development of military technology,
    83–4, 217–18
division with visual aesthetics, 8–9, 26, 35
in Duchamp's *Etant donnés*, 161–2
perception and prosthesis, 11, 215
3D images, 218–19

wandering
    diasporic communities, 171, 178
    motif, 204–6
Wankel, Harold D., 130
war on terror, 187, 188, 189, 190, 191, 216
Warncke, Carsten-Peter, 12, 23n
The Washington Post, 188
weapons
    effects of long-distance devices shown in
        Three Kings, 35
    endowed with sensory perception and
        intelligence, 26
    hiding of human damage, 34
    human–machine integration system, 189
    manufacture in Kusturica's *Underground*,
        137
    and military bodies, 126
    "reframing perception", 83–4
    see also intelligent weapons systems
weapons technology, 65
    Heidegger's reflections on, 88
    themes in Duchamp's *The Large Glass*,
        225
Wells, H. G., 28–9, 75, 137, 214
    "Argonauts of the Air", 152–5
    "The Country of the Blind", 156–8
    "The Remarkable Case of Davidson's
        Eyes", 152, 188, 216
    science and the occult in short stories,
        151–2
    The Time Machine, 74
Whitlam, Gough, 132
Williams, William Carlos, 33
Windrem, Robert, 217
Winters, Yvor, 47n
Wisdom of Solomon, 197
Wittgenstein, Ludwig, 83
Woodside Petroleum, 132
World Trade Center attacks, 192, 193
World War I, 105
    Keystone image, **3**, 22
    veterans' on killing enemy soldiers, 209
World War II, 29, 86, 205, 207
    air raids, 137
    decoy tactics, 165n
    in *Underground*, 136–7

Yeats, W.B., 33
Yugoslavia, 192

Zeno, 158